Raising Our Voices

An account of the Hearing Voices movement

by Adam James

Thanks and thoughts

Thank you Ian for the opportunity, Terry for your insight, Manchester Metropolitan University for access to your library, Anne for her reflections, Matt, Mark, Alec Jenner and Phil Thomas for the chapter proof-reads. And Alessia for her proof-reads, comments, and above-all intelligence, love, support and vibrancy.

This book goes out to all those hoping for a better deal for people who use the mental health service. It also comes with fond memories of Sharon Lefevre who died before its publication.

© 2001 Adam James

Published by Handsell Publishing

ISBN 1-903199-13-1

Cover illustration by Dave Ingram

Designed and printed by Trio Graphics, Gloucester 01452 302858

Contents

Introduction
Perceptions of a psychotic

Ron Coleman, a mental health trainer and voice-hearer – but one-time chronic schizophrenic – once described himself as "psychotic and proud". These words made a lasting impression on me as they struck at the heart of the stereotypes and prejudices which pervade our perceptions of psychosis. As well as reflecting distress, to be diagnosed with a psychotic illness, in particular schizophrenia, can be one of the most soul-destroying of human predicaments. If already feeling bad about oneself, a diagnosis of schizophrenia is unlikely to be uplifting[1]. It can leave a patient to walking the longest, murkiest corridors of certified insanity. It incities fear in the misinformed who hear of such a diagnosis. Most of those who have never set foot in an acute ward and witnessed the plight of its patients are bombarded with derogatory images of a psychotic – with its media-induced[2] connotations of violence, evil and lunacy. In our cultural mythology a psychotic is either a sinister odd-bod who creeps up on showering women, or a maniacal community care patient raiding picnicking children while swinging a machete. Also, a minority of convicted murderers[3] are diagnosed with a psychotic illness of some variety, and the media has a field day with such tragedies, tending to present them as a realisation of our most chilling of nightmares.

But the fate of the everyday psychotic in our psychiatric wards or homeless in the streets are never on our newspapers' front pages. Where are those thousands of men and women either aimlessly treading up and down wards, stiff-limbed with sedative medication, or those sheltering from the rain in the dirty doorways of our cities. We hear little of those psychotics who slash their arms and faces with razors because their voices order them to do so. Little of those who are so frantic, confused and locked in their own solitary interpretation of the world that they have no friends, nor the ability to make new ones. Such is their anguish. But yet, amidst all these degrading images, Coleman proclaims himself "psychotic and proud". He longs for the time when: "I can walk down the street and talk to my voices without being denied my freedom." Coleman's words, echoing the resistance of the black and gay pride movements, are bound to cause ripples of disapproval, and even disgust. Where is the slightest whiff of satisfaction in being psychotic? Is he saying he is proud to be mentally ill? Are these the words of a charismatic fighter for the mental health users' cause or remnants of a past delusion? If these are questions you ask yourself then great, please read on, because some tentative answers lie in the chapters ahead.

---

[1] The reaction from relatives, or even the patient, of "oh, at least we now know what the problem is" carries little credibility considering the highly controversial nature of the schizophrenia concept.

[2] For example, "Evil psychopaths will be locked up" screamed the Daily Mirror on December 9, 1998, as a headline for a report on new NHS beds for the mentally ill!

[3] In the UK there are approximately 40 homicides a year committed by the "mentally ill". This is about 10% of the 360 homicides per annum.

This book

If tuned into Radio 4's Women's Hour on November 11, 1998, you might have heard this gem of a conversational snippet between presenter Jennie Murray, and footballer Vinnie Jones of *Lock Stock and Two Smoking Barrels* fame, but more notorious for his machismo on the soccer field.

Vinnie Jones: "I discuss a lot of things with my grandfather."
Jennie Murray: "Your grand-father is dead isn't he? He acts as your spiritual guide."
Vinnie Jones: "Yes, he does."

Is Mr Jones seeking the authoritative voice of our ancestral gods which philosopher and psychologist, Julian Jaynes, refers to in this book's opening chapter? Is Mr Jones gazing up to the heavens to hear the voice of his spiritual guide, as ancient prophets were said to have done? What a wonderful vision.

I was first alerted to Jaynes' book, *The Origins of the Consciousness in the Breakdown of the Bicameral Mind,* because according to the story of the Hearing Voices Network its message offered reassurance to a disturbed voice-hearer in Holland struggling to heal her fragmented identity and inner chaos. I hope you find the gateau of intellectual delights offered by this academic as fascinating an account of the human condition as I did. You may find yourself in agreement with some of what he has to say. Even if not, you may never conceptualise the experience of voice-hearing in quite the same way.

Chapter two firstly discusses the work of Professor Marius Romme and Sondra Escher in Holland. It was they who rejected the disease connotations of voices, and set in motion within psychiatry the idea of "accepting" the reality and meaning voices of a psychiatric patient, and recognising the role the voices' content played in distress. They worked with, rather than against, the patient's explanations for their voices, and formulated pragmatic ways of enabling people to develop new strategies for reducing the negative effects of voices on their lives. Essentially this section documents the positive interventions that Romme made with his voice-hearing patients, and details the stories of others who have, to a greater and lesser extent, learnt to "cope" with their voices. One proof-reader of this chapter discussed with me how he was concerned this section could appear to be too blasé, and that with its emphasis on those who could not cope with their voices, it ignores the experience of those who can not cope. I think a better way of conceptualising this coping/not coping dichotomy is to appreciate that one is never really a coper or non-coper, but perhaps toing and froing from being closer to one end of the dichotomy than the other. The second section looks at how Romme and Escher's work was introduced into the UK, and the events which expanded and developed The Hearing Voicers Network, and more generally the "hearing voices movement". I should emphasise that the following 10 chapters reflect my interpretation of these and subsequent events.

The chapters relate my perceptions of the Network and the movement, and are laced with my own anecdotes, encounters, interviews and analyses. You may have got a different flavour to this book if it had been written by, let's say, a voice-hearer who has experienced the psychiatric system, an established academic, or a psychiatrist.

As a member of the Hearing Voices Network I support its work. So, while discussing the politics, ideas and initiatives from here onwards, it sometimes may not be clear when I am expressing my own views, those of the Network, or some other individual. But this need not be problematic because the Network itself is not bound to one unitary position. There is no official line. As an organisation the Network can be better defined as a web of self-help groups offering assistance to troubled voice-hearers, together with patients and mental health professionals predominantly united in approaching voice-hearing alternatively from orthodox psychiatry.

It is in chapter two that political comparisons are made between the hearing voices and the gay movement. Here the challenge set to voice-hearers is to as successfully campaign to depathologise and normalise the experience of voice-hearing, as gay activists did with homosexuality, which up to the 1970s was an official pathological "sexual deviation" which medicine attempted to cure by a range of physical and psychological treatments[4]. As will become clear during this book it is those individuals who hear negative or abusive voices, often incessantly over a continuous stretch of weeks or months, who end up in psychiatric hospital. It is in light of the hostile *content* of such voices that some readers may judge that to depathologise hearing voices *per se* would be more of a philosophical, political and pragmatic challenge than depathologising homosexuality. Even if the category of "auditory hallucinations" was struck off the list of mental illness symptoms tomorrow this would probably not mean there would no longer be sufferers of abusive, denigratory voices. My response is if the voice-hearing experience was to have less illness/disease connotations then, instead of only neuroleptics being prescribed to rid the voice-hearer of such "symptoms", more attention, concern and value would be given to the *content* of voices – what they are saying and why they are saying it. It is this reprioritising of method, definition and approach which, as we shall learn, is a core component of the hearing voices movement. Such repositioning would require political action as much as calls for alternative treatments.

---

[4] For example, see Feldman, M.P. and MacCulloch, M.J. A systematic approach to the treatment of homosexuality by conditioned aversion. Preliminary report. American Journal of Psychiatry, 1964, 121, 167-172.

Chapter three centres on the grass roots of the Network – *self-help*, and the pragmatics of helping psychiatrised individuals struggling through their lives. It is often via such groups that patients have the freedom, space, and time to discuss their experience. Such groups are not for everyone, and do require from its participants a degree of composure, and ability to engage in communicative dialogue. But for others their remedial power can be immense.

Chapter four moves on to document some interpretations of the voice-hearing experience and we hear comprehensive accounts by those who hear voices. I thought it important that such subjectivities are offered by members of the Network themselves, rather than me fumbling to piece together summaries of them.

Chapter five discusses the life, opinions and work of Ron Coleman of Action Consultancy and Training (ACT) which is one of the most progressive and fresh initiatives in the UK's mental health scene. It has taken the ideas from the Network into the commercial mental health arena. Coleman's "recovery" is a dramatic story, and a psychotherapist who leads a hearing voices self-help group once said to me. "You know, many of the members who attend our group are in a terribly distressed state, and they can not all be like Ron." This may be so, but "recovery" means different things to different people.

Chapter six looks at the latest developments within cognitive psychology and what it can offer psychiatrised voice-hearers. Psychiatrist Douglas Turkington, who features in this chapter, told me he sees cognitive behavioural therapy as having "really taken off, and it challenges the use of medication as the be-all and end-all of treating psychosis." Turkington, who admits he works under the banner of liberal psychiatry, is a professional who not only actively sits and engages with his patients about their life and experience, he also brings a sparky optimism to his practice. When I once asked him to what extent it was important for there to be two-way collaboration between professional and patient to make cognitive behavioural therapy effective, he replied: "It is up to the *therapist* to make the relationship work, to find a way of working with someone, and to open up a channel for communication. From my experience, I would say there really has been no one who I have not been able to achieve this with to some degree, even when someone is in the most acute stage of psychosis." Turkington's medical discourse aside, it is such confidence in the ability to communicate and open up channels of partnership with the most severely distressed that offers hope for the future of the mental health service. It is when learning of such psychiatrists not getting confined into the position of, "I am reluctant to discuss with you about how you see the world, because you are mentally ill" that we can be warmed by faith in the possibility for change.

Chapter seven documents the work of Sharon Lefevre who elucidates how radical perspectives on hearing voices can lead to equally new frameworks for conceptualising other supposed mental illness symptoms such as self-harm. Again the thread that links this chapter to the others is that of endeavouring to listen to the user/patient, rather than presuming that traditional "experts" have a monopoly on knowledge of human experience and psychology.

Chapter eight tells of a unique partnership between a psychiatrist and his patient, and it also gives us the opportunity to hear the "voice" of psychiatrists. I hope you find reading this chapter as eye-opening as I did researching it, because it reveals some psychiatrists' own dissatisfaction with how their profession works, and helps relieve any frustrations accumulated from previous chapters that this book presumes psychiatric professionals are lacking in sensitivity!

As well as encouraging a reconsideration of voice-hearing, those in the movement are also involved with the more messy and drawn-out practice of advocating and supporting patients following an admission to hospital. Chapter nine focuses on the story of psychiatric patient, Sarah Devrin, and looks at the pragmatics of advocating for a patient while challenging the assumptions and suitability of psychiatry's main treatment principles. It also exemplifies how the twists and turns of a patient's career can depend on how professionals interpret his/her life and experience.

Finally, chapter ten offers re-evaluation on the genetic research into schizophrenia. I felt a need to include such a chapter because genetic discourses permeate our readings into the causation of this dubious disease entity, of which auditory hallucinations is a primary alleged symptom.

Orthodox psychiatry
It will become evident that this book is not favourable in its judgement of the psychiatric profession. But I acknowledge there are many pockets of innovative psychiatric services carving their own niches in the UK's mental health service. For example, North Birmingham Mental Health Trust (see chapter eight) whose psychiatrists and managers lean towards *social*, not *medical*, models of mental distress. And then there is also Bradford's Home Treatment Service which rejects psychiatric diagnoses altogether. Some readers will probably identify themselves as working in one of such pockets, and distance themselves to what I shall hereinafter refer to as orthodox psychiatry. Then there are the hundreds of individuals working in the mental health service who differ in their perspective to the mainstream but who, without support, have little power to initiate change. Indeed, I recognise myself as having been one of these frustrated individuals.

I have two objections to orthodox psychiatry. My first is the emphasis given to biological determinism. As I endeavour to demonstrate in the final chapter, proclaimed success in "finding" a genetic determinant to the string of official mental illnesses, and in particular schizophrenia, has been grossly inflated. Moreover, because I side with a more cultural relativist perspective on conceptions and definitions of what we call mental illness, I fear biological determinism inadequately addresses how discourses theorising on the psychology of the human condition are locked into the cultural, political and historical dynamics of the time. For me, orthodox psychiatry s allegiance to biological determinism, particularly prevalent in the UK and America, is more a cultural, political enterprise than adherence to the truths out there in the world. For me, orthodox psychiatry is not about tracking down facts which are patiently lying dormant in the world awaiting their discovery by researchers. I prefer to understand mental distress from the frameworks of social constructionism and poststructuralism which fundamentally challenge (and deconstruct) the objective status of scientific knowledge . For example, if I were to be told: Wherever you look in the world you will find cases of schizophrenia, my reply might be something like: Coca Cola and Michael Jackson fans also exist the world over. If you construct something through language, talk about it long enough, get on board a good marketing team, then sure enough, you *will* find that before long you can find it wherever you look. From Kings Cross to The Kalahari.[5]

Texts which have been particularly informative and seminal for me, and which shape my outlook throughout this book, include *Madness and Civilisation* by Michel Foucault, *Discourse and Social Psychology* by Jonathon Potter and Margaret Wetherell, *Divided Self* by RD Laing, and Thomas *Szasz s The Myth of Mental Illness*. In particular, *Deconstructing PsychoPathology*, compiled by a collection of academics and professionals, accounts for how institutionalised cultural and political discourses inform our definitions of mental distress and the treatment of its afflicted. *Asylum – A Magazine for Democratic Psychiatry* has been both an ever-flowing source of critical perspectives on mental health, and philosophies on which to base progressive mental health practice. For an anthology of writing by key contributors to the postmodern/poststructuralist debate there is *The Fontana Postmodernism Reader*.

But whereas academic texts formalise and package ideas, other sources can present us with examples of behaviour and ways of being which orthodox psychiatry might, in certain contexts, judge as pathological due to underlying disease. I would like to present two such examples I recently encountered. The first is a photograph published in *The Guardian* on January 25, 1997, which depicted a Hindu devotee hanging from a pole by more than 20 hooks piercing the skin along the length of his body. The photo s caption

---

[5] I once hitch-hiked through Botswana's Kalahari desert, and yes, not only could you buy Coca Cola from small shacks at the side of the main "highway" that ran through the heart of the desert, some local residents liked Michael Jackson's music, and had the T-shirt to prove it.

told readers that this self-inflicted test of physical endurance was conducted during a religious procession in Madras, India. Hundreds of people went through similar hardships each year, believing they would win favour with the god Murugan and so have their wishes fulfilled. Such behaviour is defined as admirable because of the strength of the cultural meaning contextualising it. But if we were to travel from India to Europe and learn of a distraught 25-year-old man practising such worship alone in the top floor flat of a Bradford council tower block, what would be our most likely reaction? Without a culture to reinfore his subjective experience would this man receive admiration for his devotion or advise from puzzled relatives "to see a doctor"?

The second example comes from when I spent two weeks in Sardinia. On a guided visit to the remains of a Carthaginian/Roman settlement in Nora at the south of the island, tourists were told of one special room which at the time had been swarming with snakes. Sick Romans were apparently advised to spend one night sleeping on the ground with the vipers in the hope that the snakes, acting as a vessel for Roman gods, would whisper the ailment's cure into the ears of the afflicted. Again, what would have been the fate of our reclusive Bradford man if he had brought some snakes up to his flat with the aim of settling down with them for the night in the hope, inspired by these ancient beliefs he had read about, they would cure him of his existential dilemma?

I appreciate that it is theoretically thorny to compare the experiences of a fictional Bradford individual with those of a contemporary Murugan devotee in India, and sick Romans at the turn of the century. But likewise I would suggest it is equally problematic for orthodox psychiatry to argue for a universal biological determinant (stretching across space, culture and time) of the supposed pathological behaviour of our Bradford man. It is a "way of being" and behaviour which is not only *defined* by its context, it also can not be *divorced* from its context. For sure, all cultures may have a way of understanding, talking about, and dealing with aberrant or distressed individuals, or those who they have sidelined to its peripheries. But these categories will vary, dependent on the cultural milieu in which they float. In light of such a perspective, this book can not only be understood as part of a project to construct a new language for conceptualising acute distress. It also, through its call for a unity of voice-hearers, has this very potential to depathologise the experience, possibly enabling the distressed to be less distressed by the stigmatising experience *per se* of having an "auditory hallucination". Perhaps, ultimately, when someone can be "psychotic and proud."

My second objection is to orthodox psychiatry's philosophy of treatment of the severely ill. Aside from the popular complaint from users that, for whatever reason, nurses rarely *talk* to their patients in hospital, if ever readers detect contempt in my account it would most probably be due to my disapproval of enforced treatment, usually via tranquillisers, and the immense powers invested in psychiatry enabling them to proceed unchallenged with such practice. While employed as a mental health worker in Bradford and Leeds, I saw what were the results of mixing conservative psychiatry with distraught psychiatric patients. I have witnessed how psychiatrists and other professionals can react to patients, and how likewise patients can react to psychiatrists and other professionals. For me compulsory treatment (instigated by sectioning) is a main protagonist in fostering the culture of violence – originating from both parties – which sadly afflict our psychiatry wards. Unfortunately acute wards are often hellish scenes of long drawn out conflicts between psychiatry and its patients. Outbursts of physical aggression can, although not always, be desperate actions of a frustrated patient matched by ward nurses' unpleasant duty of constraint, confinement and intravenous injections. Such violence is rarely found in any other hospital ward. But in psychiatric wards we are presented with a hammer house of horrors including compulsory medication and electric shock treatment; isolation rooms; sectioned patients so angry at being denied their freedom they will retaliate; patients so paranoid, threatened and chaotic they will hit out; and staff so pressurised to take action they will inject provocateurs with tranquillisers to silence discontent and anger. Let's face it, many psychiatric wards ooze violence from all corners.

When 22-years-old and fresh from university with a psychology degree I landed my first job with Bradford's mental health services. Within one week of starting work at a residential unit across the road from the city's psychiatric hospital, there was one incident which for me demonstrated the explosive mix of a "troublesome" patient, and compulsory treatment. A heavily medicated 26-year-old schizophrenic man called Ian had thrown a brick through the staffroom's window. My manager's explanation for Ian's behaviour can be paraphrased as: "Ian is mentally ill which is why he threw the brick at the window. We should bear this in mind before deciding whether or not we should fine him for the damage." Such a reaction is far from satisfactory, because in my view Ian hurled the brick for reasons I understand without deferring to a supposed biological mental illness shedding him of responsibility for his actions. In my interpretation, Ian lobbed the brick through the window because he was angry about his predicament – and anger is not pathological. Ian was a loner, who was homeless during periods of his adult life. With a history of petty criminal activity, illicit drug taking, and a rugged appearance capped by an ugly self-shaved mohican Ian can be better described as an anti-social and paranoid pariah. In comparison to Ian, Sid Vicious was charming English gentleman. No one spared much affection for Ian, and I doubt whether he was capable of being affectionate towards anyone himself, at least not according to conventional interpretations of affection. Ian might have heard abusive voices, but I do not know of him being able to talk to anyone

11

about them. On top of all this it was difficult to assess what extent his mind and stability was muddled with neuroleptics. If not cared for by a psychiatric institution, Ian might probably have just lived on the streets or be in prison. Ian was forever antagonistic towards psychiatry which tried to order his life and compelled him to take a daily cocktail of neuroleptics. By my interpretation Ian hurled the brick at the window because perhaps that was the only bitter and feeble retaliation he could muster against constraints he objected to. And, because Ian offered no inclination of an incentive or ability to modify his general behaviour, it was left to psychiatry, equipped with a combination of sections and drugs, to survey and control this social deviant. Without Ian's acquiescence, psychiatry was asked to *control* his disruptive behaviour, while justifying its actions as appropriate treatment for a severely mentally ill patient. But for me, once you have seen through this discourse of biological illness and treatment, you enter the realm of control. Classifying Ian's inabilities and inappropriate social behaviour as a symptom of mental illness is a convenient way of interpreting Ian's condition. But when Ian was later sectioned after throwing the brick, I believe it was a desperate act of control, not treatment

The assumption of the existence of a biological mental illness makes compulsory segregation and drug treatment a smoother, less controversial practice to follow. But how do we proceed if choosing to conceptualise mental distress differently? What if people's deviancy, distress, social inappropriateness and even dangerousness is understood with more emphasis on politics, social conditions, life history and experience than aberrant DNA or brain chemistry? How does society organise itself then? Does it still invest itself with powers to curtail those suspected of being prepared to use physical violence against others? I do not object to the principle of such powers of constraint as I am not anti control *per se*. But let us stop masking control in medicine. I would prefer to see the denial of a person's freedom be conducted after debates heard in publicly accountable judicial courts as in some other European countries, rather than subject to the authority of the signatures of a social worker and two psychiatrists as, for example, in a Section Two Assessment Order. I would prefer to see a patient having the right to a solicitor in the lead up to a section order for either assessment or treatment, so shifting emphasis towards an issue of civil liberties rather than mental illness. Let's put sectioning into the realm of politics and human rights, where an innocent person's propensity for violence would be decided through open civil processes, instead of judgements behind closed doors.

When sectioning (via the civil courts) is necessary (I think it is difficult to envisage a contemporary industrialised society without it), it should be the civil liberty of a patient, however "mad", to refuse physical treatment. As a last resort physical restraint[6] or even isolation. But no compulsory tranquillisers, neuroleptics, or ECT. Compulsory

---

[6] Non-violent martial art skills can be used effectively for such restraint.

treatment incites fear, discontent and distrust, sparking scenes of violent conflicts between an unwilling patient and psychiatric authority. Most importantly, compulsory treatment opens up floodgates for abuse of psychiatry's unrivalled statutory power, which groups such as Survivors Speak Out, Reclaim Bedlam and ECT Anonymous continue to publicise. Psychiatry has been stained with stories of oppressive practice for long enough. Without compulsory physical treatment professionals would have to test out the therapeutic skill of conversation and reassurance to win over a patient's confidence. Many may find this difficult, but can the psychiatric discipline ever expect to work on par with the confidence of the rest of the medical professions if it insists on maintaining its power to inject and electrocute patients when they do not want to be? If a treatment works wonders then great, inform the patient (and the public) of its benefits, and gain their trust. If you can not achieve such a point of communication on Monday's consultation, try again on Tuesday's. Compulsory treatment is often justified "as a last resort". But this is does not reflect what is happening up and down the country. There are usually in fact two options – medication or ECT[7]. Without the well-documented horrors of compulsory treatment, the user movement would have had far less reason to rattle psychiatry throughout the profession's history.

Lastly, while this book adds to the momentum of depathologising and demedicalising voice-hearing, and deconstructing the concept of mental illness, such an endeavour could be equally initiated on the other symptoms of official mental illnesses, as listed in a psychiatric handbook. Chapter six goes some way to do this with "delusions", where such "odd" or "bizarre" interpretations of the world can be related to the experience of voice-hearing. But other so-called symptoms of, for example schizophrenia, include: "illogical thinking", "poverty of speech", "inappropriate affect", "deterioration from a previous level of functioning in such areas as work and self-care", "social isolation", "marked impairment in personal hygiene", "vague or metaphorical speech", and "unusual perceptual experiences". While the concept of "auditory hallucinations" receives the brunt of criticism throughout this book, it would be equally viable to deconstruct these so-called symptoms and in so-doing, reinterpret, redefine, and depathologise them. This would lead us to a more rounded and less rigidly biological analysis of unhappiness, discontent, and the social position of psychiatric patients.

---

[7] Campaigning group The North West Right to Refuse Electroshock Campaign has drawn up a booklet entitled 101 ways to help people suffering from severe depression without using ECT.

Chapter one

Moses – prophet or schizophrenic?

"In the beginning the voices created heaven and earth".
Julian Jaynes' suggested translation from Hebrew to English of Verse 1, Chapter 1, The Book of Genesis, *The Holy Bible*[1], as discussed in *The Origins of Consciousness in the Breakdown of the Bicameral Mind*.

"As the stag ponts after the waterbrooks,
So ponts my mind after you, O gods!
My mind thirsts for gods! For living gods!
When shall I come face to face with gods?"
Psalm 42

"In Europe maybe we should have more gods, while in India you should maybe have more neuroleptics." **Italian psychiatrist Pino Pini addressing Indian delegates at The International Mental Health Conference, 1998, Trivandrum, India.**

Julian Jaynes – everyone used to be schizophrenic
This account of the hearing voices movement aims to gnaw at the roots of traditional psychiatry, to challenge scientific psychology, and to reconsider the relationship between mental distress, religion and spirituality. While chipping away at dominant ideas of madness, its project is to promote alternatives in mental health theory and practice, and challenge established reasoning on the experience of hearing voices, or what orthodox psychiatry calls "auditory hallucinations."

I could have started with reference to one of an array of critical theoretical perspectives that the hearing voices movement has been associated and connected with during its growth. These include social psychiatry, Foucauldian deconstruction, and existentialism. Indeed, as we shall see in later chapters my account touches on an assortment of such philosophies and analyses. But to begin I would like to refer to the late Julian Jaynes' 1976 book, *The Origin of Consciousness in the Breakdown of the Bicameral Mind*. My reason for this is not because references to Jaynes' work thread through this book's entirety, or that it is some kind of bible for the hearing voices

---

[1]Original translators interpreted the Hebrew *elohim* as God. But *elohim* is plural. According to Jaynes, *elohim* does not translate as God, but *the great ones*, and hence, according to his hypothesis, *the voices*.

movement. This is far from the case. But not only does *The Origns of Consciousness* have the historical experience of voice-hearing as central to its thesis, more importantly, as the next chapter reveals, this largely neglected piece of scholarship had a dramatic impact on a Dutch voice-hearing schizophrenic patient and her psychiatrist more than 10 years later which proved significant in planting the seeds of the Hearing Voices Network in the UK.

Jaynes, who died in 1997, was a behavioural psychologist by trade, but his work stretched into other disciplines. *The Origins of Consciousness* is not only devoted to the role of voice-hearing in the development of consciousness, it also treats us to a dazzling re-interpretation of the human mind. As I will demonstrate, Jaynes' work takes us back many thousands of years to also discuss his conceptualisation of the evolution of language, and although it may feel odd that an account of a contemporary mental health movement should set off by attending to an academic's probing into the lives and culture of ancient cave-dwellers and Middle Eastern nomads, Jaynes' thesis, and the debate and discussion it sparks, is important in setting the tone to my project of offering alternatives to our more hegemonic truths. It is also a piece of work which, because of its obscurity, I imagine most readers will not have come across. Although Jaynes' leanings towards biological reductionism and his strong evolutionary understanding of human development may disappoint some critical readers, his work is characteristic of the spirit of this book. For not only is *The Origins of Consciousness* a compelling and captivating story about voice-hearing through the ages, it also invites us to ponder another framework for conceptualising human psychology and voice-hearing.

Jaynes' hypothesis is that prior to 2000 BC *everyone* was schizophrenic, and *everyone* heard voices. The Princeton academic arrived at this stunning proposal from an in-depth critique of what the West understands as consciousness. Drawing on his worldly familiarity with archaeology, anthropology, religion, philosophy, biology and medicine, Jaynes guides us on an historical tour of the world. He weaves through ancient documents and modern anecdotes to propose that consciousness is a relatively novel experience for human beings, and that in the West we have come to accept the idea that human beings are conscious because of unanimous faith in the existence of self-referential psychological constructs such as "I" or "me"; constructs which have steadily evolved in maturity since 2500 BC. Jaynes argues that it is only because we refer to ourselves as an individual "I" or "Me" that we are able to believe we are conscious. He claims that without a belief in (and subsequent experience of) these socially created phenomenon, individuals would be unable to experience a sense of consciousness because they would have no "self" to be conscious of. To try and clarify what may feel like a profound and perplexing idea let us imagine an animal – why not an iguana.

While pointing to this lizard, Jaynes might have argued that it is unable to be conscious because it is not aware of itself – it has no "I" Although contemporary humans, based on their own experience of consciousness, may *believe* an iguana has a minutiae sense of consciousness, it would be more courageous to suggest the iguana has developed a language for conceptualising itself, or describing to on-lookers in any language structure whatsoever that: "I am a lizard." And without subjectivity how can a reptile *believe* in, or in any way be *aware* of its own consciousness? Well, for Jaynes, the first homo sapiens who wandered the earth were about as lacking in consciousness as lizards were….But lest such grand ideas and analogies have been introduced too hastily, we should go back in time to when Jaynes started his analysis of consciousness – to the first Neanderthals.

Neanderthals and the evolution of language

Jaynes' premise is that these first cave people roaming the African wilderness between 80,000 and 40,000 BC were not conscious. He argues that they simply acted, with no ability to be conscious of their actions because their language was no more sophisticated than a repertoire of grunts, growls, hisses and groans. For Jaynes, there was no evidence that such wandering people, not dissimilar to apes, had any experience of subjectivity, or conscious awareness of their existence. Contrary to evolutionists advocating that language and speech was inherent to the genus *Homo* who had walked the world for a previous two million years, Jaynes claims that the little remains of culture or technology excludes the possibility that such people, including the early Neanderthals, had even the elementaries of what we know as speech. According to Jaynes, these people who treaded the savannah with no spoken language other than an assortment of noises, communicated knowledge (such as the construction of hand axes) by imitation, in the same way that chimps transmit the trick of inserting straws into ant hills to access the insects. In line with behaviourist learning theory, Jaynes insists that these early individuals were passive learners and recipients of experience. They had no sense of being subjectively proactive in the discovery and accumulation of knowledge. They were not equipped with, nor had evolution yet constructed, the psychological concepts for one of these people to leap out from their cave shouting: "*I* am fed up with the cold. *I* will discover a way to get warmer."

Jaynes' writing is sprinkled with scientific humility throughout, and with characteristic grace he calls his theory of the evolution of language and consciousness a "rough working hypothesis" rather than a definitive statement of truth. His hypothesis goes on to assert that the first basic elements of human speech would have been the sounds of the communicative calls between these groaning, growling Neanderthal cave people. He suggests that such vocal signals would have been evolutionary beneficial in the increasing cold and darkness of the Fourth Glaciation in northern climates, where inter-

17

personal communication via sound was essential to survive threats from predators prowling in the blackness of night. To reinforce this claim Jaynes, in his animated manner, proposes: "A danger call for immediate present danger would be exclaimed with more intensity, changing the ending phoneme. An imminent tiger might result in 'wahee' while a distant tiger might result in a cry of less intensity, and so develop a different ending such as 'wahoo'. It is these endings, then, that become the first modifiers meaning 'near' and 'far'".

Jaynes continues by suggesting that the next stage of language development would have been marked by a vocabulary of commands coming into use after 40,000 BC during which humans increasingly relied on group hunting in the colder climates when it would have benefited hunters to strike up effective communication with each other. Jaynes' evidence for this second stage of language development was the discovery of tools used during this period. He hypothesises that it would have been the blossoming repertoire of commands that preceded such a surge in tool making. He explains that the construction of such tools would have been largely dependent on such commands. He writes: "We may imagine that the invention of a modifier meaning 'sharper' as an instructed command would markedly advance the making of tools from flint and bone, resulting in an explosion of new types of tools from 40,000 BC up to 25,000 BC."

Nevertheless, despite this embryonic spoken language, there was for Jaynes still up to this period no justification for suggesting that these early people had mastered suitable language for identifying "things" or individuals. He believes there were no concepts for nouns such as trees, animals, tools, or fellow hunters, because they were not understood as separate entities, objects or individuals in the same way we identify them as such. These people certainly had no comparable concepts to our "I" or "self"[2]. Jaynes encourages us to entertain the idea that up to this time consciousness (and self-consciousness) still had not developed, and that these people had no more conscious ability to identify and name a berry as a 21st century dog can a bone.

The use of nouns and the first hallucination
But by 15,000 BC there *was* the first indication of a spoken language inclusive of nouns – specifically the cave drawings representing those things in their environment which mattered most to these hunters, i.e. animals, tools and weapons. Outlining the linguistic

---

[2] Such a view echoes psychoanalytical interpretations where an important stage in an infant's development is to learn, often with bitterness, that it is a separate being from other objects in its life. Melanie Klein attached particular emphasis to such a process in relation to the "good" and "bad" breast. See *Envy and Gratitude and other works, 1946-1963.*

evolutionary processes involved, and keeping to his intriguing tiger example, Jaynes says: "Once a tribe has a repertoire of modifiers and commands, the necessity of keeping the integrity of the old primitive call system can be relaxed for the first time, so as to indicate the referents of the modifiers or commands. If 'wahee' once meant an imminent danger, with more intensity differentiation, we might have 'wakee!' for an approaching tiger, or 'wab ee!' for an approaching bear. These would be the first sentences with a noun subject and a predicative modifier, and they may have occurred somewhere between 25,000 and 15,000 BC."

It was at this watershed of evolutionary development that Jaynes suggests the experience of voice-hearing – which he also calls auditory hallucinations – began. Although accepting substantiation for this claim is problematic considering the lack of archaelogical evidence, he invites us to consider the scene within an increasingly co-operative social group of 15,000 BC where a man is commanded by his chief to set up a fish weir far upstream from a campsite. Although having a basic grasp of speech and language, this man is without consciousness, a self-referential "I", and little, if any, associated sense of volition. So he is incapable of repeating the chief's command of setting up the weir "in his head", as most contemporary westerners believe they do. Instead, proposes Jaynes, he had the language of a repeated "internal" verbal hallucination which instructed him what to do. More of Jaynes' evidence for his emphasis on the pivotal role played by voices in societal organisation is discussed later in the chapter, but indicating how he arrives at what some may feel is a leap of conjecture, Jaynes argues: "If facing directly and conscientiously the problem of tracing out the development of human mentality, such suggestions are necessary and important......Behaviours more closely based on aptic structures [more 'instinctive'] need no temporal priming. But learned activities...do need to be maintained by something outside of themselves. This is what verbal hallucinations would supply." What Jaynes is claiming is that without some kind of apparent guidance these prehistoric people would not have had the appropriate faculties to succeed in carrying out increasingly sophisticated and complex tasks. Performing a duty needed to be directed by someone or something, and it was voices that took on this role because human "instincts" alone were insufficient. What Jaynes is suggesting is if, for example, a 20th century council gardener raking up leaves in the pouring rain wants to return home before 5pm she may remember "in her head" the voice of her boss instructing her to continue until her contracted hour. And so, because of her boss's instructions echoing "in her head" the dutiful gardener may continue diligently with her toils. However, Jaynes would like us to accept that ancient humans would actually have *heard* the voice of their boss, or chief, because they were not equipped with the same degree of consciousness and subjective wilfulness as our contemporary gardener.

Names

Jaynes identified the next important stage of consciousness evolution as being the age of names – when individual people as well as objects were identified through speech. The beginning of the use of names was important because, as we shall see, it meant hallucinated voices could both be attributed to someone, and refer to an individual. Jaynes proposes that the birth of names would have been during the Mesolithic era, about 10,000 to 8,000 BC, when humans were adapting to the warmer post-glacial environment. With increasing grassland hunting, forest life, and shellfish collecting, there would have been a greater stability of population. Jaynes hypothesises: "With these more fixed populations, with more fixed relationships, longer life-spans, and probably larger numbers in the group which had to be distinguished, it is not difficult to see both the need and the likelihood of a carry-over of nouns into names for individual persons." And as individuals became identified by name, so did relationships between these individuals become more intense and long-standing. Whereas previous men and women, like other primates, would have probably left their dead as they fell, hidden or eaten them, the names of these deceased Mesolithic people remained in the early "memory" of their fellows with whom they had been in relationship with while they were alive. For Jaynes the evidence for this higher "respect" and recognition for others was the more elaborate ceremonial graves for the dead as built by, for example, the Mesolithic dwellers of Morbihan in the Middle East who buried their deceased in skin cloaks fastened by bone pins, sometimes crowning them with stag antlers protected with stone slabs. Other graves from the period showed burials with little crowns, ornaments, or flowers in carefully excavated places.

The first town and the first god

So in Jaynes' vision, at around 10,000 BC these ever evolving, but essentially nomadic humans with still no consciousness, had enough speech sophistication to create nouns and names, and the voices played their role in guaranteeing people stuck to the tasks necessary to maintain the functional cohesion of the social group. But what of the names given to these voices? Who were they understood to be or represent?...It is now that Jaynes ushers in the gods! Because it was the gods (initially deified human rulers or kings) who came to be associated with these voices, and Jaynes points us to how and when he conceptualises that gods *first* came into existence in humans' lives. It was around this 10,000 BC period with the momentous transformation of civilisation from hunting-gathering economies to the food-producing economies and domestication of plants (wheat and barley) and herd animals (goats, sheep, cattle and pigs). This was the beginning of the agricultural age. And the most fully studied Mesolithic culture by archaeologists – the Natufians in Israel – provided evidence for Jaynes of the voices of gods which proved to be so instrumental in the social control in these more stable populations.

Jaynes explains that by 9,000 BC the Natufians, named after the Wadi en-Natuf, were burying their dead in ceremonial graves and adopting a settled life, indicated by the first signs of structural buildings, such as the paving and walling of platforms with plaster, and cemeteries spacious enough for nearly 100 burials. Discovered in 1959 at Eynan, this site was about 12 miles north of the sea of Galilee overlooking the swamps and pools of Lake Huleh. Three successive permanent towns dating from about 9,000 BC have been excavated showing each town to have consisted of 50 round stone houses with reed roofs. With a sense of excitement, Jaynes writes: "Now here is a *very* significant change in human affairs. Instead of a nomadic tribe of about 20 hunters living in the mouth of caves, we have a *town* with a population of at least 200 persons."

In his touching style, and with a literary hand stretched out to the reader, he writes: "I beg you to recall, as we try to picture the social life of Eynan, that these Natufians were not conscious. They could not narratize and had no analog selves to 'see' themselves in relation to others. They were what we could call signal-bound, that is, responding each minute to cues in a stimulus-response manner, and controlled by those cues. And what were the cues for a social organisation this large? What signals were the social control over its two or three hundred inhabitants?".......Answer: voices. It was the "hallucinated" voices, either of an individual him/herself or the chief, that kept people at their tasks, and maintained social control essential in a town with such a large population. Explaining that the first voices could well have been similar to verbatim recordings of what the chief or king had commanded, and making insightful comparisons with contemporary voice-hearing experiences, Jaynes elaborates: "After a time there is no reason to suppose that such voices could 'think' and solve problems, albeit, of course unconsciously. The voices heard by contemporary schizophrenics 'think' as much and often more than they do. And thus the voices which I am supposing were heard by the Natufians could with time improvise and 'say' things that the king himself had never said. Always, however, we may suppose that all such novel hallucinations were strictly tied in consistency to the person of the king himself. This is not different from ourselves when we inherently know what a friend is likely to say." And so it was that each worker, perhaps gathering shellfish or trapping small game, had the guiding voice of the king to assist the continuity and utility to the group of his/her labours.

For Jaynes there was also at Eynan the first signs of the voice of a king being re-interpreted after his death as the voice of a *deified* king. His evidence was in how the king's tomb was circular, about 16 feet in diameter, where inside lay two skeletons in the centre extended on their backs, with legs detached after death and bent out of position. One, presumed to be the king's wife, wore a head-dress of dentalia shells. The other, presumably the king, was partly covered with stones and partly propped up on

21

stones, his upright head cradled in more stones, facing the snowy peaks of Mount Hermon, 30 miles away. Years later, the entire tomb was surrounded by a red-ochered wall or parapet, and two large flat stones were paved over the top of the tomb, roofing the bodies in. On the roof a hearth was built. Another low circular wall of stones was built still later around the roof-hearth, with more paving stones on top of that, and three large stones surrounded by smaller ones set in the centre. Continuing his hypothesis Jaynes surmises: "I am suggesting that the dead king, thus propped up on his pillow of stones, was in the hallucinations of his people still giving forth his commands, and that the red-painted parapet and its top tier of a hearth were a response to the decomposition of the body, and that, for a time at least, the very place, even the smoke from its holy fire, rising into visibility from furlongs around, was... a source of hallucinations of the commands that controlled the Mesolithic world of Eynan."

Jaynes then presents his evidence for the on-going generational cycle of heard regal voices. The fact that the royal tomb contained previous burials which had been pushed aside for the dead king and his wife suggests its former occupants may have been earlier kings. The skull beside the hearth on the second tier above the propped-up king suggests it may have belonged to the first king's successor. Jaynes claims: "Gradually the hallucinated voice of the old king became fused with that of the new." It is with this particular sentence that the reader can begin to scent the significance that Jaynes attaches to the role of gods' voices in the subsequent history of humanity. Kings once dead were recreated as gods, and the voices of kings became the voices of gods. And what better example of this spiritual metamorphosis than the Osiris myth which was the power behind the majestic dynasties of Egypt.

The world-view blossoming from Jaynes' interpretation of the significance of deities' voices drifts tantalisingly under the reader's nose, as he lauds that the findings at Eynan represented the birth of modern civilisation, with gods (and their voices) playing a central role in the growth of the civilised town-dwelling populations. Gods, their blessing and their guidance were implicated throughout the unfolding of history up to the present day. And whatever culture you care to focus on (Ancient Egypt, Aboriginal Australia, Middle Age Catholic Europe, Indigenous Americans, Islamic Middle East, or European Protestantism), how relentless and unsurpassed was the influence of gods, in all their colourful creeds and manifestations, throughout civilisation for the next 10,500 years.

But still no consciousness
Yet, in Jaynes' analysis, ancient people up to about 2,000 BC – including the 9,000 BC Natufians and the 5000 BC colonies of the Tigris-Euphrates and Nile valleys – still did

not have what we in the West experience as subjectivity. They still had no comparable concepts to 20th centuries' "I", or "ego", and no intentions, motivations or desires stemming from some inner "self". Hence they had no ability to think via the same "inner" network of systematic cognitive processes as contemporary cognitive psychology suggests we do. So, when faced with a "dilemma" or "decision" to make, these people did not "think" their way logically through to another decision – they acted on voices they heard. It could be said that the voices were a substitute for our thoughts. An essential feature, therefore, of Jaynes' hypothesis, was that up to the second millennium BC people had a *bicameral* mind consisting of an executive part – the voice which gave instructions and orders; and a following part – an individual man or woman who did as the voice commanded. And, emphasises Jaynes, they *really* did hear these voices, no less real than when we hear the voice of someone speaking to us. If bitten by a snake on the banks of the Nile and "wondering" whether to walk home or shout for help, these bicameral people would not have decided themselves on what action to take because they were unable to. They had no sense of themselves. It would have been the hallucinated deified voice of the leader who would have made that decision for them.

The Iliad
But what other evidence does Jaynes put forward to support what he himself calls the "preposterous" hypothesis that these ancient bicameral people led their lives according to the guidance of voices? To bolster his case he turns to documents collated at a time when "writing" first began. The first signs of such literary practice dates back to around 3000 BC, and Jaynes calls it a "curious and very remarkable practice (involving)....a transmutation of speech into little marks on stone or clay or papyrus so that speech can be seen rather than just heard, and seen by anybody, not just those within earshot at the time." The Judaeo-Christian bible (which I shall refer to later) was one of the earliest known pieces of writing, but Jaynes argues that the first writing in human history in a language of which there is enough certainty in translation to consider in connection to his hypothesis is the Greek Iliad.

"There is in general no consciousness in the Iliad," asserts Jaynes with characteristic audacity. He claims that this story of the ancient Greek heroes – believed to have occurred at around 1230 BC, and not written down until between 900 and 850 BC – is an epic documenting the minds of people who acted on the instruction of voices of gods, and not on any notion of free will. For Jaynes there is no suggestion of self-determination in the Iliad, and he proposes that the voices of gods played the role of subjective consciousness. As the Iliad clearly expresses, it was the gods who advised Hector, and spoke to Achilles, Agamemnon and Helen. Although the reader may presume it was the men and women themselves who were responsible for their own behaviour, what was it like for the person him/herself? Where is the testimony that Iliadic people had subjectivity, conscious plans, reasons or motives? As the story narrates it was the voices of gods who sparked off quarrels among men which really caused war; it is a god who grasps Achilles by his yellow hair and warns him not to strike Agamemnon; a god who rises out of the sea and consoles him; a god who whispers to Helen to sweep her heart with homesick longing; a god who hides Paris in a mist in front of the attacking Menelaus; a god who leads armies into battle. "They were voices whose speech and directions could be distinctly heard by the Iliadic heroes as are heard by schizophrenic patients, or just as Joan of Arc heard her voices.....the gods are what we now call hallucinations," continues Jaynes. He states that in these days of the bicameral mind any action which required a decision was sufficient to bring on an auditory hallucination, or voice[3]. So, Hector faced with the decision of whether to go outside Troy's walls to fight Achilles or to stay within them, under the stress of the decision hallucinates the voice that tells him to go out.

Of course we can accuse Jaynes of entertainingly concocting a charming theory from what might have been the Illiad's story-tellers mere literary style, and that the roles of the Illiad gods were hyped up to create a riveting and dramatic fairy-tale. The part played by the gods could have also reflected the Illiad's story-tellers (*aoidoi*) unfamiliarity with expressing psychological dynamics. Jaynes's emphatic response is: "Not only is there no reason to believe that the Aoidoi had any conscious psychology they were trying to express, such a notion is quite foreign to the whole texture of the poem.....And as for the gods, the Iliadic authors and the Iliadic characters all agree in the acceptance of this divinely managed world. To say the gods are an artistic apparatus is the same kind of thing as to say that Joan of Arc told the Inquisition about her voices merely to make it all vivid to those who were about to condemn her."

The Bible
For Jaynes' second source of written evidence for his hypothesis he returns to the Middle East towards the end of the second millennium BC with its half-nomadic people with no fixed grazing ground. Many were refugees from the Thera destruction, and Assyrian and Dorian invasions. Jaynes states that to the established city-states these refugees were desperate outcasts of the desert wilderness, demonised as robbers and vagrants, occasionally organising into whole tribes raiding the city peripheries for cattle and produce. He narrates poetically: "The word for vagrants in Akkad, the language of

---

[3] I do not think such an experience is far removed from ours. When faced with a difficult, soul-searching decision we tend to assess all the options/voices "in our head". But what is the source of these inner narratives? Further discussion of this theme in chapter six.

Babylon, is *khabiru*, and so these desert refugees are referred to on cuneiform tablets. And *khabiru*, softened in the desert air, becomes *hebrew*." And of course the story of these particular nomads is retold in the bible, a bestseller throughout the history of Western civilisation. It is this text that Jaynes next turns his intellectual attention to.

The first four books of the bible – Genesis, Exodus, Leviticus and Numbers – are, for Jaynes, stories reflecting human psychology from the ninth to the fifth century BC. Importantly, it was a time in history when the voices of bicameral people were being replaced by a subjectivity which was increasingly culturally necessary for town-dwelling people. Jaynes explains that with their large number of fixed people, towns could function more harmoniously via a permanent authority rather than the less organised and idiosyncratic nature of voices. Through the process of evolution, these settled people began to increasingly lead their lives according to centralised written law, and less from the guidance of the prophetic few who could still hear voices.

But during this watershed era, when subjectivity was proving evolutionary beneficial for the social cohesion of towns, Jaynes concludes that the writers of these first four books of the bible were nostalgically harking back to the days of the bicameral mind, when God – the authority above all man-made law – spoke directly to his people. The books recount the history of the Hebrews, enslaved by the "civilised" town-dwelling Egyptians, who are led by voice-hearing Moses out of bondage and onto The Promised Land. Moses, and other Hebrew fathers like Abraham and Jacob, were all directed by the voices of their particular god – Yahweh, He-Who-Is. For Jaynes, the Hebrew story is an insight into the experiences of its bicameral leaders whose decisions were made according to voices. Abraham almost killed his son, Issac, on the orders of his voice (Genesis, 22); Jacob led his family to the land of his kindred after the Lord spoke to him (Genesis, 31); and Moses heard, through a burning bush, the voice of God instructing him to "bring forth my people the children of Israel out of Egypt" (Exodus, 3). These first four books are quite clear in their message. Never did Moses, Abraham, or Jacob *think, feel or believe*, they acted on what God *said, commanded, instructed or ordered*. Never did they *feel* his presence, they *heard* him. This is in tune with Jaynes's hypothesis that the Hebrews were one of the last tribes led by a voice-hearer, even though Moses, under 20th century medical scrutiny, was a deluded chronic schizophrenic with auditory hallucinations[4]. In the same vein, Jaynes points out that the voice which told Abraham to beget a son, then sacrifice him, and finally to spare him, is how a criminal psychotic might be directed today.

---

[4] You can click on connected discussion groups at Jaynes' website (http://www.home.sprintmail.com/~marcel1/essays.html) to read of views that Christianity was founded on the basis of visual and auditory hallucinations and delusions of severely mentally ill individuals.

The bible also tells how, when the Hebrews became nomadic after their exodus from Egypt, they encountered societies led by other gods. These societies led the Hebrews astray, as documented after the death of Joshua: "And they forsook the Lord God of their fathers, which brought them out of the land of Egypt, and followed other gods, the gods of the people that were round about them, and bowed themselves unto them, and provoked the Lord to anger. And they forsook the Lord, and served Baal and Ashtaroth," Judges (2:12-13). This reflected the conflict between different voice-hearing societies over whose god was the True One, which precursed the demise of bicameral societies and encouraged the advent of the less ephemeral authority of written law and subjectivity. For example, Gideon heard a voice which he identified as Yahweh who instructed him to tear down his father's altar to the bastard god, Baal, and build one to himself. Gideon, guided by this voice of Yahweh, then proceeded to deliver the Israelites from the oppressive Midianittes, and ushered the story of the marginalised Hebrews forward to its next chapter

Nevertheless, up to 400 BC as culturally beneficial subjectivity took hold, so voice-hearing societies fade into the distance, their numbers dwindling, their authority doubted, their authenticity questioned. And as bicameral voice-hearing people declined, the authority of subjective Hebrew moral teachers such as Ezra and Ecclesiastes who studied the written law of Yahweh without hearing him directly took their place. Although groups of bicameral people roaming the wilderness were now scarce, these prophets were consulted at times of strife, as Ahab king of Israel did in 835 BC, when he "rounded up 400 of them like cattle to listen to their hue and clamor." (I Kings 22:6). But it was also a time when groups of voice-hearers, for perhaps the first time in history, were victimised and even purged. From time to time they were hunted and slaughtered as Elijah did to the prophets of Baal (I Kings 18:40). Although some individual prophets such as Amos and Jeremiah, who did still hear voices, survived without the group support of other hallucinators, by the time of Zechariah (13: 3-4) parents who caught their children chattering with voices were advised to kill them. By their pathologisation of voice-hearers perhaps Elijah and Zechariah were the forebears of 20th century psychiatry.

"Once one has read through the Old Testament from this point of view," Jaynes writes, "the entire succession of works becomes majestically and wonderfully the birth pangs of our subjective consciousness. No other literature has recorded this absolutely important event at such length or with such fullness. Chinese literature jumps into subjectivity in the teaching of Confucius with little before it. India hurtles from the bicameral Veda into the ultra subjective Upanishads." The Old Testament reflects a time when "evolutionary selection helped move the gene pool of humanity towards subjectivity." For Jaynes, the Fall of Adam and Eve, when "they knew that they were naked" (Genesis 3:7) represents itself the myth of the demise of gods and the beginnings of (self) consciousness.

World view

Jaynes' theorising grows in grandeur as each page is leafed. He asserts that all religion is a "search for authorisation". Commenting on the present day, he writes: "All about us lie the remnants of our recent bicameral past....we have our house of gods which record our births, define us, marry us, and bury us, receive our confessions and intercede with the gods to forgive us our trespasses." Even the scientific revolution failed to prevent our fascination with a human relationship to a greater and wholly other. Not only did pioneering scientists such as Galileo, Newton and Locke see their role in the Age of Enlightenment to write down the natural laws of God, but the godless grand theories of Marxism, psychoanalysis and Darwinism, Jaynes argues, are in themselves representative of the search for The One Truth or The One Voice. Finally, Jaynes admits with ever pervasive modesty that his own theory is no exception to this quest. "The very notion of truth is a culturally given direction, a part of the pervasive nostalgia for an earlier certainty," he writes. It is this humility which falls cosily into the lap of the postmodern era and cultural relativity which, as we shall see in subsequent chapters, cradled the hearing voices movement.

Schizophrenia

Jaynes heard voices once himself – during one afternoon while lying on his couch in a half awake/half asleep hypnagogic state. He also has a lucid appreciation of the voices of a person diagnosed schizophrenic. "They converse, threaten, curse, criticise, consult, often in short sentences. They admonish, console, mock, command, or sometimes simply announce everything that is happening. They yell, whine, sneer, and vary from the slightest whisper to a thunderous shout.....They call from one side or another, from the rear, from above and below; only rarely do they come from directly in front of the patient. They may seem to come from walls, from the cellar and the roof, from heaven and from hell, near or far, from parts of the body and parts of the clothing."

Jaynes' biologism (much of *The Origins of Consciousness* is devoted to an analysis of the evolutionary development of brain structure) and deference to orthodox medical discourses on schizophrenia may be anathema to some readers, but what Jaynes did for the schizophrenic diagnosed voice-hearer was not only pre-empt the normalising of the experience of hearing voices, but in associating the experience with figures such as Moses, Jesus and Joan of Arc he drew parallels, made connections, and threaded a story for the voice-hearer which the schizophrenic had never been a character in before.

Voice-hearing, although framed as a remnant of an evolutionary past, was painted as much a historical consistency as a pathological abnormality. The schizophrenic's voices were equal in their reality to those that Paul the Apostle referred to in his letter to the Corinthians: "There are, it may be, so many kinds of voices in the world, and none of them is without significance." (Chapter 10:14).

Although Jaynes' account dabbled in the supposed biological defects of schizophrenics, such as overactive dopamine systems and enzyme deficiencies, he accentuated the *social* role of the voices which can plague people with a diagnosis of schizophrenia. In cultures, such as the Hebrews, where voices were attributed to the word of gods, their influence on the hearer was, as Jaynes suggests, immense. In addition, he recognises that while the voices of distressed schizophrenics may have less religious authority in our secular age they still play the same commanding role as they did for bicameral people. Using an example fittingly in tune with the following chapters of this book he says: "Occasionally the voices are recognised as authorities even within the hospital. One woman heard voices that were mainly beneficial which she believed were created by the Public Health Service to provide psychotherapy......They constantly gave her advice, including, incidentally, not to tell the psychiatrist that she heard voices." The modern schizophrenic, for Jaynes, is lost in a cultural time warp. With tyrannical, overwhelming and authoritative voices, any sense of an "ego" "self" or "I" which the modern Western conscious being is so indebted to, can be threatened or dissolved. "With no cultural support and acceptance for the voices, the result can be the social withdrawal of the hearer. Compare this to the *absolutely* social individual of bicameral societies," says Jaynes. "The modern schizophrenic is an individual in search of such a culture....in effect, he is a mind bared to his environment, waiting on gods in a godless world," he concludes.

Jaynes' critics
Jaynes's conceptualisation of the human condition is rarely discussed within academic circles – it is small fry compared to Freudian psychoanalysis or Darwinian evolution. We do not talk about, or refer to, our "remnants of bi-cameral mind" as we do our psychoanalytical "unconscious" or evolutionary "survival instinct". Discussion of Jaynes' work appears to be more confined to obscure Internet chat-groups than included in essential reading lists for psychology and philosophy degree courses. Jaynes' ideas have simply not been developed or expanded by any mainstream academic discipline, and I have yet to locate a comprehensive critique of his work, perhaps because it does not fit neatly into any one particular discipline. Certainly, it appears that no recognised scholar has tackled in depth Jaynes' hypothesis of the bi-cameral mind, and the concept of voice-hearing in human consciousness. As an indication of the silent rejection of Jaynes' work, *The Oxford Companion to Philosophy,* for example, does not mention Jaynes once, neither does 1997's *The Contemporary Philosophy of Mind,* apart from a reference in a footnote. The most

credit given to Jaynes by mainstream American and UK philosophers of mind/consciousness appears to be Daniel Dennett's praise in *Consciousness Explained* for his "boldly original speculations". The Americanised discipline of the philosophy of the mind is dominated by the "mind as machine" analogy, where cognitive models are favoured above all others. And some of its philosophers, who endeavour to reduce the phenomenon of consciousness to computer-like cognitive processing in the brain, can not accept Jaynes' non-cognitive approach. For example, in *Consciousness Reconsidered*, Owen Flanagan, Professor of Philosopher at Duke University, criticised with arrogant disdain Jaynes' colourful descriptions of consciousness. He wrote: "Such descriptions seemed like a good thing for a psychologist interested in gaining a reputation, *not to study*...as appealing as they might be to mushy-minded mystics they hold no interest to the scientist of the mind." Ouch! For such reasons, it appears that despite Jaynes' scholarship there has been little whole-hearted and serious critical discussion of Jaynes' work in mainstream philosophy, and certainly not in psychology or psychiatry.

But such neglect from the mainstream should provoke a critical inquisitiveness, and suffice to say, Jaynes' work is a story of the human condition which challenges our own dominant conceptualisation of consciousness, subjectivity and psychology. Another reason for the little coverage by mainstream academia of Jaynes' work could be that it's protagonists have little interest in the phenomenon of voice-hearing. This, of course might be different if you were a voice-hearer, or had an interest in how the experience relates to our theorising about human psychology...When is a voice a thought? When is a thought a voice? Is there a "self", or have we just been led/persuaded to accept that such a thing exists? Even if you find deficiencies in Jaynes' vision it may be different if you hear voices yourself. The next chapter reveals how significant Jaynes' theory proved to be for at least one voice-hearer.

Chapter two

Freedom to hear voices and the birth of the hearing voices movement

You believe in a God we never see or hear, so why shouldn't you believe in the voices I really do hear?" **Dutch voice-hearer Patsy Hage, diagnosed schizophrenic, to her psychiatrist, Professor Marius Romme.**

Imagine losing your mind. Uncontrollable and relentless voices bombard you from all angles. Distressed and unable to comprehend who the voices are, what they are, or why they are directed at you, you become locked into a world where no one else lives. You swiftly end up with a diagnosis of schizophrenia – one of the most stigmatising labels of western industrialised society. But unsatisfied with how medical psychiatry labels your experience, you shift and search through old and new writings on psychology, the mind, philosophy, spiritualism and religion. Looking for an alternative answer, a reason that makes sense. A solution, other than biology, that can authenticate and legitimise your experience. After all, you can't really be mad?

Patsy Hage and Marius Romme

In 1986 Patsy Hage, from Maastricht, Holland, was hearing 20 different voices, and she had heard voices since she was 14-years-old. During her childhood Hage's voices were mixed – both troublesome and amicable. But she managed to get through school OK[1]. "The voices were nice to me in the beginning when I started hearing them," said Hage. "They protected me against quarrels at home and at school. When there were situations which I didn't feel comfortable with they comforted me as well. They kept me busy with conversations and with jokes. It was pleasant then, and I had quite a lot of conversations with them. While I was taking a shower, or on my way to school."

But as Hage reached adulthood the voices took on a more sinister role, testing her strength by their dictatorial nature. They forbade her to leave the house or to have visitors, and did not allow her to open the door when the doorbell rang. Her voices instructed her not to attend her singing lessons or sporting activities. They messed up her job and her friendships. Over time, Hage reached the point where for periods the voices captivated her, and she could not resist their commands. Even though they had

---

[1] See Asylum – Magazine for Democratic Psychiatry, 1994. Vol 8 (Nov) for report on *Congres voor Kinderen die Stemmen Horen* (Trans: A conference for children who hear voices) Amsterdam, 1993.

such an influence on her life, she did not tell anyone about her voices for years – mostly because they forbade her to. She developed her own conceptions of who the voices represented. "I used to think they were all-knowing and all-powerful gods who managed and determined everything on earth," she was to say in public later. She tried to ally herself with her gods, and, like all devotees, brought her gods offerings. But Hage's gods did not abate, and she then concluded that the voices were connected in some way to home, so she ran away. It was no surprise that she ended up at the juvenile section of the Department of Social Psychiatry in Maastricht with a diagnosis of schizophrenia. She then just feared she was insane.

Up to this time, even though Hage believed she was the only one who heard voices, she did have a keen intellectual curiosity. Therefore, when she was lent a copy of Jaynes's book it was bound to cause a stir. Let us remember what this pioneering American psychologist wrote: "We could say that before the second millennium BC *everyone* was schizophrenic." What a personal discovery this must have been for the inquisitive Hage, who had felt so adrift with the lack of validation for her experience, and what a message it was to later prove to be for voice-hearers. Hage was absorbed by Jaynes's swashbuckling theory and discussed it with her psychiatrist, Professor Marius Romme, who had lent her the book in the first place.

Romme was attentive to what his distressed patient had to say – especially as he was concerned about her increasing talk of suicide. Nevertheless Romme still felt Hage was on a road from which she would never return. "Neuroleptics had no effect on her voices," wrote Romme later. "They did reduce the anxiety induced by the voices, but they also lowered her mental alertness. The only positive element in our communication at that time was a theory she developed about the phenomenon of the voices." That theory was, of course, based on what she had learnt from *The Origins of Consciousness*. But Romme's background was still that of a physician. Although throughout his professional career he had always taken an interest in a social model of mental distress, Romme's medical training told him that voices were symptomatic of acute disease. So it took Hage a whole year, during her consultations with Romme, to make in-roads into her psychiatrist's framework and gently persuade him that the "medical disorder" she was said to have was not such a signed and sealed issue. In fact, Romme said: "Hage played a large part in persuading me that the voices were not necessarily pathological, but had in fact been with her on-going for a period of approximately eight years." The effect of Hage's literary discovery on Romme's outlook was a milestone as he began to ponder how her theory of voice-hearing would be accepted by others who heard voices, and he wondered whether she would be able to communicate empathatically with such people. "If she could, it might have a positive effect on her isolation, her suicidal theory, and her dependent reaction to the voices," concluded Romme. From that point on, matters accelerated."

Sonja on Monday

"I hear voices and I am glad of it." **Speaker at voice-hearers' meeting, Maastricht 1987.**

When Romme and Hage appeared on *Sonja on Monday*, a Dutch afternoon chat show, the medicalised historical script of the *schizophrenic* set off on a new tangent, and the emergence of the newly defined *voice-hearer* began in earnest. Science journalist Sondra Escher, Romme's wife, organised the increasingly confident Hage and her psychiatrist to appear on this live broadcast, where Hage, who still lectures periodically on the international mental health circuit, chatted informally with Sonja about her experience. One of the show's aims was to initiate contact with other voice-hearers in Holland, whether or not they had contact with psychiatry, to find out in what ways people could or could not cope with their voices. Sonja invited voice-hearing viewers to phone in and leave their name and address, and it succeeded in being an unprecedented media coup in bringing together 450 voice-hearers, some with successful strategies for dealing with the experience, others without. All of the 450 voice-hearers were sent a questionnaire asking them about their experience and ways of dealing with voices. Another positive response to the programme was the organising of 300 voice-hearers to attend a Maastricht congress in October 1987 to share their thoughts and experiences with each other. Foundation Response, a user's movement endeavouring to break the taboo of voice-hearing, was formed, as was Resonance, a self-help organisation. The following year, the Chief Inspector for Mental Health from the Dutch Ministry of Health and Welfare opened another Maastricht conference, *People Who Hear Voices*, organised by Foundation Response and the Department of Social Psychiatry. This represented a chance for voice-hearers to take to the podium, and share their experience with an attentive professional audience.

Copers and non-copers.

Almost 200 of the 450 dispatched questionnaires were returned, and then used by Romme and Escher to formulate an "emancipatory" way of working with psychiatrised voice-hearers. Over the next 10 years their work was published in a range of medical and mental health publications in America and Europe, including the *British Journal of Psychiatry* and *The Schizophrenia Bulletin*. Their 1993 edited book *Accepting Voices* is the most extensive elaboration of their work and ethos. Published by MIND, UK's leading mental health charity, it was awarded its book of the year prize. But while progressives and radicals welcomed the sparkling fresh ideas in *Accepting Voices* this can be contrasted to the frosty reception the book received from the UK's medical establishment. In the *British Medical* Journal, Birmingham Professor of Psychology Raymond Cochrane, wrote a damning critique, even claiming the book's message was "potentially dangerous" to voice-hearers, because the philosophy of "accepting" voices meant colluding with delusionary beliefs. In fact Cochrane found the book's message so spooky that when he read what Romme

33

himself wrote it sent "a chill down the reader's spine." Nevertheless and ironically, at the same time Cochrane was demonising *Accepting Voices*, psychologists working in his own city and just further up the M6 in Liverpool were incorporating Romme's work in to their own practice (see chapter six). So what was it exactly about Romme and Escher's work that got such approval from some quarters, but raised such hackles in others?

Based on the 1987 Maastricht conference, the replies to the questionnaires, and Romme's own clinical experience, they defined three chronological phases experienced by those who had learnt to cope with voices.

1. The startling phase

"It was 2.20 in the morning. I awoke suddenly. It was pitch black in the bedroom, but what was that noise? Who was crying so pitifully? It sounded like Marie – but she lived four miles away, so how could it be? How could I possibly hear her whimpering and sobbing in my room, when she lived so far away? The sound seemed to be registering in the middle of my brow. I was thrown into utter confusion. I didn't understand what was taking place. Then, at once, I realised...2.20 a.m. Now I knew why Marie was crying out, screaming to me, 'I'm frightened! I'm frightened! It's back in the room again!' She was being haunted.' **Stephen O'Brien, medium, in** *Visions of Another World – The Autobiography of a Medium.*

Complete fear, panic and mental chaos. Such is the terrible state people can be thrown into after hearing their first voices. Romme called this the "startling phase", and more than 80 per cent of Romme's sample heard their first voice after the age of 20. In a society where hearing voices is likely to be perceived as evidence of madness, who can you turn to after such a startling but taboo experience? Keeping it to yourself, or seeking religious/spiritual or medical help are the main options facing someone distraught by the intrusion of voices, particularly those of a negative nature. Wales' Stephen O'Brien, who has inherited the position of the UK's most famous spiritualist medium since the death of the popular Doris Stokes, sought the guidance of his grandmother when he first heard voices as a child. With spiritual leanings herself she validated her grandson's experience, consoling him that in her view he was blessed with a special gift. She could just have easily arranged an appointment for her grand-son to see a GP, and this may have had very different repercussions for O'Brien. But with support from his family O'Brien appears to have sailed through his own startling phase, and now he is internationally renowned as a clairvoyant and medium, who by his own accounts has heard the voices of hundreds of spirits.

But O'Brien's experience is in stark contrast to one of the speakers at the Maastricht conference who said: "At ten o'clock one Sunday morning it was as though I had suddenly received a totally unexpected enormous blow on my head. I was alone, and there was a message. A message at which even the dogs would turn up their noses. After that, the voices gave me no peace. They were everywhere – inside my head, behind me, in front of me. It seemed as though I had telephone lines inside my chest. At first I was even silly enough to look inside my shirt to see where they came from – perhaps there was a microphone or something. I thought that it was unbelievable – it seems as though I had a complete built-in telephone exchange." "Startling" almost understates such a ferocious and disturbing first encounter with voices. Because of the devastating short-term effects on one's state of mind we might compare the impact for some of hearing such voices as being told you have cancer, or receiving the news that a loved one died in a car crash.

2. The organisational phase

"For some, the period of confusion [of hearing voices] only lasts a few weeks or months, whereas for others this phase continues for years," wrote Romme in *The Schizophrenia Bulletin.* "Most describe this period as one of great fear, panic and a feeling of powerlessness." Orthodox psychiatry might understand it as acute psychosis.

Romme listed the various methods people used to cope with their voices. Some, he wrote, are more effective than others. For example, one possible reaction is to become irritable or even infuriated by the intrusive behaviour of voices. This is the kind of response we all might have towards someone who persistently harasses or bothers us. Because they frustrate us we shout back. But the problem is that this may aggravate them more, reinforcing the battle lines. The voices of a voice-hearer may adhere to the same kind of logic. One Maastricht speaker believed his voices were of people telepathising with him, and he became annoyed when they kept intruding on his privacy. So he finally decided to confront the people he suspected were telepathising to him. When they denied such communication, the speaker went headlong into the conspiracy theory that every one was against him. Such a reaction is not often fruitful – psychiatric wards all over the world entertain thousands of variations of conspiracy theories, with a patient often sensing they are a central character in the plot. Although magazines such as *Fortean Times,* and the activities of Mulder and Scully in *X Files* parade conspiracy theories as entertainment, to see individuals agonising in the terrors of a conspiracy theory is harrowing to witness let alone experience. (See chapter six for more on conspiracy theories)

Another strategy of dealing with someone, or a voice, that relentlessly bothers you, is to ignore it. Romme stated that about a third of his sample were able to achieve this. But there is a limit to how long you can keep your head buried in the sand. Romme said that for most voice hearers this is not a wise solution, and ignoring the voices can have unpleasant repercussions. Another of the Maastricht speakers related her story: "Finally I decided to ignore the voices and asked them to leave me alone," she said. "In my ignorance I chose the wrong way to handle the problem. You can't just set aside something that exists within yourself and manifests itself so strongly. Moreover, it would lead to the voices losing their right to exist because of lack of attention and energy, and of course this was not what they wanted. Until then the voices had always been polite and friendly, but they changed in the opposite way; they said all kinds of strange things and they made these things that were important to me look ridiculous. It was a full-blown civil war, but I was determined to win, and I continued to ignore everything. And I did so by keeping myself busy the entire day. In that period I solved a lot of crossword puzzles, my house had never been cleaner, and the allotment garden was never taken care of better. The result was that life became more peaceful, but in a constrained way; I nearly couldn't relax anymore." So it seemed that blanketing out all voices may also mean ignoring your friends as well as your enemies. Then again, selectively listening to positive, amicable voices is a useful strategy for some. The above speaker mentioned that whilst she tried to ignore all her voices, she had two voices that endeavoured to assist her. They persistently tried to convince her that she needed them, and so she entered into dialogue with the voices. "As a result I began to feel better," she told delegates.

From their questionnaire sample Romme and Escher compared those who claimed they were able to cope with their voices (70 of the sample had never consulted a psychiatrist) and those who were not. Romme summarised that people able to live with their voices felt stronger than their voices i.e. they had more control over them. They also experienced more positive voices than those less able to cope. Their voices were also not as commanding. "Copers" were more able to listen selectively to their voices and set them limits, for example, only communicating with them during the evening. This contrasts to the "non-copers" who tried to flee their voices in some way. They were also less able or inclined to set limits to the voices.

3. The stabilisation phase
According to Romme those who had learnt to cope with their voices had developed an equilibrium with them. This he called the "stabilisation" phase when a voice-hearer feels more at ease with their voices, and can accept the experience as an essential part of themselves. Romme went as far to say: "one can say they are even glad to hear voices". He explained: "The voices are felt to be part of life and they have a positive influence. In this phase the individual is able to choose between following the advice of the voices or his or her own ideas." Another speaker from the conference exemplified

this phase of stabilisation: "They [the voices] show me the things I do wrong and teach me how to do them otherwise, but they leave the choice to me," she told the audience. "They think the way I listen to music isn't right. I lose myself in music and they think I shouldn't. I tried the way they think I should listen to music but I didn't want to make the effort, I didn't see the use of it. Such a decision is taken in mutual consideration but I have the final choice and the voices always resign to it." Stabilisation, for Romme, is a very different concept to orthodox psychiatry's remission or cure, because it implies developing a balanced, workable positive relationship with voices, rather than being healed of a disease symptom.

Romme's challenge to psychiatry
"At the first conference I attended, some people thought I had lost my mind, and asked me if I too heard voices. Lots of people like to feel professionally safe and like to keep to what is already known. It is not safe to think differently, as is necessary to understand schizophrenia." **Marius Romme, 1988.**

Accepting the subjective reality of voices was to become a cornerstone of the hearing voices movement, and Romme set the ball rolling by directly challenging the logic of medical orthodox psychiatry which might consider "accepting" voices as tantamount to accepting disease. As with Laing in the seventies, mainstream psychiatry was challenged by the ideas of someone from their own ranks. Still now, establishment psychiatry has paid scant attention to Romme's work because of the radically different aetiological angle he approaches the experience of voice-hearing and the concept of schizophrenia. It is to these differences in approach that I now turn to.

Firstly, like Jaynes, Romme appreciates that throughout European history the hearing of voices has been conceptualised as a spiritual experience. That is not to say this was all fine and cheery, because to hear voices could have been either a blessing or curse. For example, during the Middle Ages the Roman Catholic Church may have canonised you for "hearing" the word of God[2], whereas others might have been exorcised to free them from possession. Witches, also suspected of hearing voices, were burnt at the stake. Nevertheless, as Jaynes had documented so extensively, Romme conceded that prior to the birth of medicine and its psychiatry sibling, the hearing of voices had historically been connected with spirituality of some creed.

---

[2] Teresa of Avila (1515-1582) heard voices and experienced visions after prolonged prayer; Joan of Arc (1412 – 1431) was said to have heard voices when she was 13-years-old; Francis of Assisi (1181 –1226) while praying heard the voice (of Christ?) say to him "Repair my home which is falling into disrepair"; Bernadette 1844 –1879 had visions of, and directions from, The Immaculate Conception. As in Saints by Alison Jones, W and R Chambers, 1992

Secondly, Romme emphasised that today an unknown number of perfectly "sane" citizens who have never been psychiatric patients have experienced voices. As well as Romme and Escher's own work, an American study in 1991 reported that 600 out of 15,000 members of the general public heard voices to the extent that it could warrant a psychiatric diagnosis. But only 200 of these individuals admitted being distressed by the experience. In addition, there are also eminent voice-hearers, who are supposed to include Gandhi, Beethoven, Jean-Paul Sartre, Charles Dickens and Carl Jung. (If seeking a contemporary celebrity voice-hearer there is actress Zoe Wanamaker who, speaking on Radio Four's *All in the Mind,* told of a voice which speaks to her as if it is sitting on her shoulder.) Be it as a consequence of "enlightenment" aggravated by nutritional deprivation (Gandhi), a state of drowsy hypnagogia (Beethoven, Sartre and Dickens), "nervous breakdown" (Jung), or maybe for no obvious precedent at all (Wannamaker), all such eminencies are said to have heard voices, if not ever with as over-powering intensity to become concerned enough to seek psychiatric help. But they have been recorded in history not as survivors of an undiagnosed "brief psychotic episode", but icons or celebrities from their respective fields. So, while the bulk of orthodox psychiatry lends its weight to pathologising voice-hearing Romme publicly equated it with the revelatory experiences of some of the most famous names in history.

Thirdly, Romme noted that medication fails to affect the voices of 40 per cent of psychotic patients: the "drug-resistant", difficult-to-treat or chronic schizophrenics. He argued that as medication is not a complete panacea it would be in the mental health profession's interest to try non-physical interventions with such patients (see chapter six).

Fourthly, and perhaps most importantly, Romme argued that the onset and experience of voice-hearing is related to circumstances in a person's life. These may include an intolerable situation in daily life such as harassment or bullying[3]; recent trauma such as bereavement, the end of a relationship, severe physical illness, isolation, torture or physical deprivation; or childhood trauma such as sexual, physical or emotional abuse.

So, Romme understood voice-hearing not as a biologically aberrant misfortune, but a socially meaningful and decipherable phenomenon, where the content of an individual's voices can mirror their social world. Going beyond orthodox psychiatry, which might

---

[3] I remember a 26-year-old man, diagnosed schizophrenic, whom I met at a MIND drop-in centre in Bradford, He related the torrid time he had while being bullied at school. His self-image was rock bottom, he had few friends and suffered from paranoia. He spent the Christmas of 1991 alone in his flat in a council tower block, sitting on a chair watching TV with baked beans on toast as his Christmas dinner. His voices were forever denigrating him, like his bullies.

readily admit that a stressful situation may "trigger" schizophrenic symptoms such as hearing voices, Romme argued that the quality of relationship a person has with her voices can be a reflection of how she is relating to her environment and other people. Therefore, to understand and assist people with their voices involves a reflection on their nature and content. This is the first step in developing a healthy and proper attitude towards the voices, said Romme. Describing his personal practice in Holland, Romme explains: "We begin with a wide inventory of the number of voices, their sex, age, recognisability, who they belong to, how they are organised and what influence they have on the person who hears them. We find out what the voices say and how the person who hears them reacts to what the voices say. We also look at what has happened since the first time the voices were heard."[4]

Voices and the social world

Occasionally the relationship between the voices and a person's environment is relatively straightforward to a third-party observer. Romme offered an example of a 67-year-old woman whose voices continually issued instructions in the patronising tone adults can have with children, such as "be careful you don't stumble" and "button up your coat". When Romme first met this woman she was accompanied by her two daughters. One had her arm around her mother as if she was unable to walk alone. The other was gently pushing her into a chair whilst unbuttoning her coat. Their mother looked uncomfortable with this over zealous attention. After they were all seated, the daughters discussed with Romme their mother's problems, as if she was not in the room. But when the woman herself spoke out about her experience she told Romme how the voices had begun after her husband stopped work, and had taken over the domestic activities and roles which previously had been hers – she was being treated more like a child. "When I friendly told the three family members my impression about what the voices might be expressing, they were all astonished," said Romme. "By exploring, they started to recognise the relationship between what the voices said, and the way the family treated the mother." The voices were an echo of those around her.

Another of Romme's patients, a 24-year-old man, heard voices whom he understood as fascistic powers, which gave him law and order instructions. But what the voices instructed him to do mimicked the authoritarian manner in which he was treated both by his parents and in hospital, and he had never managed to oppose these stifling relationships. So, when aged 18, he first left his parental home to live on his own, he lacked the confidence to make his own decisions – and so he let his voices do it for him. However, by doing so he became dependent on them to the point where they subsumed

[4] The UK's Action Consultancy and Training (see chapter five) offers such a detailed inventory.

his self-control. Then again voices may provide a lonely person with the social stimulation they yearn. "Like one of our patients who takes the voices from people he likes with him to a cafe and drinks coffee with them," recalled Romme. "Or a man who is living on his own. When he has to make important decisions he seeks the voice of a good friend to give advise."

Freedom to hear voices

But Romme and Escher had a more ambitious vision than advertising a new toolbox of coping strategies for those in trouble with voices. They also talked about "emancipation" for voice-hearers, promoting a society where to hear voices, even if they are unpleasant, is an acceptable rather than an insane and awkward-to-discuss-around-the-table experience – a future where people can be out-and-proud to hear voices. Romme made parallels with homosexuality, and draws inspiration from the gay movement: "When I started my education psychiatrists tried to find all kinds of therapy for homosexuality, but they did not solve it. The problem was solved by organisations of homosexuals," said Romme in interview. As a social psychiatrist Romme broadens the perimeters of analysis promoting emancipation over medicalisation. "Science has a democratic background, and it was the political activities of the gay movement, not psychiatry, that removed homosexuality from being classified as a psychiatric illness. Therefore we must organise groups of people hearing voices so that they can help themselves – psychiatry cannot help them," encouraged Romme. This political stance on voice-hearing was to be followed up by some in the UK which we shall turn to later.

Accepting spiritual voices

"How much longer is psychiatry going to rule the roost labelling first one thing, then another, as mental sickness? Look at the record of psychiatric blundering that has quietly been crossed off with no apologies, let alone any compensation for the many victims. Masturbation, homosexuality, having a child out of wedlock, poverty stricken people stealing a loaf of bread to feed their family. These are but a few of the many natural ways of human nature, that in Britain at least, no longer qualify for diabolical forms of treatment psychiatrists inflict upon those they are empowered to label mentally sick." **Bill Warwick of the Liverpool Hearing Voices Group, 1992. Warwick appealed to spiritualists to challenge orthodox psychiatry's pathologising of voice-hearing.**

"If spirituality had not existed, people in psychosis would have invented it," **Edward Povell in *The Seduction of Madness*, 1990**.

A gypsy at the bar

In April, 1997, I was working behind the bar at the GMEX, Manchester's exhibition centre, during the World Table Tennis Championships. We were particularly busy, so more staff were called on to deal with the workload. These included 28-year-old Vicky. We were working at the same bar, and while chatting I explained to her how I was writing a book on the hearing voices movement, and started informing her of the Hearing Voices Network in Manchester. She seemed interested, so I went on to mention how some spiritualists and mediums would recognise the experience of hearing voices, while calling it clairaudience. At this point Vicky became animated, telling me how she herself heard voices. "I have heard them since I was a child," she said. "The mother's side of my family comes from an Irish gypsy descent where fortune-telling and clairvoyance are all part of our background." I was very inquisitive and quizzed Vicky more about her experience, including asking her where exactly she heard her voices. She replied: "On my brow mainly. Sometimes if I walk past someone and brush them I might be told something about them – it is like a wave of electricity."

We hit an instant rapport, and in between serving cokes to table tennis champions from all over the globe (and whiskies to their country's bureaucrats) we chatted about voices. Vicky explained to me how voice-hearing, or clairaudience, was recognised by her parents as a special skill, and they did not see it as unusual, although Vicky's friends and husband found it all a bit "weird."

As well as hearing voices, Vicky offered an example of the clairvoyant skill she also believed she possessed. "My husband and I were with some friends who had just had a baby. As I held the baby I just felt that something terrible was going to happen to it. I didn't dare mention it to the mum and dad – it would not have been right. But on the way home I said to my husband how I knew this baby was to become very ill. My husband did not know what to make of it, and just ignored me, but later my friend told me how they had to take the child to hospital with a serious infection!"

On the second and last day that we worked together, Vicky served coffee to a Swedish champion and they exchanged pleasantries. "He is going to lose his match tomorrow," Vicky asserted to me with confidence. In anticipation I watched the game the next day on the TV overlooking the bar. Sure enough the Swede lost. Interestingly, Vicky is to start training as a mental health nurse.

The Church and madness

Before discussing Romme's stance on the role of spiritual voices, let us take a brief look at the Christian Church's view of its relationship with psychiatry and the mentally distressed. Because interestingly, although Jesus was judged by the influential chief priests of his day to be a blaspheming heretic, he was also one of our most famous voice-hearers[5] (who by all accounts definitely could cope with his voices). However, as the story goes, the price Jesus paid for his confident forthrighteousness, his alleged voices and subsequent blasphemy of failing to publicly deny he was the Son of God, was to be nailed to a wooden cross. It is worth noting that although Jesus was ridiculed by the established clergy of his day he was also supposed to have healed those unable to cope with torrents of unpleasant voices – outcasts such as "lunatiks", and those "possessed with devils" (St Matthew 4: 24). Today, in Europe[6] at least, these "lunatiks" face medicine, as they have in various forms since The Renaissance.

The Archbishop of Canterbury represents the Anglican church's official line in Britain. And in 1996 this is what Archbishop George Carey had to say to the Royal College of Psychiatrists about the uneasy relationship between psychiatry and

---

[5] See Jesus's conversations with the "Devil" after his 40 day, 40 night fast in the wilderness (such as. "And when the tempter came to him, he said, If thou be the Son of god, command that these stones be made bread." Matthew: 4: 3) Based on Julian Jaynes' reasoning discussed in chapter one, is Matthew revelling in poetic licence, or did Jesus really hear such a voice precipitated by a lengthy period of physical deprivation?

[6] At The International Mental Health Conference, 1998, in Kerala, Southern India, delegates heard how medical psychiatry is increasingly building bridges in the more rural areas of the state, complementing the area's indigenous healing methods. Delegates were told of the more extreme methods of controlling/healing the sickest of individuals. These included being tied to a tree outside a temple for up to a week in the hope that the temple's gods would heal the afflicted. Of course, subsequent debate questioned whether it was preferable to tie the most seriously distressed to a tree or forcibly inject them with medication, or whether either were legitimat options.

religion: "Some clergy have resented the way in which parishioners now turn to counsellors and psychiatrists when they might have come to them in the past." Acknowledging that "there are millions of people on this planet who are not materialists, agnostics or atheists", Mr Carey called for a closer partnership between psychiatry and Christianity, and he lamented psychiatry for not being prepared to take account of the religious or spiritual realities of patients.

Interesting as it is that the archbishop makes this criticism, I wonder what he would have to say about the *voices* that many of these patients hear? Would he accept that they are spiritually valid, or would he defer to the psychiatric view of labelling them as evidence of disease? Whatever the case, contemporary Christianity like all other Western religions, has not been noted by its commitment to publicly recognise the spiritual meaningfulness of the voices of those inside psychiatric wards.

Romme and spiritual voices

But while contemporary organised religion is conservative in its thinking, Romme was bolder, and publicly trod on territory that no psychiatrist before him had ventured onto. Whilst most of his medical psychiatric colleagues declined to respect the spiritual voices of their patients, labelling them as a disease symptom, or even an illness in its own right (Spiritual Disorder is now a DSM[7] IV category of Mental Illness) Romme accepted the subjective spiritual reality of voices, and advocated that the first step in assisting a person to cope with problematic voices is for their understanding of them to be validated. As mentioned earlier, this derived from a recognition that historically voices have been conceptualised as a spiritual experience. Whether it be the voices heard by ancient biblical prophets, to contemporary Brazilian Umbanda healers, or world famous European mediums such as Stephen O'Brien, these voices arc all regarded as a spiritual phenomenon of some variety. Romme and Escher's message to professionals was to acknowledge this pattern, to break out of their own materialist cupboard and accept, however difficult it may be, that the spiritual experiences their patients can be very *real* and meaningful to them. *Accepting Voices* is packed with accounts of people who live with the understanding that their voices are spiritual experiences. Parapsychological, Jungian, Karmic, religious and mystical perspectives are all accommodated, and as part of the *Victim to Victor* series published by UK's Handsell Publications (see chapter five) Escher and Romme wrote *Working with Spiritual Voices* advocating that to relate and engage most positively and cooperatively with psychiatrised voice-hearers meant working within their own belief system as to what the voices represented. Also, to spend time listening to the carefully elaborated belief system of such a confused or

---

[7]The Diagnostic and Statistical Manual of Mental Disorders.

distressed voice-hearer can make the whole, perhaps perplexing experience, clearer and more comprehensible to a third party[8] (see chapter six).

For example, one woman who wrote of her spiritual experience in *Accepting Voices* used the hearing of voices as a spring board to develop as a medium. As her son was dying, she had visual hallucinations of his death, and after his passing away she started to hear his voice giving her messages. "To my own surprise I had to conclude that I really started to receive messages from the other world, where my son was in residence," she wrote. After this communication with her dead son she was visited by the spirits of other deceased people, but she had to learn how to seal off her "aura" from these sometimes disturbing "lower level entities". Despite their medical background, Romme and Escher do not patronise concepts such as "layered realities" and alternative "time/space dimensions". People who suffer a great loss such as the death of a partner or child may describe hearing the voice of that person, and such an experience is more likely to be regarded as normal and socially acceptable. It may also take time to end the material contact with the deceased. "It is possible that emotional trauma may rupture the familiar boundaries of our field of existence, creating a hole through which voices from another dimension may take hold of the person concerned," hypothesised Romme and Escher with philosophical open-mindedness.

Unfortunately Romme's attention to the *spiritual* subjective reality of his patient's voices was no more attractive to orthodox psychiatry today as it was to the church establishment when Darwin preached that humans all evolved from apes. It is not necessarily in medicine's materialist scientific repertoire to feel comfortable with concepts such as "super" or "higher levels of consciousness", "spiritual paths", "awakenings" or "regenerations." As mentioned earlier it has not been easy for Romme to get his work published in psychiatric publications.

Romme is also in many ways a post-modernist and multi-culturalist. While not expressing allegiance to any metaphysical corner, he validates alternative perspectives on the voice-hearing experience, and recognises, for example, that in the cultural transfusion of Western society, belief in reincarnation has spread beyond Asian societies. The West has its own ever growing adherents, and Romme was meeting them in his workplace. One example which he wrote of in *Working with Spiritual Voices* was that of a 28-year-old woman who for many years had been pursued by three voices. They effected her life

---

[8] As many mental health workers would reinforce, madness can often be de-mystified by asking someone what their voices are saying, and acknowledging how the voices' content relate to a person's experience and conceptualisation of the world.

terribly as she had to obey their orders. She had even slashed her face with a knife at their commands, and had been hospitalised for many years. After feeling that psychiatry had nothing to offer she received help from a therapist who worked on the principles of reincarnation[9]. It was revealed that the most hostile voice represented that of someone who was initially her friend but a serious conflict had turned them into enemies. This animosity reached a haunting conclusion on her friend's deathbed when he said he would pursue her with his revenge. It seemed that he did just as he pledged, because that was when the hostile voices started. The therapist helped the woman return to a former life where she met the voices in person. The aggressive voice of her former friend was the most difficult to bear, and it proved to be the hardest to deal with. But, during her return to the past, her friend's voice explained the root of their conflict, and both parties managed to form an understanding of each other's point of view, and they made steps to reconcile their differences. They were also able to say good-bye to each other, and the voice disappeared.

Despite his accommodation of alternative explanations, Romme did not preach mental health professionals to become born again spiritualists, but encouraged them simply to accept different philosophical frameworks to their own – to be more liberally responsive to models of mind other than the medical one. To replace the white coat of medicine with a cloak of philosophical courage. Telepathy is another explanation for voices that Romme took seriously, because despite years of traditional psychiatric intervention, many patients will cite a telepathic ability as being the most acceptable reason for the voices they hear. "Telepathy is the only explanation that is most accurate," wrote one of Romme's patients after 10 years in the Dutch psychiatric system. "It is the only explanation that I can live with easily – I prefer it to being a nut. I have telepathic communication with living and dead people. Sometimes I hear my grandmother's voice which has the same sense of humour as my grandmother when she was alive." Romme encouraged his colleagues to work with the concept of telepathy. This may mean evaluating with the voice-hearer whether telepathic communication is only achievable with people to whom they are especially close, and attending to what role stress plays in the experience. Coping with telepathic voices may mean building a mental shield to prevent being overwhelmed by voices – known as "psychic defence". It is not a necessity that Romme himself believes in reincarnation or telepathy to recognise that the therapies derived from such beliefs can be of benefit. Indeed, with Romme's back-ground in psychodynamic psychology as well as

---

[9] American psychiatrist Judith Orloff, also Assistant Clinical Professor of Psychiatry at UCLA is a psychic, and is willing to send her patients to consult with other psychics. She aims to teach other therapists and psychiatrists psychic therapies. See her book Second Sight.

psychiatry, his own personal interpretation of voice-hearing is to relate it to the psychological effects of trauma. So, Romme assessed that the woman hearing the voices of her dead friend was going through a consequence of the deathbed trauma. In his view the therapist helped her "face up to her negative emotions" and to resolve the conflict that inflicted such torture on her life.

But, really, all this talk of telepathy and reincarnation! Is it not all hocus-pocus I hear some readers ask? Telepaths? Mediums? Are they not at best misguided, at worst con artists? Are Mystic Megs best confined to the commercial showbiz playground? Guardian journalist Simon Hoggart and paranormal expert Mike Hutchinson wrote *Bizarre Beliefs* in 1995 which is a damning critic of everything from crop circles, astrology to UFOs, and also contains a concerted attack on the work of the late Doris Stokes and spiritualism that puts the movement up against the wall. Whether it be Buddhism, New Ageism, shamanism or Doris Stokeism a whole list of spiritual doctrines are confined to the reality dustbin. This was just the latest comprehensive attack on such beliefs which are publicly ridiculed with regularity. (One suspected reason for spiritualism's reluctance to ally itself with the hearing voices movement is because adherents feel it would not benefit their cause to be associated with psychiatric patients.) But firstly, we must remember that the orthodox psychiatric model of mental illness itself can be criticised as, if not hocus-pocus, at least a model of dubious scientific legitimacy by its most fierce of critics (see Mary Boyle's work in chapter ten). Secondly, when psychiatry medicates or therapises a bewildered sectioned psychiatric patient by compulsion, with the hope of bringing them back into a more conventional reality schemata, is this sound psychiatric treatment or crude cultural elitism? The point at which you fall on this dichotomy will depend to what extent you accept the medical model of mental distress. But whereas The Archbishop of Canterbury may appeal to the psychiatric establishment to move over and give conventional Christianity a place in the treatment stakes (and, as an establishment figure, preaches to an attentive audience) a panic-stricken inarticulate patient in a consultant's office has no such powers of influence in persuading their consultant of the existence of spirits. Moreover, it is often not the more accepted Christian constructs of God, the Devil and angels that patients present to psychiatry, but beliefs and discourses imported from Romany gypsies (telepathy), Asia (reincarnation) and Africa (possession). The demonisation of indigenous healers was a hallmark of the European domination of Africa, Asia and South America when they were often denigrated as "witch-doctors" or practitioners of "black magic". Are we still seeing the remnants of such conquest in our psychiatric hospitals?

"The voices didn't fade as I got older, but as the years passed I came to regard them as fantasy and paid little attention to them. Then, when I was in my teens, they became clearer and started telling me things I didn't know. They were only trivial things. Once, for

instance, they told me that a particular aunt was coming to stay. She wasn't expected, but a few days later she turned up on the doorstep with her suitcases. I started to get frightened then. Either I was going insane or these voices were real and, if they were real, who did they belong to? Still I didn't tell anyone. I went to the library and read all the psychic books I could find, hoping they would shed some light on the matter. One day I picked up a book about mediums. I say picked up; in fact, it just seemed to fall into my hand as I was taking another book off the shelf. It was a revelation, I sat up most of the night reading it. At last I knew what was happening to me." **Linda Williamson, medium, and author of** *Mediums and their Work,* **1990.**

The beginning of the Hearing Voices Network in the UK and abroad.

Manchester as the international gateway

Because of Romme's innovative ideas, and his status as a professor, news of his work was likely to spread. In 1988 an important link with the UK was established in Italy when Paul Baker, a mental health worker with the Manchester Alliance for Community Care, attended a conference in Trieste which was holding celebrations for the 10th anniversary of the Italian psychiatric reforms to close down the country's asylums. Ironically, it was actually by fortune that Romme was speaking at the conference at all, because the key note speaker had dropped out, and a student of Romme's who was on a six month placement in Trieste, suggested that his tutor be an adequate substitute for the missing speaker.

Baker had been personally touched by mental distress in his own family (his brother had been a psychiatric patient), and so was open to innovative ideas in mental health practice. Therefore, he found Romme's message particularly powerful. "Paul was absolutely astounded by what Romme was saying," recounted Baker's colleague Mark Greenwood, then manager of Creative Support, Manchester's leading mental health charity. Greenwood, affected by Baker's enthusiasm, later organised a trip to visit Romme in Maastricht and was equally impressed. "We could see why Paul was getting so excited...we immediately grasped the significance of it." Nigel Rose, another mental health worker from Manchester MIND, followed suit: "It was pretty clear that it was something important. The particular thing that stood out was it was the only thing we had come across that actually looked at so-called psychotic symptoms in a different way, and that was quite radical."

Greenwood, Rose and Baker had been involved in radical mental health politics throughout their careers – they were on the editorial collective of *Asylum – The Magazine for Democratic Psychiatry*, which had been a debating forum for alternatives to orthodox psychiatry since the seventies. The trio decided to take practical action on what they learnt in Maastricht and began presenting talks to audiences varying in number from three to 100 at institutions and groups around the north of England. Romme, Escher and representatives from Resonance were also invited to spread the word and attend conferences which eventually lead to preparations for the UK's first National Hearing Voices Conference.

After placing adverts in 120 local papers asking people who heard voices to contact them, Rose and colleagues received more than 100 replies, including 20 from Manchester. As it turned out 14 people attended the conference. "It was an extraordinary experience," remembered Greenwood. "For most of the people there it was the first time they had managed to have a place where they could talk about their voices without it being medicalised or being problematic in any way – it was fantastic to watch. A lot of the things that Marius Romme had said and experienced were replicated." For the first time in the UK, two important landmarks were made at this conference. Firstly, schizophrenics were redefining themselves as voice-hearers, and so making the first collective attempts to depathologise their experience, and secondly their voices were being validated as real and meaningful experiences rather than an "auditory hallucination." The media also picked up on the newsworthy innovation of the growing Network, with the Independent on Sunday taking the lead by publishing a feature article on the new ideas blossoming around voice-hearing.

Radicals and hearing voices

Not only was redefining the nature of a psychotic symptom empowering some voice-hearers, it also offered mental health radicals a new vantage point from which to criticise psychiatry. Although psychotherapeutic understandings of psychosis had, ever since Laing, been the main counter to biological explanations for "auditory hallucinations", voices still tended to be conceptualised by psychotherapists as some kind of dysfunctional experience or dynamic. However, Romme's idea of encouraging people to talk freely about their voices flew in the face of the notion that voice-hearing was, *per se*, a psychotic symptom (whether viewed medically or psychodynamically) that needed to be cured. For Network member and Asylum executive editor, Terence McLaughlin, simply just spotting the advert in a newspaper for a voice-hearing conference indicated a new angle from which to build a unified critique of orthodox psychiatry. McLaughlin, from Stockport, has been involved in advocacy work since the seventies, and the effect of seeing the advert in the Manchester Evening News was no less dramatic and revelationary than the influence that Patsy Hage had on Marius Romme earlier in Holland. McLaughlin said: "It was Patsy's insistence that was a breakthrough for Romme, and I'd shared that experience without even meeting him by seeing this advert in the paper. Simply seeing the advert that voice-hearers were talking about their voices was an immediate clue to what had been the failure of radicals before."

The Manchester self-help group

According to McLaughlin, the decision to form Manchester's first Hearing Voices self-help group was governed as much by the need for Mike Grierson, a sociology student from Manchester University, to attract funding for his PhD research, as it was to provide a new service for voice-hearers. Nevertheless, the first meeting was in February, 1991, in Baker's office. From then onwards the group met fortnightly, and then once a week, later moving to a nearby Methodist hall. Self-help groups played, and continue to play, a hugely important role in the Network and the hearing voices movement particularly as a source of strength for isolated psychiatrised voice-hearers. Although we turn to the nature of self-help groups in more detail in the next chapter it is worth noting that, ironically, the first group in Manchester was facilitated for its first nine months by Greenwood, a psychiatric nurse, the most medically orientated of all those involved in the Network at that time.

The Network's development

Anne Walton, who has been hearing voices since she was 25-years-old, was involved with the Manchester self-help group and the Network as a volunteer ever since she attended the first Hearing Voices Conference. Diagnosed schizophrenic, and with experiences as a sectioned patient of being pinned down while injected with neuroleptics in hospital, her outlook symbolised the Network as it was then developing. "I believed the voices I heard were a form of telepathy. I was not convinced that what I had was a mental illness," she said. "Neither did I believe that it needed to be treated like a mental illness – I certainly did not feel as though I had schizophrenia. At the time of being diagnosed the only symptom I seemed to have was the voice-hearing, and although it caused me to become slightly displaced in what I was thinking, it was all due to what I was hearing and nothing else really. I was not convinced that you could call it schizophrenia." Walton, who went on to become chair of Manchester's Schizophrenia Media Agency which challenged the media image of schizophrenics as deranged machete hackers, hoped the Network would provide a national exchange between non-psychiatrised and psychiatrised voice-hearers of ideas on how to cope with the problem of hearing voices. This would involve learning "how to deal with labels and psychiatry, with medication, everyday life, and the whole gamut." Conferences would then be the platform to disseminate new ideas.

Increasingly it became voice-hearers themselves who would spread these ideas, presenting talks or holding training seminars. In the early nineties Walton was joined by Ron Coleman (see chapter five), to do most of the Network's training and present Romme's work to a wider audience. "Each time they went out and did a talk they would get requests to do five more," recalled Rose. The Network began to organise conferences and training days all over the UK and abroad, and self-help groups sprung up nation-wide, often via local MIND groups, demonstrating the enthusiasm with which the Network's message was being received. Important contacts were also forged with user groups in London, particularly with Peter Campbell and Alan Leader of Survivors Speak Out.

In the spirit of Romme, the Network also accommodated and validated the reality of spiritual voices, and recognised their importance in people's lives. Not only did those who gave talks on behalf of the Network in the north of England, such as Walton and Susan Clarkson, from Keishley in Yorkshire, believe themselves to be communicators with a "spiritual world", religious/spiritualist figures began to initiate contact with the Network. Representatives of the Deliverance Ministry, which deals with "possession", were requesting meetings between themselves and the Network, and Carl Williams, an Edinburgh professor of parapsychology, was invited to conferences. By July 1995, when the Discourse Unit of Manchester Metropolitan University held a hearing-voices conference, spirituality was the most emphasised explanation for the experience of hearing voices. This conference was also important in bringing together the most diverse, non-medical, theories around voice-hearing. The papers presented discussed voices as a sign of "telepathic communication", "unseen energies", "unconscious sub-systems", "dissociation", "ideas insertion", "ESP" and "clairaudience". Of the 24 speakers many were voice-hearers. There were physicists, philosophers, drama therapists, healers, hypnotherapists, psychotherapists, nurses, shamans, psychologists, Christians and parapsychologists. Interestingly, there were also two psychiatrists who both distanced themselves from the ways of orthodox psychiatry. One talked about hearing voices as a "growth-promoting" experience. The other, Dr Phil Thomas (see chapter eight), then a consultant at Gwynedd Community Health Trust in Wales, marked the day by becoming the first psychiatrist to go public about having experienced voices himself, when he stated he had heard them during a half asleep/half awake state.

Users taking over

The subsequent power shift between the Network's management committee and the self-help group was an important development in the Network's history, at least as far as Manchester was concerned. In the early nineties, according to McLaughlin who was by then facilitating the self-help group, its members regarded the professional non voice-hearing members of the management committee as defining the Network, and making all its decisions. Led particularly by the increasingly dynamic Ron Coleman, there was a positive move towards voice-hearers taking over the role of the mental health professionals both on the committee and increasingly in the HVN office at Creative Support's offices. Coleman's role in this power shift was ironic considering that, according to McLaughlin: "he was perhaps the most chronic and sad case of a schizophrenic that I had ever seen. Certainly in the case that he had no good voices." But, Coleman's recovery and energy in paving the way for the management committee to become more voice-hearer led was more than being politically significant, it was also a step of a personal journey for Coleman which was to form the basis of his *From victim to victor* slogan that he subsequently advocated in his training. As McLaughlin recounted provocatively, there was also another message to be heard by Coleman's rising status and influence: "He was almost becoming living proof that the voice-hearers definitely were not that mad, which meant that professionals were not that professional.[10]"Coleman's view of the Network was: "It was not that the professionals were abusive or were holding us down. But the fact was that the Network was still controlled by people who were not voice-hearers, and I think that all started to change when we managed to get our own office, equipment and Mental Health Foundation Grant. We then became a user-run, user-led office, although we still did not have a user-run, user-led organisation." Nevertheless, Rose dropped out of the committee in 1992, Greenwood in 1993 and Baker moved to Spain in 1994.

Where do we go from here?
As the Network was (and still is) largely run by volunteers, all those involved were committed to its general philosophy. But its development did fester dissatisfaction. With self-help groups nestling under the wings of MIND, academic institutions, and the National Schizophrenia Fellowship, the Hearing Voices Network began to resemble a new mental health service for psychiatric patients. As we shall see psychology (and psychiatry) began to appropriate the work of Romme and the ideas of the Network into their own disciplines. Rose pointed out that: "the hearing voices movement has become a survivor movement far more than an emancipation movement...I believe very strongly that you are not going to radically alter the experience of people who hear voices by adopting new treatments and new coping strategies. What you need to do is to bring about an acceptance of hearing voices in our culture." Although the Network has members with radical political agendas, Rose, echoing Romme, said pertinently: "Look at homosexuality, it was not a curative thing that made a difference, it was the gay liberation movement." And, in a paper addressed to a German academic audience in 1996, McLaughlin demonstrated the political aspirations the hearing voices movement could choose to follow. "To the fight against sexism, racism and homophobia we should add the practice of psychophobia in the provision of mental health," he wrote. One incident he recounted to exemplify his understanding was when, following a Manchester self-help group meeting, all its members went off to the pub for a drink. The evening turned sour when they got involved in a brawl with some men shouting abuse. Recalling the event McLaughlin said: "Discussion in the group later revolved around how the incident could have resulted if the police had become involved – almost the entire central committee of the Network, as it was then, could have been sectioned. It

---

[10] I am reminded of Lowon's polemical article in Asylum, 1994, 8, (2): 29-30, entitled *Understanding professional thought disorder: a guide for service users and a challenge for professionals*, where he draws up a list of symptoms of what he calls PTD (Professional Thought Disorder).

was quite clear that the hearing of voices remained an issue of democratic rights, through the concrete reality of schizophrenia as a legal mechanism."

Nevertheless, it appeared to be unanimously accepted that self-help groups enabled many psychiatrised voice-hearers to improve their quality of life and overcome to some degree a sense of powerlessness. But, for some individuals, self-help is quite simply not sufficient. For example, community worker Mike Grierson, from Levenshulme in Manchester, became involved with the Network in an effort to help a friend, Thomas Brooke, who arrived in Manchester from Uganda in the seventies to pursue his education in the "gold-paved cities of Britain". While Thomas was enjoying his privileged English education, his family members, friends and neighbours were being killed under the Amin regime. Grierson put it frankly: "Whilst he was having a good time, Thomas' family were being killed." In an alienating environment and burdened with guilt, there was little mystery in Thomas's breakdown. A culturally isolated immigrant, living off benefits, he heard offensive voices from morning to night, particularly "white voices" swearing at him, calling him a "fuckin' scrounging nigger" who did not deserve his benefits. For two years Thomas went to the Manchester self-help group and, concluded Grierson: "it did not help my friend, and still now the Hearing Voices Network has not helped him because his problems were too great, too big for amateurish self-help....The weakness of the Hearing Voices Network is that it is overly preoccupied with how people cope with the voices, where the problem actually is how people cope with their *lives*. The voices only make sense in the context of people's lives." Thomas's life could only be addressed by social, political and economic transformations, suggested Grierson.

Chapter three

Voice-hearers helping themselves

Self-help groups

As discussed in the previous chapter the Hearing Voices Network was largely founded upon the notion of "self-help" – when voice-hearers can use their collective power and abilities to improve their relationship with voices, and support each other by suggesting ways to cope with voices or affirming each other's experiences. The mushrooming of self-help groups in the eighties and nineties was intricate to the policy of community care when the old Victorian asylums and long-stay psychiatric hospitals were closed and replaced by services in the community. Although economic factors were a driving force behind community care, the growth of self-help groups were also consistent with the liberal concept of "empowerment" which presumes that psychiatrised voice-hearers (or other mental health service users) providing each other mutual support offers benefits beyond a once-a-month appointment with a doctor.

Self-help groups are popular across the mental health spectrum. Hundreds of patients have gained from self-help groups, and some have used them as a starting point from which to end their relationship with clinicians altogether, or to develop a more informed and balanced relationship with them. Nevertheless, we should remember that self-help developed under a clinical umbrella, reflected by the fact that hearing voices self-help groups are almost all funded via statutory services or MIND groups. Therefore, I think it is doubtful whether self-help groups can ever transcend the stigma of being associated with mental health and madness. In addition, so long as they are run by mental health professionals, and for as long as mental health workers are responsible to social service or health managers, the empowering achievements of self-help groups will always be curtailed by the boundaries set by their more powerful clinicians who oversee such groups. For example, a self-help group organising itself to advocate for an end to compulsory drug treatment may land itself in an awkward relationship with any more conservative professionals on board, and their payroll masters. The hearing voices self-help groups dotted around the country, although differentiated by different roots and founding personalities, are generally another community care service. I feel it is important we note that this is a far cry from those aspiring to see the movement as something detached from the mental health services, with more ambitious political and social concerns.

Nevertheless, I would like to convey a sense of the real benefits many voice-hearers reap, and continue to reap from self-help groups. So I wrote to some of the groups asking them to send me details on how they started, and what their activities are. I received some replies which are printed below. Written by voice-hearing members themselves, and mental heath professional "facilitators" or "allies", they give a flavour as to each group's composition, expectations and functions. The extracts give an indication of what is happening on the ground level of self-help. Their position should not be understated in the movement.

Paddington Hearing Voices Group.
Address: *The Day Hospital, Paterson Centre, 20, Wharf Road, London. W2 1PD.*
– by allies Kate Augarde and Helen Thomas, July, 1997.

The Paddington Hearing Voices group started two and a half years ago. We had noticed a lack of information provided on voice-hearing, and of independent advice/support for clients experiencing the mental health system for the first time. A nurse and an occupational therapist employed by an NHS Trust approached the day hospital where they worked, and were allowed to run the group in the evenings. Originally the day hospital was used because it was free, and at the time there was no independent funding available.

Since then, the group has become part of the Extended Day Care Service in the area, and we have moved to a room at a local day centre. Group members find this more acceptable as it is away from a medical setting, which was found to be very off-putting. Originally we began with one member only, and the numbers have steadily increased (roughly one enquiry per week). The current membership is 18. The same people don't attend every group, although there are usually five or six people per group plus two 'allies'. We decided that it is important that there is no pressure to attend, as a desire to attend often depends on how someone is feeling on the day, what sort of week they are having, and whether the voices are particularly bad. We run as a self-help support group, sharing experiences, asking questions, and discussing coping strategies. We provide leaflets on mental health issues and medication, and we also operate as a social group, originally meeting to chat, but we have moved onto looking at more self-help/support issues. We usually try to have social events around Christmas and summer. We are limited with not having independent funds, so we try to do some fund-raising activities. We also apply to Extended Day Care Services for additional funds if need be. They have paid transport fees to conferences.

The group has a lot of discussion around the diagnosis of schizophrenia – what schizophrenia means, medication, hospitalisation, whether doctors listen, what it means to have the "label", what society thinks of us ("that we are frothing at the mouth"), coming to terms with, or rebelling against the medical diagnosis, and side-effects of drugs.

The group's views on why voices occur vary from spiritual explanations, possession, negative experiences from the past, representations of parts of our personality, cultural differences, "pay back", and stress. People cope by shutting them out, shouting at them, getting drunk or stoned (this may make them worse but you may be happier), talking to someone you trust (not always a doctor or CPN who may discuss increasing medication), taking medication because it helps, accepting the voices, avoiding stress or arguments, or coming to the group. People may read a book, meditate, listen to a walkman, focus on a candle's flame, or use crystal healing. People deal with abusive voices by trying not to listen to them (although they can be so intrusive that this is impossible), and checking out what the voices say with other people (although sometimes you do not believe that person is telling you the truth).

The Edinburgh Hearing Voices Group
Address: *The Stafford Centre, Edinburgh.*
- by John Matthews, group member, January, 1997.

The group was started in 1992 by a user of the Stafford Centre, a mental health drop-in facility in Edinburgh run by National Schizophrenic Fellowship Scotland (NSF(S)), and is funded by Lothian Social Work Department, and Lothian Health. The user experienced voices, and was feeling isolated as a result. She was able to talk to a member of staff about her problems, but wished to share her experiences with other users with similar difficulties. Another user who knew of her interest in starting a group gave her a copy of the Manchester Hearing Voices Network newsletter so she wrote to Manchester and was sent an information pack telling her how to go about starting a group. She sent fliers to CPNs, doctors, nurses, day hospitals, the Royal Edinburgh Hospital, other mental health projects in Lothian.

In the beginning the group consisted of only herself, and the staff member. And it was six months until others started to come along. Initially users were reluctant to talk about the actual content of their voices (some experienced voices which threatened them with dire consequences if they were to reveal anything about them) so discussion centred around problems due to voices, the distress caused by them, associated problems, coping strategies and medication.

The numbers in the group varied from one to four plus a staff member. The founding member often attended even if she did not need the group's support, as she thought it important that the group should continue even if she was the only user at times. This determination really paid off because other users came to the group who were able to talk about the actual content of their voices, and the nature of the group changed and gave people confidence to share their experiences more freely.

Being the first hearing voices group in Scotland it received visitors from other centres who wished to start their own groups. The Stafford Centre runs a variety of groups for users and the hearing voices group became another group open to users at the centre. The group meets weekly, and is usually led by a member of staff, but is user led if this is not possible for some reason. Meetings last for an hour an a half, and it should perhaps be stressed that the rules are not imposed on members from above, but have been formulated and agreed by the actual users of the centre and the group.

During the group people are free to leave if and when they wish. This happens if somebody finds certain subjects too disturbing, or does not find the discussion interesting, or to their taste. This is important because some users of the group may be feeling quite fragile, and if they have had enough they feel free to leave without any embarrassment.

Membership of the group is constantly changing, and although the founding member no longer attends as she doesn't feel the need for support any more, the group now numbers as many as eight. Members are a mix of people who are, or have been, inpatients or outpatients, and most, but not all, are on neuroleptics. All members experience, or have experienced mental health illness as only such people my use the centre. This is necessary to provide a safe environment for the more vulnerable users.

The members' experiences of voices include those which talk to them directly, sometimes abusively, sometimes neutrally; some are commanding; and others are of well known people who talk to them. Sometimes the voices talk about the hearer to one another, for some a voice may report everything that the hearer is thinking, seeming to echo their thoughts. Or they may seem to be another person's thoughts, making the hearer think that they are telepathic. Voices may seem to belong to devils or spirits. Two hearers have heard a dalek voice which they both reported as particularly frightening. The voice may belong to a person who the hearer knows i.e. their mother, and if this voice commands them to do something they immediately do it because they trust the voice and are used to obeying it. Voices often denigrate a person in an abusive way. Voices may be heard which are so real that they may appear to be real people in the room, street, bus, or wherever, the hearer acting on them as if they are real.

People react to their voices in different ways and hearers who have lived with them for years have developed different methods of coping. Coping strategies include talking back to them, ignoring them, listening to headphones to drown them out or stop them, focusing on them by writing them down, relaxation, humming, taking more of their prescribed drugs, drinking alcohol, smoking dope etc.

Discussion of the causes of one's voices is another frequent topic. Is it all in the brain? A genetic condition? Environment? Or bit of both? How is stress a major factor which brings the voices on? Some people believe that abuse of various sorts during their childhood may be to blame. Other cite suffering from some other illness which seemed to precipitate the hearing of voices. Many have no theory and they just wish that the voices would go away. This subject usually causes considerable disagreement, and people end up agreeing to disagree.

The treatment of voices, and whether they are symptomatic of an illness, is a popular subject, with much criticism of psychiatrists, doctors, hospitals, police, sections, injections, and of course the drugs and their side effects. Some members of the group are trying counselling or psychotherapy privately in an effort to help themselves, finding that the NHS will not give them any sort of 'talking treatment' – just the 15 minute interview, and a prescription of neuroleptic medication. Staff members, while very sympathetic to people's feelings on this subject, point to the fact that all the users they know who have come off their medication have had relapses. They do however tell people that what to do is up to them. Some members of the group have heard voices for years and have managed without any medication, so it is a very controversial issue, as some members clearly can not seem to manage without medication while others feel the medication is much worse than the voices. Warnings of the brain damage caused by neuroleptics is greeted with horror by members who do not wish to know this sort of thing. Some people who become free of their voices admit to missing them. The primary resource is the members themselves and their experiences, but the group is building up a collection of articles and papers on voices, and the centre possesses a copy of Marius Romme's book. Clearly, due to the constraints on membership of the group, there are no members who have not been considered as mentally ill. This may be seen as a failing of the group as the healthiest voice hearers are by definition excluded and can not therefore share their experiences, problems, or coping strategies with the very people who might most benefit from them.

Oxford Hearing Voices Group
Address: *c/o Gordon Claridge, Magdalen College, Oxford. OX1 4AU.*
– by Dr Gordon Claridge, teacher of psychology at Oxford University's Department of Experimental Psychology, January, 1997.

The Oxford Hearing Voices Group started in autumn, 1991, and is affiliated to Oxford Survivors and the National Hearing Voices Group, to which most of the members also belong. Present membership is about 15.

A unique feature of the group is its informal connection to Oxford University. This comes about through the involvement with the group of Dr Gordon Claridge, a former clinical psychologist, who teaches Psychology in the University Department of

Experimental Psychology, and at Magdalen College. Gordon has a particular interest in all manner of unusual mental states, including their relation to such things as creativity, and it was through this that he became involved with the group at its inception. He has the status of associate (non-voting) member, since he is a non voice-hearer (though he has been known to admit to various visual, and occasional brief auditory, hallucinatory experiences, "derisively" dismissed by the proper members of the group as "probably hypnogogic"!)

The group meets fortnightly on Sunday afternoons in Gordon's room in Magdalen College. Attendance varies, but there is a core of people who almost always come, and there have never been an occasion over the time that the group has been running that a meeting has been cancelled for lack of support. The format of the meetings is that, after dealing with any business matters, members take it in turns to bring the group up-to-date on their voice and voice-related experiences, as well as any additional personal matters they wish to share with the others. This will sometimes include a brief summary of their history of voice-hearing, for the benefit of any new members present. Needless to say, such individual participation is entirely voluntary, though a lively interchange always ensues, to which everyone contributes. The atmosphere of this discussion, is, and is intended to be, primarily one of emotional support; but, as befits the setting and the intellectual accomplishments of the group members, it often becomes a more academic debate, about the nature of the voice experience, and so on. (Indeed, Gordon admits he would be hard pushed to distinguish it from the more usual tutorial encounters he has with his students).

The academic connection has also had the consequence of stimulating research. Inspired by an idea proposed by one of the group's members, Gordon organised a research project, funded by the Medical Research Council, to examine the day-to-day influences on the frequency and nature or voices. The work, undertaken by Mary Coombs – a medical student acting for a year as a research assistant – has recently been completed and will eventually be published.

Outside the fortnightly meetings, the Oxford Hearing Voices Network acts as an emotional support group (many of the members meet on a social basis at other times), is involved in advice and training, and acts in an advocacy capacity, mediating between the voice hearer and professionals with whom they may be involved.

Salisbury Hearing Voices Group
Address: *Greencroft House, 42-46 Salt Lane. Salisbury. SP1 1EG.*
– by Tony Evans, social worker, December 1996.

In March, 1996, six people got together at Salisbury Arts Centre to begin an experiment. Three of us were mental health professionals, three were people who hear voices, and this experimental meeting was the first of a series of fortnightly gatherings where people could talk about voice-hearing – about its affect on their lives, and the way their experiences were dealt with by mental health services, and about finding different ways of coping with voices. Professional helpers have long been reluctant to discuss voice-hearing, for fear of stirring up a hornets' nest. Would this open the floodgates? Would it trigger off other overwhelming mental problems? Would it reinforce the hearer's delusions, making the voices "real" by talking about them? Far from helping people, this wariness about tackling a major day-to-day experience has been more likely to frustrate and alienate the hearers.

This silence denies many hearers part of their own identity, as well as the opportunity to seek help and advice. Many hearers have found their individual experiences ignored or treated as 'a psychosis' on the psychiatric equivalent of an assembly line, and have been left to cope with them as best they can.

The idea of establishing a voice-hearers' group was first mooted in Salisbury in the early nineties, but this came to nothing. By 1995, a small group of hearers and professionals with a common interest in the project were ready to try again. During our discussions it emerged that we had all been inspired by the work of psychiatrist Romme in the Netherlands. Interest in voice-hearing began to spread, and organisations such as the Hearing Voices Network were set up in the UK to help hearers establish self help community groups.

When the Salisbury group was first set up, my colleagues and I were rather worried about the reactions of other professionals. We contacted social work teams, nursing teams, and psychiatrists to publicise the group's work, and explain its purpose, expecting a dismissive or negative response. But we were surprised at how positive more respondents were: some had even advised their clients to contact our group and were prepared to support them in using it. Membership has fluctuated since the group's establishment: meetings involve anything from two to six voice-hearers, and one or two professional facilitators. The group opted to have professionals there to take on the day-to-day administration and to acknowledge that they were working as allies in helping them to manage their voices. Meetings cover ideas about the nature of voices, discussed by members in relations to their experiences; aspects of hearers' own particular voices, and how they have affected their lives; exchange of strategies to minimise the negative effects of voices – and so on. Professionals and carers are also invited to attend, to gain an understanding of the voice-hearing phenomenon, and of ways to help. Catherine Herrod, a community development worker for mental health, has found that "patterns can emerge and be recognised in their voices which help increase the sense of control rather than being out of control and swamped..." She has also learnt the importance of acknowledging even the most disturbing experiences. "Even members who say they've been punished later by their voices for talking in the group have said it's worth persisting with the group and continuing to come."

The Salisbury group has now been running for over a year, and continues to provide support and a positive focus for voice-hearers. It has been a source of growing recognition among mental health workers of the contribution that voice-hearers themselves can make, in the management of their own care, and in giving professional helpers an insight into their skills and experience. Sarah Gouldbourne, one of the contributors to a tape the group made about voice-hearing said: "I hope my fellow hearers can take comfort for this; you're not alone. Reach out for help – it's there. Be strong. You can overcome."

Talking about voices
For a psychiatrised voice-hearer to spend an hour and a half per week in a self-help group with other voice-hearers discussing their voices could, possibly, have very little benefits. Members may leave still harassed by negative voices. They may still go through more crises, and remain under the surveillance and care of the statutory services. As voice-hearers shouldering labels such as manic-depressive and schizophrenic, their standing in a democratic state may still be threatened as they continuing to experience the force of mental health sectioning. Self-help may never contribute enough to enable these voice-hearers to escape the status of psychiatric patient. On the other hand, group discussions about voice-hearing can offer voice-hearers ideas on how to understand their experience, and give it validation. A discussion about the voice-hearing experience will not only refer to established ideas within psychology, psychiatry, mental health, philosophy, religion, and spirituality – it will also venture into new territory. When discussing self-help, ideas can blossom which can challenge all of these disciplines in some meaningful way – this is the power of collective discussion and debate.

Below is a transcript of such a discussion on self-help I had with Salisbury's Hearing Voices Group. I think it demonstrates the value of group discussion on voice-hearing.

While covering issues such as the relationship between recreational drug use and voice-hearing, the role of visions, psychiatry and psychiatric drugs, interpretations of experience, and coping strategies, members not only discussed their own experience, they also had the space to elaborate their understandings of it. My purpose in publishing our discussion is to convey some of the day-to-day concerns of the psychiatrised voice-hearer, and the pertinent issues in their life. I do not want to add my comments or analysis to the discussion because I feel the transcript is complete in itself.

Kath is the non voice-hearing mental health professional. Geoff, Janet, Dave, Andy, and Matt, had an assortment of psychiatric diagnoses between them.

Adam: What are the most effective ways of dealing with the voices?

Dave: My experience in hospital has been one of being controlled, and simply left alone to discuss problems with other patients. Everything is discussed with them. What I would like to see is more talking therapy on offer. I think talking therapy is very useful in dealing with voices because they are not clearly treatable by drugs. Voices can either genuinely upset people, or make them euphoric. To have experts with experience of working with 50 or 60 voice-hearers would mean they could suggest coping strategies. All the coping strategies that I have heard of have come directly from patients. In a way this is unusual because patients generally keep quiet about hearing voices because it is still – at least in our rural mental hospital – a major factor in the diagnosis of psychosis. So, most of my coping strategies have been picked up from other patients and from the Hearing Voices Network, rather than from nurses with a course in hearing voices or something similar.

Adam: What kind of coping strategies, for example?

Dave: By and large it has been self-help and the hearing voices group that has passed on various strategies for coping. For example, I now try to accept positive explanations of internal phenomena – which I call imaginary phenomena – rather than negative explanations which only lead to a downward spiral. What I mean by this is if I am having problems with paranoia – such as believing that social workers are the police or the secret service – someone might say to me, "look, they are not actually policemen, they are social workers," which might help change my attitude towards these imaginary policemen. Therefore the voices will probably not pick up on my suspicion and antagonism, and may even disappear. Whereas if a voice says to me, "well, the social workers are just the plods, and behind them there are some CID inspectors who want to talk to you," this might feed into this mythology-of-the-police type thing.

Adam: So, the voices are saying things that arouse suspicion?

Dave: They might say things like: "You do realise that you can be done for this", or "all these questions will go back to the inspector".

Kath: But you can look at both explanations and choose one? Is it you that does this?

Dave: Well, I seek advice from disinterested parties, or third parties. If a third party says something like, "the social workers are just doing a routine check," it may make me feel OK.

Adam: So it's about talking with other people about this experience?

Andy: With me it helps to keep quiet about the voices. But if there is someone who does not know you – who is disinterested – they can sometimes give you a bit of advice that no one else can give, because they are looking at it freshly and through a more balanced outlook.

Dave: Yes, it's a disinterest in reality isn't it? I should add that the third party I was talking about were actually imaginary voices themselves.

Andy: But if you are hearing voices of any sort they do not always induce paranoia do they? Maybe they do with you. Geoff, I read something you wrote. You said that if you have a friendly, or a good voice, playing around with it can make it into a bad one, and visa versa.

Geoff: I did not mean that. What I meant was if you have a good voice, *use* it. Use that voice to prevent others from coming in. Trade on it.

Andy: But you also said that a good voice can change into a bad voice. I find that this is true, because if I have this very nice, loving voice going around my head too much then it can revert into a bad one.

Dave: Like any personality in other words. If you hammer on at somebody they might change for the worst – the voice is just like a real personality....I find the whole process of hearing voices slightly annoying actually.

Geoff: I do too!

Dave: I find it annoying because you might be in a room with somebody, or in a pub, and the person who has been talking to you for the last five minutes might ask, "what do you think about what I have just said?" And because your mind was elsewhere you are left picking up the pieces. The voices impinge on your reality.

Adam: Are you able to have a relationship with your voices where you can switch them off and come back to them later?

Dave: Yes, but the voices are a very seductive medium because you are often dealing with voices, or people, whose personalities are far more mature than the people you are socialising with in the pub. You are getting more interesting insights out of the voices, and I see them as a better world. But in my case the drug, Clozapine, which is a serotonin inhibitor I think, completely knocks out the voices. I did not take the drugs for about two weeks recently and all my voices came back. Now I have been taking them regularly for a month or so, and the voices are disappearing again.

Adam: Does that make it easier to engage socially?

Dave: Yeah.

Adam: Is anyone able to develop a sense of control over their voices, so they can give time to speak or communicate with their voices at one time, and put them off at another?

Andy: I have a voice before I go to sleep – a voice I hear in my bedroom which is a loving voice, a kind and flattering voice. It's a sort of love affair that I have with it. Whereas the voice I hear outside makes me paranoid. For instance, one evening I was walking and wearing my dead father's coat. I thought I heard people talking about this. As it was dark I could not really see. But when I got home to my girlfriend she said to me, "you have been hearing voices – remember you are paranoid and remember you hear voices." And then I thought, "well, of course, it was a voice," which makes me feel better.

But also, if I find that if I'm having trouble with my paranoid voice in my bedroom, I will take more pills to get me hearing a nice voice.

Dave: Does that work?

Andy: No, it sends me to sleep! And I wake up confused and not remembering what the voice was about in the first place. I am very confused at the moment.

Dave: When I go to bed and lie my head on the pillow I may stay awake for an hour or so just talking to these personalities in my mind. The next morning there is this continuity when I wake up and remember, "yes, of course, such and such was happening in my head," and the whole thing carries on. But if I wake up late at midday or 1pm the voices will say, "no, it's all changed, everybody else woke up at 9am. Since then this and this has happened." So it's like a world where I have missed out on a couple of hours, another world which carries on with or without my prescence.

Geoff: Maybe you are the ego talking to these personalities.

Dave: No, I do not understand what this "ego" thing is – I never have.

Geoff: What I mean is that *you* are talking to these personalities. You are the colonel of the whole lot.

Dave: No, because if I wake up at 11am or midday, instead of 9am, the world of voice and visions has moved on. So, for example, one evening I may be getting off with so and so, and when I wake up she is 20 miles away with somebody else.

Geoff: But it is still you yourself who is conversing with personalities or voices or characters?

Dave: Yes, but it is still an independent world – or at least it seems to be an independent world. It is like a real society. I am a participant in a real society. But as for controlling them, in my mind I have large crowds and these crowds have, historically, against my wish, been segregated, and one of the ways that they are segregated is into groups of men and women. The idea being that I would have all the women, and none of the men. And all the men were hidden somewhere near my parents' house, and all the women were somewhere else. And I said to myself, "right, I will unite the men and women." So I put both crowds together and told them that what I want from this united crowd was to stop hearing voices.

Geoff: But are you doing this from your own will?

Dave: Yes, I said to them that I had had enough. My girlfriend thinks that I am an arrogant, self-centred person with my head in the clouds, and that I never have any time for real life. So I said, "OK, I want to get out of this situation." And so these people positioned themselves at Salisbury Leisure Centre, and they said to me that everytime I went there in my mind they would ask me whether or not I had somebody with me, the general rule being that I could only fantasise if somebody was with me in reality. If I was on my own they would tell me to go back. But they said that when I fantasised with somebody, bring them to Salisbury Leisure Centre and talk to them there, as well as talking to them in real life. I found this too difficult to do – but it was a centring thing. Most of my voices or personalities do not represent people from my everyday life. They are people I would not otherwise be able to contact.

Anyway I have this clear image of a central figure in white bringing together all these crowds, and I have this image of the crowds receding and disappearing. Two weeks later I smoked a joint, which seems to bring on this telepathic, "other world" experience, and all of a sudden there I was talking to this woman's relation. The whole thing came back.

Adam: So, the marijauna did not help?

Dave: That's correct. Because up to then the whole imaginary experience had gone. For the first time in the ten years that I had known this person in my mind she was actually receding and the crowds were receding with her. There was the pain of loss but at the same a real sense of relief because I am out of the milieu from where the person came from.

Geoff: You seem to be encouraging them Dave. You are encouraging them as far as I can see.

Dave:	No, I was asking them to stop, and they said that they would stop me from hearing voices and imagining things by not allowing me to imagine when I was on my own, only when I was with other people.
Geoff:	Do you see you own self as an imaginary image?
Dave:	Yes, I can do. Yes, I have an imaginary personality.
Geoff:	That's superadded to the personality you've already got?
Dave:	It's a much more happy, confident person that I actually am.....but the dope actually brought all the crowd back – the whole thing, the whole razmattaz.
Geoff:	Do you think you were wise to take dope?
Dave:	I haven't smoked it since.
Geoff:	It was an unwise move wasn't it?
Andy:	I find smoking dope very negative. I smoked every day for five years without missing a single day without at least one joint.
Geoff:	Do you crave for it Dave?
Dave:	No.
Andy:	It's not addictive.
Dave:	I know people who smoke and I never smoke with them.
Andy:	It's not addictive – but I still have problems without it. I have to transfer that on to the pills that I have been given for my head. And I don't have anything to do with dope anymore.
Dave:	There was a period when I had a lot of legal highs, using drugs such as Guarana, and then I went back on to hash. But now I would rather go out for a drink.
Andy:	I can not go out for a drink because I am twice as bad. First of all I can not stop drinking once I start because I find it so pleasurable, and the next day I am at an all time low with guilt and with wondering what conversations I had because I was so pissed I can not remember.

Matt: I think hearing voices runs on a spectrum. There are some people who are driven to trying to kill themselves, and there are others who don't really suffer, and the voices are assimilated into one's imagination.

Dave: I really feel sorry for those people who have voices which introduce themselves as gods and then say, "slit your wrists," or "jump out of the window." I am not like that. If I have God in my imagination it's a benevolent God, rather than a terrible one. There are people who are not here today who have really negative experiences.

Matt: Yes, I remember with interest Samantha, the actress from Southampton, who told us very graphically about this voice which told her to kill her baby. She told us it was her father's voice that was telling her to do this, but, if you remember, it became a school mistress on the tape that we recorded. She mentioned that she was very fortunate in having a lady doctor who had suffered this kind of post natal psychosis herself. Another woman who has not come for ages has thrown herself under a bus rather than push someone else off the pavement under it. She had been given the choice of either to push someone else under a bus or to do it herself. It can be pretty hard at this end of the spectrum.

Dave: Then there are other people who have attended this group who have totally positive experiences; who have never been to hospital but who still hear voices.

Adam: What about support from relationships and friends? Is this important?

Matt: Of course, very important if it's available. The only thing, of course, is that, sadly, most forms of mental instability can lead to distance being created between people. Basically, one can be a real pain in the arse. But yes, support is invaluable.

Dave: I think that by and large you can pick positive voices to hear. In my experience they do do some good if you are on a downward spiral of fear and paranoia.

Andy: I've got a positive voice but when it comes to reality it is no good at all. The positive voice may egg me on but when it comes to physically doing something I am on cloud cuckoo land – it is just not very apt at the time. So the positive voice is actually harming me. I would prefer to say, "shut up! Just shut up!" But I do not do this because it's a positive voice, and it is better than the bad voice which makes me paranoid.

Dave: I think another cause of mental illness, certainly for me, has been taking imaginary voices literally. For example, some guiding writing voices that I have, said they would compose a letter for me to write to a woman. Of course, they meant a letter in my mind, a mentally constructed and delivered letter. But I wrote this letter out for real and this woman was, of course, totally mystified, and the whole thing was not very clever! But it seems to me that the cause of the actual psychosis which precede hospitalisation is to take literal those things that are meant exclusively for the imaginary world. The only time that taking things literally can work for me positively is in writing when I get mental muses who dictate to me. As far as I know, the word "inspiration" means "dictated word by word" or "being dictated or channeled from the spirits".

So, going back to that incident when the woman had the choice of chucking herself, or someone else, infront of the bus. If you keep it in your imaginary world, letting it just be a mental choice, you will be OK. It is when it is taken literally that the problems start. And this has been true for most of my breakdowns. They have involved the literal interpretation of imaginary suggestions or instructions.

Some people have heard voices since their childhood haven't they. It is said that only children have an imaginary play friend and I have tried to trace mine back. My first contact was when I thought I saw a tall woman in my grandmother's larder. I asked my grandmother about this woman, and she told me that this was my "second sight." The next time was when I was twelve, and I kind of predicted a coach and horses haunting of a particular house. I was walking past this house at half past nine at night when lo and behold they appeared. That was the first time I consciously saw anything from another world or from my imagination. But I know my grandmother had this special facility which I may have inherited in some way. My mother says her only experience of hearing voices was when she was crossing a crowded street in Rome, and she was not looking where she was going. All of a sudden an angel's white hand stopped her and ten scooters passed by. She knew that she had been saved from death by this imaginary white hand.

One time when I was very depressed I was suffering from a delusion which made me suicidal, and I was walking out in front of cars and willing them to run me over. One time I was just about to walk in front of this car when, again, a white hand grabbed my shoulder, and a voice said, "no, not this time." So I drew back, and I was saved from death by something from my mind – so it has been positive in some ways.

Janet:	Is it possible to have a relationship with someone who does not hear voices?
Dave:	Yes, I have. Although I might sit for quarter of an hour in silence with my girlfriend Ellen, and she will say, "oh, you are hearing voices again."
Kath:	But that happens in normal relationships doesn't it – where you're sat down with someone, and they're thinking about what they're going to do at work the next day. It's a similar experience isn't it.
Dave:	Yes, well apart from the fact that she will be divulging some fantastically emotional thing to me, and I will just sit there doing nothing.
Kath:	I know the feeling. I can really feel for her!
Dave:	After a couple of minutes she might ask whether I heard what she said, and I would say, "yes, yes," and then she would ask, "well, what is your answer," and I would reply, "oh, I'm not too sure!"
Andy:	There was one thing that got to me about having a relationship and hearing voices. This concerns Peter, my friend, who lives in a different bedroom to me. Often I hear a voice and equate it to a voice in his room, and I will jump out of bed and run to open his door as a result of paranoia. Of course, there is never anyone in the room but I can not get the idea out of my head. This was something that used to happen to me – I am less strung up about it now.
Dave:	In my opinion the interface between the real and imaginary world is the root of psychosis. Your voice will instruct or suggest you to do something like slash your wrists and you may end up doing it for real instead of in your imaginary life. It is when the real crosses into the imaginary that the danger can start.
Andy:	When I was very ill I was walking in North Wales on a hot summer's day, and I was convinced that I was being persecuted by hundreds of bikers who were passing me. I thought that I was being tracked down and that something horrible was to happen to me.

I borrowed a pair of scissors from a pub and sat in a hedge, and this voice was saying, "Hari! Hari! Commit Hari Hari." I was trying my best to cut |

out my stomach with a pair of scissors and I just couldn't physically push them into my stomach. If it had been a gun I think it would have been very easy to do.

Dave: What the voices meant was do it in your imaginary life.

Andy: That was an intense moment of change in my life – it was a real cross-roads. Before this I had been taking a lot of drugs – mushrooms, LSD, and Coke, and I was smoking dope everyday. God knows what state my head was in. But when I got home my mum called a psychiatrist. I was being very contradictory and conflicting. For example, someone in the hospital asked me if I was hearing voices. I replied that I heard them on the telly and the radio. I was psychotic, burnt out, and completely off my head.

Matt: Yes, I can be very high or very low. At the high end I have done the most absurd and impossible things which I could not do in a normal state. Some of them have been to do with self-preservation. I made an amazing self-preservation escape about five years ago which I know I could not do if I was in a sane state..

Dave: A literal escape?

Matt: Yes, a literal escape from a very bad situation.

Dave: Yes, the voices always say run don't they. I remember that once I had the choice of staying in a bathroom for five days or running.

Matt: At the other end of the spectrum I tend to become incredibly paranoid, when literally everyone is against me in a gang. They all have it in for me one way or another. It is only in the last few years that I have actually been able to realise these things. I think I could handle them better now because of the things I know, but before, this state of mind was the status quo. It is like the cliché that I am OK, it is everyone else who is mad – I am right, it is everyone else who is wrong.

My father was a manic-depressive. He was never diagnosed as such because he was very old and there was not Lithium in his day. By and large I think that these are inherited conditions, a bit of nature and nurture. But as for you Dave – just in the time that I have known you, I have noticed how

70

much control you have been able to insert over a number of things that have been bearing down on you. Quite seriously.

Dave: When I am bad I do not come to the meetings.

Matt: Of course, this is an important matter. If people are really feeling bad they do not come, and if they are feeling really good they do not come because they have something better to do. This is one of the ways in which I think we work very well because it is quite a pleasant social interlude. It is something that I quite look forward to once a fortnight. That is one of the reasons why I think it works so well, apart from the fact that we all learn from each other.

Chapter four

Who or what are the voices?

As has become apparent, the hearing voices movement incooperates a more varied understanding of voices[1] than orthodox psychiatry's "auditory hallucinations". As chapter two endeavoured to highlight, the philosophy of the Hearing Voices Network has been marked by an acceptance of a *diversity of explanations* for what voices represent, why one experiences them, and the role they play in an individual's life. Because of an acceptance of the subjective reality of spiritual voices, and the recognition that ways of referring to and talking about voice-hearing are both rooted in and mixed with cultural discourses, the hearing voices movement has fostered alliances with academics in psychology and psychiatry interested in "deconstructive" approaches to mental health. *Deconstructing Psychopathology*, compiled by academics and mental health professionals, with its attention to the ever-changing politics (including race, class and gender) of psychopathology, is perhaps the most comprehensive account of such an approach. The book also devoted considerable space to the ideas of radicals within the Hearing Voices Network, and represented the links between the academic methodology of deconstructive analysis and critical mental health practice. By proposing that truths, norms, and categories are located in language rather than any objective world, such work elevated the authority and legitimacy of "mystical", "non-scientific" or "parapsychological" experiences for voice-hearing. It also allowed us to reflect on how the most dominant ways of talking about hearing voices *suppressed,* through their powerful institutional positions, these other web of ways of discussing them.

Three members of the Hearing Voices Network have contributed their insights below in order to further convey a sense of the multi-faceted discourses on the voice-hearing experience. Each one documents a different meaning for voices, including what brings on the experience, the role voices play in their life, and how voices relate to the world in general. The *experience* of the writers can not, in a sense, be argued with. We could also advocate that none of the personal explanations for the voice-hearing experience are more *factually* true in a scientific way than any other, and that each explanation is

---

[1] While discussing my research with friends, two of them have also, quite casually, told me of the voices they hear. One is a journalist and the other works in the advertising industry. Neither has previously discussed with me about their voice-hearing, and neither has had contact with psychiatry. Interestingly, both understand their voices to be a reflection of their own thoughts (see chapter six). But as the voices have always been with and alongside them, they have never felt a pressing need to treat them as an experience requiring prolonged self-reflection and analysis.

as valid as the next one. Readers may judge one or some of the accounts to ring with more clarity and be consistent with their outlook. But I would argue this is more a reflection of the reader's philosophical allegiances than a question of one reader being more in tune with "objective reality" than another. I should add that I have not included a medical psychiatric account of voice-hearing because the movement, as this book documents, is generally antagonistic towards its modernist and biological reductionist framework.

1. Creative Voices
by Maxwell Steer

Maxwell Steer, musician and composer, is a former BBC radio producer and Deputy Director of Music with the Royal Shakespeare Company. In 1993 he produced a radio programme about his pilgrimage to visit Saibaba, an Indian holy man. He hears voices, but conceptualises the experience differently from orthodox psychiatry of which he has never had a need to consult. "Creative Voices" puts the voice-hearing experience into a historical and cultural context, and makes a link between a "creative voice" and the psychotic voice. It compares the discourses of the psychiatric framework with that of eastern religions and philosophies.

The artists' voices

Max Bygrave's famous catch phrase, "I wanna tell you a story", reflects one of the elemental aspects of the human psyche[2]. For more than being an impulse to communicate one's identity, it signifies the universal subconscious urge to excel, to be able to hold other people's attention, to spell-bind. This is echoed in a line from the theme song of the TV series *Fame*, "I want them to know my name." At some level each of us wants *them* to know our names. We want respect – even if it is only from the person behind the counter in our local convenience store. When we do not get the attention we feel we deserve we get angry or, if inhibited from expressing anger, we get depressed.

By adulthood most of us will have found a balance between our aspirations to communicate, and what others respond favourably to. Those on whom "the blind watchmaker" has scattered genetic gifts enabling them to talk, sing, paint or write, have a socially approved means of expressing this impulse. Paradoxically, while millions

---

[2] I use the words *psyche* and *psychic* to denote the human personality taken as a whole. It should not be taken in the popular sense as implying something communicated to human minds from an external source, but on the other hand the term would include extra-sensory faculties as subjectively experienced, since those are aspects of a fully-developed consciousness.

strive hopelessly for their "15 minutes of fame", many have found their success an intolerable burden. Leaving aside the never-ending parade of burnt-out popular icons, there are much more puzzling enigmas behind the creative desuetude of, for example, Baudelaire, Strindberg, Elgar, Mahler, Salinger, Sibelius, Pound, Pinter....just a handful of those who successfully "told their story" yet became dumb at the height of their success. Did they lose their voice? Or did the voice lose them? What *is* "the creative voice" and where does its territory overlap "the psychotic voice"? Is it something that can be turned on and off at will?

Ronnie Scott

According to an obituary of jazzman Ronnie Scott, found dead on Christmas Eve, 1996, his daughter "found it hard to divert Scott from the urgent demands of voices within him". "I am old," he told her. "I am nearly 70. I can't play. What's the point?[3]" Scott had suffered from depression most of his adult life, but, as the obituarist reminds us, he lived and worked in a culture dedicated to spontaneity. What Ronnie Scott's death reveals is that the creative impulse contains both wanted and unwanted elements. He was driven by a *wanted* desire, or voice, to communicate musically. But when his psychic energy imploded due to depression, alcohol and old age, he was left with only the impulse itself, which, because he could no longer satisfy it, became *unwanted* and ultimately psychotic. Coming to terms with the wanted and unwanted aspects of the creative impulse, or voice, is often complex for any artist. Not only is there no vocabulary supporting the positive attributes of voice-hearing but there is enormous professional danger in admitting to experiences of this kind, no matter how benign, since it is likely to lead to being singled out as a weirdo.

For many artists their life journey and creative journey are aspects of the single attempt to resolve or make sense of the discrepancies between their creative sense and the responses echoed back to them by the public. Van Gogh, Kafka and Charlie Mingus are three out of thousands for whom the creative voice was both inspiration and curse. Creative artists are also frequently every bit as obsessive about their craft and as antisocial in their behaviour as the mentally unstable. However, it is my observation that no matter how "uncontrollable" their creative impulse becomes, it rarely causes anything approaching the distress experienced by psychotic voice-hearers because the experience is "answered" by the appreciation of others.

Religion and voices

Partly because psychoanalysis emerged during the age of scientific materialism, it does not consider voices to be a normal feature of religious or moral clarity. In a 1996

---

[3] John Fordham, *The Guardian* 3/1/97.

collection of essays, *Psychiatry and Religion*, one writer notes that three classic textbooks of psychiatry either "ignore religion or treat it as a delusion[4]". In one sense this is a reflection of the toppling of "irrational" religion by the West's Enlightenment. But, an unfortunate side-effect has been that creative and psychotic voices/impulses are now viewed as independent manifestations. I would propose, however, that they are offshoots of a central numinous voice.

The Bible itself, the core text of Western culture, is permeated by ideas of the existence of a voice which exists partly in an individual's subjectivity, and, partly in an archetypal collective experience. The idea of "hearing" and "being obedient to" the "voice of the Lord" lies at the heart of all religious awareness [see also chapter one]. This idea is not unique to Judaeo-Christianity. The idea of guidance through life by some inner, but independent, moral force, is also implicit in the Vedic concept *dharma* – the idea that each individual has a dynamic which both propels and attracts the propulsion along an ideal course. In fact, this concept is not so foreign to us – does not the very word, *vocation,* sum up the same idea[5]?

According to Buddhism, originally a reform movement within Hinduism, *dharma* stills an individual's ego so that the underlying cosmic voice may be heard. This voice is imaged as a radiant silence. In merging with this silence, or voice, the individual achieves *nirvana*, the state of being and nothingness in which the ego is reunited with the inner voice or conscience. In such a highly sensitised state the conscious mind is no longer closed off from the subconscious, and so has access to the wealth of experiential knowledge to which the conscious mind only has access as feelings. (Indeed, a sense of personal resolution or inner reconciliation is the goal of all religious traditions.) When all the dimensions of the personality are brought into harmony, the creative impulse or voice is attuned to the maintenance and development of this concord. This is the true meaning of *sattva,* the pursuit of enlightenment which liberates the mind from the restraints of the mundane consciousness.

The idea of *dharma* is also invoked by the Old Testament prophets. How *could* their listeners hear "the word of the Lord" if not as an internalised voice? The borderline

---

[4] ed Dinesh Bhugra, *Psychiatry and Religion*, Routledge 1996. Quote from a review by Julian Candy in Network #61, 1996

[5] One aspect of this idea of *dharma* is expressed in remarks by the retiring broadcasting executive Sam Chisholm about his success at BSkyB [Guardian 23/6/97] "It does require sacrifice, because you have a sense of duty. You've got to learn to put everything ahead of yourself." Plainly this "sacrifice" was before the altar of a Golden Calf rather than the pursuit of anything profound, and the quote reveals one of the things Chisholm sacrificed was his own family, yet it shows what can be achieved by single-minded application towards, here, a simple-minded goal.

between the creative and the psychotic affects of the inner voice is beautifully illustrated by this passage where the prophet Jeremiah, in a veritable mid-life crisis, speaks of his utter dejection that appeals for his fellow countrymen to heed the authentic voice of their national religious identity have failed: "The word of He Is (Yahweh) has meant for me insult, derision, all day long. I used to say, 'I will not think about him, I will not speak his name anymore.' Then there seemed to be a fire burning in my heart, imprisoned in my bones. The effort to restrain it wearied me. I couldn't bear it." (Jeremiah 20:9)

It would probably be true to say that the *tremendous* effect of being in tune – even if momentarily – with this inner power has conditioned the attitudes and culture of every human civilisation, not least in the belief of how such contact could/should be made. The crux of the issue is that in a post-religious world an irruption of this elemental phenomenon of hearing voices can be extremely alarming to someone who has neither consciously sought spiritual experience nor has even rudimentary religious knowledge by which to contextualise it.

The philosopher Carl Jung carved on the gateway of his lakeside villa at Kusnacht: *Adebit sed no adebit Deus aderit* – Bidden or unbidden God will be present. This is the heart of my thesis. Just because we can dismiss the word *God*, does not banish or replace the experiential reality it encapsulates. I would argue that by replacing God with the phrase "my inner self" in references such as prayers and oratory, we could recover a meaning that has almost been totally lost in consumerist culture.

Artists as mediums

The image that I am trying to develop is of the rewarding nature of voice-hearing. The broad mass of the populace is scarcely conscious of either creative or psychotic impulses, nor do most people hear voices. But supposing that someone from that broad mass was to experience voices then their response could be anticipated as fearful and negative. This is borne out with Jung's observation that "the Self often first confronts a person in a hostile manner[6]".

In my working life as a composer and writer I have become convinced that creative gifts have something essential in common with mediumistic gifts. That is to say, the greatest exponents of either faculty have a clear sense that there is a transpersonal quality to what

---

[6] *The Philosophical Tree*, CG Jung, Collected Works vol 13. I explored these issues in my play *The Watcher In The Rain* (1990) whose plot revolved around the treatment of James Joyce's schizophrenic daughter by Jung.

they are communicating. In *Present and Past: Intermediaries and Interpreters* Wilfrid Mellers, formerly Professor of Music at York, comments: "Independent of human particularities, music is beyond the arbitration of the artist, who is simply a medium, a vessel for truth. Artists are therefore in essence anonymous...[7]" Many composers, from Beethoven to Birtwistle, have stated that at times they felt themselves merely to be the agent of a composition seeking to come in to existence through them rather than a composer. This would certainly be a function of hearing voices. Mellers refers to this later in the same article: "With very great music...matters of personal identity may seem to efface historical considerations. John Lill, for example, seems to believe that, playing Beethoven, he may be 'possessed' by the composer's spirit, and even that discreetly superb Beethovenian, Bernard Roberts, confessed, when I marvelled at his performance of the *Appassionata*, that just possibly, very occasionally it *is* Beethoven one is hearing."[8] Psychoanalytically one might say that when direct contact is made between an individual's consciousness and a deep point in his\her subconscious, the uniqueness of this experience is projected onto or perceived as something external. S/he may suppose him/herself to have been in direct communication with a god or spirit.

The balanced, well-focused psyche is characterised, in a word, by coherence. Those who achieve an exceptionally high degree of coherence we call a *saint*. To those who are incapable of achieving even the barest minimum we assign the term *mad*. Most of us lie somewhere towards the middle of the spectrum and regard either extreme with equal suspicion. In the literature of clinical psychology a connection is often made between voice-hearing and low self-esteem. The universal assumption of conventional medicine is that by suppressing the voice-hearing, usually with a chemical cosh, the patient's poor self-image will improve.

While the recent foundation of international Hearing Voices Networks has received widespread publicity Professor Romme was in fact not the first clinician to explore this avenue. In two perceptive books published in 1971 and 1973 the Canadian clinical psychologist Wilson Van Dusen recounts his experience of paying detailed attention to the voices of his patients at Mendocino State Hospital, California, from 1964 onwards. In *The Natural Depth of Man*[9] he concludes: "There are two distinct orders of hallucinations. The lower order appears to be much more common [about four to one] than the higher order. Many patients only experience the lower order. Some experience

---

[7] W Mellors *Present and Past: Intermediaries and Interpreters* in Companion to Contemporary Musical Thought (Routledge 1994) Vol 2, p921. James Joyce said very similar things.
[8] *op cit*, p929
[9] Wilson Van Dusen *The Natural Depth of Man*, Swedenborg Foundation, US 1973, p143.

both orders, which must be something like between heaven and hell. The lower order has *less talent* than the patient. The higher order is *more gifted* than the patient. There are no hallucinations roughly at the patient's own general level of understanding. Any explanation I could give of this would be mere theorising. The lower order talks a great deal but its vocabulary and range of concepts, ideas and knowledge are less than the patient's....These hallucinations lie, cheat, deceive, pretend, threaten etc. Dealing with them is like dealing with very mean drunks. Nothing pleases them. They see the negative side of everything...Their general aim seems to be to take over the patients and live through them as they please. The higher order is just the opposite. Whereas the lower attacks the patient's will, the higher order acts out of great respect for the patient's will....The higher order is highly symbolic. It can produce thousands of highly complex symbols, many of which have an ancient historical or mythological base. Voices in the higher order are extremely intuitive of either the patient or anyone else present...They tend to be non-verbal and much more internal, feeling related and subtle."

Van Dusen describes the hallucinations of a schizophrenic gas fitter of limited education, whose voice had introduced herself to her host as "an emanation of the feminine aspect of the divine". The man felt himself being undermined by "mean critical voices working...and she came to cheer him up". It was Van Dusen's practice to engage in direct dialogue with his client's voices, and on one occasion in a therapy session the "emanation" suddenly began to describe quite esoteric Buddhist symbolism. Van Dusen was so intrigued he...."went home and studied some obscure part of Greek myths and asked her about it the next time I saw the gas pipe fitter. She not only understood the myth, she saw into its human implications better than I did. When asked, she playfully wrote the Greek alphabet all over the place. The patient couldn't even recognise the letters, but he could copy hers for me." He also discovered the "emanation" gave the gas fitter extrasensory powers: "She was the most gifted person in the area of religion I've ever known. She reflected the seriousness of my query [answering lightly or seriously accordingly]. She knew the depth of my understanding and led gently into very human allusions that reflected a profound understanding of history...The patient didn't understand my conversation with her. He had no religious interests. I remember once his turning in the doorway as he was leaving and asking me to give him a clue as to what she and I had just talked about."

Later the man was transferred to another hospital and the "emanation" ceased to visit him. Van Dusen wrote: "There is no doubt in my mind that some patients are shown things of great importance in hallucinations, though they are not often able to use them. I recall a black, alcoholic burglar [whose voices gave him] a very intimate tour of minority group experiences down through history...He came out of it feeling he had to

79

do something for minorities, but instead returned to drinking and more bouts of madness...I found patients concealed higher-order experiences. They assumed a psychologist would be more interested in the plentiful sexual elements of the lower order. They also feared the power and mystery of the higher order...One naturally meets Jesus Christ in this inner world. Fake Christs of the lower order are easy to see through. They brag about their powers and the wonder they can do. When criticised they easily become defensive and threatening. The real Christ-like figures from the higher order are just the opposite. They often say nothing, yet their radiant presence has an intense effect on the patient. They lead gently with a profound understanding of the patient's inner potentials. They do good."

Van Dusen recounts how he encouraged a psychotic criminal to become acquainted with an inner sun that appeared to him. "As he joined with the sun he went through a series of religious experiences that required temporary seclusion and supervision. He had been a prison tough guy and the numinous religious experience was a bit much for him. He went down a tunnel in the ground until he came to doors holding creatures in hell. He was tempted to open the doors when a powerfully impressive Christ-like figure, all in radiant white, stopped him. Just looking into the figure's eyes had a profound influence on him. He knew he was understood and loved. He knew the figure was wiser than him. The figure guided him out into the daylight. There he saw a gigantic golden trumpet that signalled he was to become musical. He did. He wrote about four songs a day and kept two other patients busy writing down the music, since he didn't know how."

The man was soon well enough to be discharged from hospital although Van Dusen comments that he did not think this would be the man's final encounter with mental illness. Van Dusen noted that higher order hallucinations would often manifest ESP, whereas lower order hallucinations would claim to be able to do so, but rarely could. "Occasionally I could see some relationship between the individual and his hallucinations. Persons who had violated their own conscience seemed to be mercilessly tortured by conscience-like lower order figures...repressed, "good" people were often tormented with sexual fantasies...Conversely, some people who had been criminals had spiritually elevated hallucinations from the higher order. One man had religious visions in solitary confinement that many ministers would give their left hand to have."

Humanising science
Western society values linear (masculine) logic and the manipulation of the physical world. Correspondingly, it places little value on metaphysical aspects which do not relate directly to material concerns. For several centuries this had led to the down-

valuing of "feminine" attributes – no aspect of which is more unmanly than heeding an inner voice. In any case rationalist logic denigrates the validity of the psychic functions because their operations cannot be subjected to materialistic criteria.

To most people, and most doctors, the very idea of hearing voices is a sure sign of madness. I think the opposite – not to hear voices is a sign of incurable dullness! In fact, as I am seeking to demonstrate, nearly everyone *does* hear them, they don't necessarily perceive the intuitional guidance as auditory, nor do they necessarily see it as originating outside their consciousness. Yet who has not known a moment of sudden insight or revelation – perhaps when a career choice suddenly came into focus, or when we suddenly realised someone loves us? A tragic side-effect of scientific thought forms is that we in the West have been programmed to discredit out own spontaneous subjectivity. The medical community in particular is obliged to absorb so much materialistic information that the essential *scientia* (knowledge) of healing becomes obscured. As alluded to earlier, in connection with Ronnie Scott, a climate of fear exists, as much in medicine as elsewhere, about deviation from bourgeois social norms. People who consider themselves "as understanding as anyone else" rapidly lose patience with friends who can not explain or rid themselves of conditions such as depression. Even a very fine mental nurse confessed her own fear "that associating with people who hear voices may make me hear them".

Despite our multi-cultural society the dominant thought form of Western public life still suffers from the scientific fallacy that only *one* answer can be correct. Just like an individual wrestling with voices in his own head; by denying the lesson the *whole* personality is trying to teach the ego, so the West's ruling elites are still rooted in the monotheistic thought forms of a God they no longer believe in. In public life all we have left is words. The voice is no longer heard.

The conceptual problem is that while we have a grammar for acts associated with consciousness we have little or none for acts connected with the subconscious. The two-dimensional linearity of the conscious mind (subject-verb-object) lies at the heart of all our traditions of articulacy. The existence of a vocabulary normalises a set of experiences. The history of the 20th century has been the gradual penetration of linear thought processes by the multi-dimensionality epitomised in quantum science – namely that subject and object can no longer be viewed as discrete because the act of observation materially affects the behaviour of what is observed. This transmutation of collective awareness has made those who cannot understand what is happening extremely uneasy, and they have responded to their fears by clamping hold of traditional vocabularies and trying to prevent them from altering.

The lucky ones now, as always, are those who can communicate their inner sensations, who can "tell their story", who can link their web of personal meaning with that of others in this confusing era. As a society we now need the collective compassion to look at those who struggle with flashes of insight into other worlds of thought which they can not explain, and experience feelings they can not contextualise

Like two golden birds perched on the selfsame tree
Intimate friends, the ego and the Self
Dwell in the same body. The former eats
The sweet and sour fruits of the tree of life
While the latter looks on in detachment.

As long as we think we are the ego,
We feel attached and fall into sorrow.
But realize that you are yourSelf a Lord
Of life, and you will be freed from sorrow.
When you realize that you are the Self,
Supreme source of light, supreme source of love,
You transcend the duality of life
And enter into the unitive state.

The Lord of Love shines in the hearts of all.
Seeing him in all creatures, the wise
Forget themselves in the service of all.
The Lord is their joy, the Lord is their rest;
Such as they are the lovers of the Lord.
Mundaka Upanishad

It is hard to believe these words were written over two millennia before Christ, or that it's taken the West another two millennia to rediscover the psychological language they embody. But then the holistic logic of the subconscious has always been to be learnt afresh by each person setting out to penetrate its mysteries.

This is an edited version of a longer article.

2. Mind as computer
by Mickey de Valda

Mickey de Valda is the present chair of the Hearing Voices Network in Manchester. He was diagnosed schizophrenic, and has been an in-patient in three psychiatric hospitals and a secure unit. He is also author of "Schizo", a 700-page autobiographical account of his travels in Europe in the 1970s and 1980s, and his experience of fringe religious groups, voice-hearing, delusions and psychiatry. "Mind as Computer" uses the analogy of the human mind as computer to develop his understanding of voice-hearing. His writing rejects the world of deities and spirits.

It is not my intention in writing this to undermine anyone's beliefs, or to take anything away from them which may have helped form their life or lifestyle. My intention is simply to help people who may be diagnosed as mentally ill.

Sources of knowledge

When I first became ill, a whole file of knowledge about telepathy was already in my mind. This file, built up from material I had encountered in the past, came from sources such as sci-fi movies, novels, mediums and spiritualism. But the most influential item in my file was an article I read which mentioned the Russians had invested a lot of money into the investigation of Extra Sensory Perception (ESP). It was a scientific investigation involving the use of cards. Each card contained one of five signs, and people, supposedly gifted with a sixth sense, would try to predict the card's order. However, this Russian superpower involvement lent credibility to the other more sensational contents of all the rest of the things that I knew about ESP. When there is that much information around, the layman is bound to give the possibility of clairvoyance, mediumship and telepathy at least a second glance. I gave telepathy a second glance. I even gave it a third glance.

When I heard voices, the first thing I noticed was that they were extremely realistic. I do not just mean that they *sounded* real, but the voices' content fitted, and was appropriate to, whatever subject they addressed. They were logical. Here is one example...Now, I am aware of the less well off people in the third world, and one day, as I was pissing in the toilet, I heard an African voice say: "Who's that pissing in the water? I will fuckin' kill him." Now that *could* seem like a third world person who is angry that we in the West have so much – he was obviously having a go at me for pissing in a couple of gallons of water, when for him water is a matter of life and death. At the time that was exactly what I took it to be. That is to say I took that voice to be an act of telepathy. I then told everyone that I was a telepath, and tried to make something of it, adopting a matter-of-fact attitude, and acting in a positively pro-telepathic manner. In retrospect it was rather foolish.

But this attitude was also influenced by my knowledge of the work of Carl Jung, and his ideas of levels of consciousness below the personal. My understanding was that there was even a national consciousness, below our personal level, along with a tribal and animal consciousness. I used to fake up ideas such as the French national consciousness was raged against me during the international rugby matches. I believed this because at the time I was working on a French farm and the husband of the farmer's daughter actually played rugby for France. The voices (which I thought were the French national consciousness) said that I got into the daughter's pants. She had actually just lent me a pair of jeans.

Aldous Huxley was the second writer who influenced me. In one of his books he theorised along the lines that the "mind" was not in the brain, but was something "out there" in the world. He wrote that the brain was in fact a filter which only allowed useful information into consciousness: that is, the information necessary for our survival and normal everyday functioning. When Huxley experimented with mescaline he thought that the drug impaired the proper working of the brain (by affecting the supply of sugar) so that one stared, spellbound, at the sights and sounds of the world, but was unable to get on with anything practical and necessary.

Both Jung's and Huxley's theories could explain this voice I heard whilst urinating in my clean, drinkable toilet water. A Jungian interpretation could be that for some reason the anger of an under-nourished person somewhere in the third world found an opening to communicate with me, like an electric current running to earth, and the anger surfaced in my personal consciousness. I suppose that Huxley's idea would be that the raw emotion and anger of such a person was "around" in this sea of mind, and that I somehow latched on to it.

The computer analogy
Up to the seventies scientists and philosophers of the day had difficulty with the fact that the human brain did so much, so fast, and so efficiently. It was inconceivable that the grey matter in the head could control the heart and breathing, and at the same time get us from A to B while having a conversation and scratching an itch. The scientists of today have a lot to do to explain the tiny micro processes involved. But before we had the camera it was difficult to understand the eye. Now that the computer has been invented it is within the grasp of anyone to realise that man is in fact a machine. Now

that my word processor can arrange and rearrange this text at the touch of a key it is obvious that no mixing of our "levels of consciousness" is required to enable you to spontaneously answer a question which you were unaware I was about to ask. For example, if I asked you whether your partner had any red shoes, then I think that within a second or two you could answer yes, no, or don't know. Obviously our response times can be quick. It is equally obvious to me that we can get our wires crossed, and so create a little voice or other amusement – call it a malfunction if you like. I think that if our psychiatrists told us reassuringly that our minds are able to do such things, though we are not able to fully understand them, then people would go home feeling better than being diagnosed schizophrenic. If medicine calls people schizophrenic we ought not to be surprised if they fight tooth and nail to prove that they are mediums or receiving messages from God.

Of course, this does not explain why some people hear voices sometimes, others all the time, and most not at all. From my experience of the people involved in the Hearing Voices Network, trauma seems to set off the voices in a majority of cases. If some kind of trauma triggers the voice-hearing experience, does that then mean that sufficient trauma will produce voices in anyone subject to it? I think that such a question is more interesting than to ask, say, why are some people telepathic and others not?

Most of the ordinary folk that I spend time with have no idea that man can be viewed as a machine. Instead of this knowledge flooding out to release man from his enslavement to religion and its devils and demons, the purveyors of this and that temple of worship are out in even greater force. It seems to me that more people than ever before are chanting mantras and twisting their legs into almost impossible positions.

I am concerned that many people who hear voices do not seem to be aware that a good case can be made for those voices emanating from within their own mind. The advent of high speed data processing introduces more plausible theories than telepathy. It is dangerous to go around believing that someone else has access to your thoughts. If the boundary of yourself is understood to be your physical body then, at least, you understand that you are responsible for your own actions.

To return to pissing in the water. An everyday thought could be: "Oh God! I have to piss in this water which could save the life of someone in the third world." What is wrong if I beef it up a bit and use my brain to give a more creative and dramatic representation of my thought. I resent any attempt to explain the functioning of my own self-entertainment machine as mystical or in any way outside of my control.

3.   Violence and voices
by Kati Meadow

Kati Meadows is a graduate of Latin American studies. She has never been a psychiatric patient but has participated in group therapy for two years, and consults a cognitive psychologist. Her moving contribution, reflects how the content of hostile voices can mirror a person's earlier experiences of abuse.

Professor Marius Romme stressed the link between hearing voices and the experience of trauma which included psychological, physical and sexual abuse. Many men and women who hear voices do report such experiences. For women in particular, abuse is a common phenomenon; a recent survey found that one in 10 women are currently experiencing violence from a man they know, and one in eight has suffered from violence at some time. Around 60 -70% of women in psychiatric care have suffered some form of abuse.

Domestic violence can include rape, assault, torture, imprisonment; psychological or emotional abuse (this includes continual threats, sleep deprivation, constant undermining of confidence and displays of total power). This violence is carried out by husbands, boyfriends, fathers, brothers, sons and other relations. In many cases this violence is similar to conditions experienced in concentration camps, which is known to cause hallucinations and thought disorders. Women who experience violence often have to endure many episodes of trauma carried out by men that are known to them. These events can re-occur at any time that the woman is in contact with the man, and so they can have the constant threat of this violence hanging over them which is extremely stressful.

In the case of psychological abuse, women can be kept under total control of the man, by various rules and threats and conflict, which can be like living under a dictatorship in an authoritarian regime. The constant emotional and/or physical battering a woman has to endure affects her confidence and the belief in herself. It can also be a very isolating experience, and something that she is unable to relate to another person. Because violence is such a part of our society the suffering incurred is not always taken seriously or the extent of the damage recognised.

The fact that such a large proportion of women who use the mental health system experience, or have experienced violence, seems to indicate that violence is often a direct cause of mental health problems. Hearing voices telling you what to do can be a continuation of the control of the man who has been controlling you all the time. The voices that tell you to kill yourself, or that frighten you, or ridicule you can also be an echo of this man. These words may be spoken by different voices, splintered inside yourself, which are memories and beliefs implanted by such constant abuse. If you were to replace the words *abuse* or *violence* with the word *schizophrenia* this would become an accurate definition of the effects of long-term physical, psychological and sexual violence.

I myself am a woman who hears voices, and have experienced violence from my father. My father is a man with a temper and a drink problem. He was a company director when I was a teenage and had a very stressful job and brought that stress home with him. He took it out on me, not my mother, and made my teenage years a misery. I wasn't allowed out at night. I wasn't allowed to have a boyfriend or wear make up. I wasn't encouraged to bring friends home. I was kept as a child although I was growing physically into a woman. Most of the time he humiliated me with verbal abuse and kept me under control by threats of violence and orders. If I disobeyed I knew what to expect. He would become very aggressive, swear at me, calling me a bitch, a slag etc...and then he would grab me and hit me, strangling me as he banged my head against the wall continuously, still swearing loudly as if in a frenzy. On one occasion my brother and mother had to pull him off me as it looked like he was set on killing me.

Once this pattern was set it wasn't surprising that when I left home I jumped out of the frying pan into the fire when I moved in with a boyfriend. I was so used to being humiliated and tormented that it was normality, expected behaviour. He used to dictate what clothes I wore, trying to make me look "sexy", like the women in the pornographic magazines he kept insisting on showing me. He raped me and buggered me a few times. This wasn't like making love, this was a total power game, and there was no affection on these occasions. It was like masturbation and I felt violated.

He was also good at verbal abuse and ritual humiliation, so I believed I was "thick" and "fat" when I was only a size 12. He finished the job my father had started, diminishing any confidence I had in myself, and clouding my perceptions and making me completely dependent upon him. When we eventually split up I was so insecure and damaged that I became totally psychotic. I have been hearing voices constantly and have been very paranoid and depressed for five years, and am having psychotherapy now. The voices that I hear are abusive. They say that I am a loser, a scrounger, a cow, a bitch, a prostitute, that I'm ugly, mad, weird, lazy, fat, pathetic, soft, crazy etc. They comment on my clothes, saying that I look a mess and am too fat. They are always ridiculing and humiliating me, or frightening me. These words are spoken in different voices, but they are the words of my father and my ex-boyfriend, and they describe how I feel about myself because my mind has been distorted by their twisted thinking. I am also very paranoid now. I can not go out alone and am fearful of being killed by other people. I often hear people plotting to kill me in the middle of the night. I have also heard the voice of my ex-boyfriend outside my window planning to rape, murder and rob me. I am terrified of aggression and violence, and can not watch violent films and find watching the news too horrifying. If a man shouts at me I fall to pieces and expect him to be violent towards me. It is only a short jump from shouting to hitting.

I have not had a boyfriend for several years. I can not imagine ever meeting a man who would not try and control me, be aggressive or violent, or make me feel worthless. I think that our culture is responsible for promoting violence and aggression, and teaches men to express their emotions as anger, and sees women as sexual objects and victims. These cultural stereotypes are reinforced by the media, in films, TV, books and magazines. It will take a long time and a lot of effort before we will see any change. Men have to get in touch with their feelings and express their pain and frustration in more acceptable ways, and see women as people. Women have to educate themselves and stop being victims, take a stand against verbal and physical aggression. We need to promote awareness to teach the next generation so that they do not make the same mistakes.

Chapter five

Psychotic and proud

"A psychotic is someone who believes that he has been cured by psychiatry," **Bill Martin,** *Asylum* **Magazine, 1997.**

"To refuse diagnosis is to take the side of the client and to challenge the relationship between those who think they know and those who are attempting to become experts on their own lives. In the process we can deconstruct psychopathological practice," **Professor Ian Parker in** *Deconstructing Diagnosis: psychopathological practice*

Cured by a leucotomy

I once played chess with Peter, a 70-year-old man who had had a leucotomy operation. He had undergone this brain surgery in the sixties whilst an in-patient in an old Victorian asylum in Yorkshire. The slicing of Peter's frontal lobe did not seem to have effected his chess skills, but curiously I asked him whether he thought the surgery had done him any good otherwise. "Oh yes," he replied positively, and proceeded to tell me of his role and life in the asylum, in particular his work as a scorer for the local cricket team that played on the square in the hospital's grounds. I was tempted to question him further about how he thought the surgery specifically had benefitted him, but then thought it fruitless as well as tasteless. Nevertheless, it seemed he was happy to accept that psychiatry had cured him, because 40 years later he was no longer distressed as he had been, and was only on a "maintenance" dose of medication.

Peter was sent to the asylum all those years ago because he had been psychotic and used to hear voices. He had set himself alight and thrown himself into a river under their orders. "What did the voices say to you?" I asked. He looked at me with the air of someone who preferred to forget such memories, and replied: "Oh, I can't tell you. They were terrible. So blasphemous. They swore at me like you can not believe." I asked him a second time to let on to me the awful content of his voices but, being a religious man, he declined. The voices were just too scandalous he said. For all the 40 years he had been in an asylum I wonder whether he had talked to anyone in detail about his voices which commanded him to take such destructive actions, and which had a stranglehold over his life. Peter was a chronic schizophrenic whose brain was electrocuted, medicated and cut with a surgeon's knife while in the asylum. Now he is a contented community care patient supported by a Leeds charity, and the only evidence of a "mental health problem" is residual symptoms of chronic institutionalisation.

Ron Coleman

Not all chronic schizophrenics end up like Peter. Ron Coleman, for example, who as mentioned in chapter two was a charismatic individual involved in the development of the Hearing Voices Network in Manchester. Like Peter he heard voices that ordered him to burn himself, and he dutifully complied. Like Peter he was diagnosed with a severe mental illness, and was medicated and electroshocked (on 40 occasions). But, although it was a painful and arduous struggle, he found a way out of the acute psychiatric wards. Not only was there the problem of his fiercely hostile voices, which those in the Network during the early nineties helped him to resolve, there was the psychiatric service (backed up by the police) whose interventions he continually fought. The service not only used its sectioning powers on him, but compelled him to take neuroleptics, including Clozaril, and other medication such as Lithium. The psychiatric service felt no option but to maintain and treat Coleman as a schizophrenic, because, of course, as a bewildered voice-hearer that was how his "symptoms" and behaviour were interpreted. A big man unafraid to match punch for punch he might have been doomed to a secure unit if unsupported in his efforts to find ways of challenging orthodox psychiatry without digging a hole deeper for himself to fall in. But with the backing of those in the Network, his story is more than a tale of recovery, and more than one of empowerment. As Coleman says – it is about freedom and slaying his "own personal dragon of schizophrenia."

I think it worth looking at Coleman's story in some detail because following Kati Meadow's piece in chapter four it reinforces the link between abuse, self-esteem and negative voices. It also tells of the obstacles facing a patient refuting their diagnosis to an all-too-often inflexible psychiatric service. In addition, and perhaps most importantly, his story is worth recording because of the work on voice-hearing that Coleman has developed since his days as a patient.

Later on in this chapter I turn to Coleman's political, psychological, and philosophical ideas as we discussed during an interview. Towards the end of the next chapter Coleman also explains some of his principles he uses when working with distressed voice-hearers. But before this, I have included an edited version of a tape *From Victim to Victor* where Coleman frankly, and angrily, narrates his own experience of voice-hearing and his years as a patient. The listener is drawn into the account with more intensity when listening to the tape itself, because Coleman narrates with both passion and sadness. Nevertheless the written account is as revealing in its honesty, and one can not but be both astonished and moved by its tone. Coleman's story is once again a credit to the impact that hearing voices self-help groups can have on some individuals' lives.

From Victim to Victor

"I was born and brought up in Dundee by working class Roman Catholic parents. Like every good Catholic boy my dream was to be a man of the cloth. Together with my schoolmates I attended instruction classes run by my local priest, and it was here that I learnt about the scriptures and the bible. When this priest retired he was replaced by Father Adrian, a young, lively man who me and my mates thought was a laugh. Mysteriously however, the children started leaving one by one, and not turning up for classes. Then, aged 11, I was to find out why, and it was the day my dream turned into a nightmare.

I was asked to come to the vestry by Father Adrian, and did not think anything of it. He asked me if I had anything to confess, and knelt down beside me. His hands went up my leg, and in that instance my faith was destroyed...The abuse continued until buggering became a regular occurrence.

I left the church and became a rebel at school. But if there was one thing I could do, and do well, it was to play rugby. Big and strong for my age, I was soon playing for my local men's club. It was in the pub after one Saturday match that I met Susanna, an artist nine years my senior. We got on well, and having plucked up the courage to ask her out we went for a meal together. Before long we were happy and in love. Susanna introduced me to a new world – a world of opera and classical music, which I grew to enjoy and appreciate. She taught me how to be a real man, not a hard man. I felt I had got through my earlier experience – because of Susanna. I became a whole person again.

By the time I was 17-years-old Susanna became pregnant, and it ended up being the happiest yet saddest day of my life. One Saturday, my rugby team was playing locally. Susanna said she did not want to go to the match as she did not feel up to it. After suggesting that I would not go either, Susanna told me not to be silly. After the game, and the usual trip to the pub, I bought some chips and returned home. Susanna was lying on the couch, asleep. I shouted to her: "Do you want a coffee with your chips?" There was no reply, so I went over and gave her a little shove. Still she did not move, still she did not say anything – it was then that I realised something was wrong. Susanna had overdosed, leaving a note saying she could not take it anymore. At 17-years-old I found myself having to arrange the funeral of the two people I loved most – Susanna and my unborn baby daughter. I immediately fled Dundee and joined the Pay Corps of the British Army.

I became a real loner in the army, but still got a degree in business and accounts. I still excelled on the rugby field, playing every Saturday during the season. But I had no real friends and did not want any. One day, however, I received a letter from a former officer who I got on well with, who asked me to go and work for him. I accepted, and was soon in charge of a London company's finance department. I devoted my whole time to the two things I could do best – work and rugby.

When at work I enjoyed making people redundant – it gave me a kind of buzz, made all the more easier by the fact that it was not people I was making redundant but figures I moved around on a computer screen. I did not care about people, I cared about figures. On reflection I wondered how I could have done what I did. From being a young socialist I had become one of Thatcher's children, meaning every word of it, living it and doing it. I did not give staff working under me in the office any peace, continually driving them to work harder. I was even known to come in on a Thursday afternoon, instructing staff to cancel their weekend plans because I had work for them to do.

When I was not working, I was playing rugby with a London club. When the season ended I just trained. These were sad days. Of course, I did not know that my new life was not far away now, it was just around the corner – I was soon to start my life of a madman.

One cursed Saturday afternoon the scrum went down. But this time it went down on my hips. I was unable to get up. I broke my hip and pelvis, and when the doctor came to tell me never to play rugby again it was like passing sentence. With my rugby finished where was I to go? Without my coping strategy what was I to do? Rather than sitting at home all day, I went back to work on crutches, and one night at about 7pm, whilst sitting in front of a computer screen, I heard my first voice. "You have done that wrong," I heard someone say to me. Startled, I glanced around the room – where I saw no one. "Jesus, you're shattered, it's time to go," I thought. So I went to the pub and got blitzed.

But who was that first voice? Although I was unable to recognise it at the time, I later came to see that it was, in fact, the voice of my beloved Susanna. I used to say Susanna came back to haunt me that night in the office. Now I say it was the night that I started to haunt myself.

Over the next few weeks the voices became worse and worse – and within six months I had lost my job and sold my house. I was, by then, hearing voices all over the place. They were everywhere. Day-in day-out they screamed at me, shouting, telling me I was evil, telling me I had asked for it, telling me it was my fault, telling me I should die, telling me to harm myself. I drank, and smoked cannabis, but still the voices abused me. I began to neglect myself, not washing or shaving for weeks. By the time I went to see my GP I was in a complete state. The GP immediately recommended that I saw a "specialist", and so it was that I had my first encounter with a psychiatrist.

"I think you are suffering from a treatable illness," said the psychiatrist, after interviewing me for an hour. "Why don't you come into hospital for a week or two?" I badgered the psychiatrist to tell me what illness he was referring to. "I think you have schizophrenia," he replied. "We can treat it." I snapped back to the psychiatrist that he was off his tree, and walked out of the consulting room. Three days later I was sectioned under the Mental Health Act, and the police arrived to take me to a "place of safety". I had been labelled mad, and this was just the beginning.

"Ten days and you will be fine," said the psychiatrist. After 10 weeks I still felt like shit, and told the psychiatrist I would not take the medication, only to find out what the Mental Health Act was really about – Section Three, the right to forcibly inject you. But I fought. I had freedom, I had liberties, I had rights. But no, I did not – my rights were gone. I was forced to take drugs that made me feel like a zombie, that took away my independent thinking. I became stiff and started to shake. I drooled and shuffled – just like a madman. When I became depressed, the staff wanted me to have ECT. I told them to get lost. ECT? No way.

I had turned into a happy vegetable. Ron Coleman had been taken away. In addition, I was put on a "special" which meant I was continually supervised by nurses. By now my life was controlled by doctors, nurses and occupational therapists who told me when to get up, when to go to bed, and when to eat, toilet and bath. To top it all the voices were still there and I had started to burn myself. I was a proper mess.

But could I give up? No, I had to fight back. So I threw chairs through the hospital windows. The nurses would ask me whether I had done it, and I would, of course, say no, only to then go and brag about it to other patients in the smoke room. I was planting the seeds for my own madness, I was maintaining my victim status, and reinforcing an illness I did not even believe I had. How can you expect to win when you become the only casualty of your fight-back? Becoming schizophrenic was certainly not a good career move – from accountant to schizophrenic in one easy lesson. I had lost everything. Even when I asked the nurses to talk with me about my voices, I was recommended to play Scrabble instead. Where was I going?

I tried to kill myself, but I could not even succeed at that. I was the ultimate failure, failing myself, failing Susanna, failing everybody, and now I had even failed to kill myself. I was a total waste of space. But I then met an approachable doctor who *suggested that I try a therapeutic community in Manchester. This community worked on very different principles to the hospital. Clients could leave if they wanted to, they were not forced to take medication, and they were encouraged to talk through and work out their problems. I tried, but I was not very good at talking about my problems. Moreover, I was now entertaining some delusionary ideas about why I was there and what was wrong with me. Nevertheless, another good thing about the community was that clients were allowed to sleep with each other, and were encouraged to be open about it. Driven just by the need to be with someone I used to sleep with a woman who later announced that she was pregnant. Against the advice of the community's staff, she did not have an abortion, and left. I followed her after a disagreement with the staff, and was by her side when my baby daughter was born. That day was the second time I fell in love.*

My partner and I were two vulnerable people thrown together by circumstances, and now, with a baby to feed and a woman to support, I did not have time to be schizophrenic. I took all sorts of jobs, from cleaning to designing kitchens. I continued to take my medication to keep me going. But then, my partner told me she was pregnant again. Unable to handle this news, I walked, and kept on walking. For three months I walked, becoming a tramp, my life and thinking chaotic. I was now the kind of man you see at the end of a railway station, shouting and bawling with a tin of beer in my hand. And who was I bawling at? My voices.

Eventually I was picked up by my sister and went home with her to Dundee. But my voices were still screaming at me – the same things over and over again. I believed that what my voices said were true. One day I went to Dundee's bus station, asking where the first bus was going. At quarter to four in the morning I walked off the bus in Manchester again.

After living on the streets for a while, I was taken to a hostel, where I was given my own room. I just became madder. I was soon seen by a community psychiatric nurse who convinced me to visit the day hospital. The psychiatrist I saw prescribed me a months supply of medication. I could not believe my luck – a month's supply of drugs given to someone who felt like committing suicide! I took the tablets all at once, and if it had not been for a cleaner's vigilant eye at the hostel, I would have been pronounced dead at casualty. As it was I came round after a few days, and who was there, at the bottom of my bed? The psychiatrist. (After getting to know me later, I was to find out that he was quite a good lad.) He invited me into hospital, but I declined, and so was compulsorily detained for 28 days on a Section Two.

The same things happened in hospital, and I lost all my appeals against the sections. This time I also had ECT. I did, however, get on better with this new doctor who did talk to me...sometimes. But the big difference was that I was introduced to a worker called

Lyndsey, who visited me in hospital. Although I have never thanked her for it, she probably saved my life. One day she said: "Ron, there is a new group in Manchester called the Hearing Voices Group. Do you want to go?" I did. Not because I thought it might help me, but it would get me out of the ward. It was there that I met Anne Walton who said to me – "Your voices are real, accept them." For so long I had been told that my voices were not real, and yet here was someone saying that because you hear them they are real. I thought this was revolutionary. It now meant I could do something about it. If something is real you can do something about it, it is unreal things that you can not do anything about.

Over the next few weeks I started working on my voices. I met various other people in the Hearing Voices Network who were to play an important part in helping me. Life was changing, I was becoming a real person again. The reality was that I had not grown up since I was 17 – I had done nothing since I found Susanna dead on the couch. But, now, slowly and surely, I started looking at my voices, asking who they were, why they were there, taking them apart, realising that underneath those voices there was the real Ron Coleman. I learnt to let go, to grieve – I grieved for Susanna and my unborn child for the first time. I also grieved for myself, for this pathetic creature I had become. I attended to the voice of the priest, and I realised that it was not my own fault for what had happened, that I did not ask for it, that I was not the evil one. It was the priest who was the bastard. I was just a victim. The priest was never the man of God he pretended to be. And I dealt with the priest by taking him on. I phoned a bishop to tell him what the priest had done to me. As a result the priest never went to prison – he went somewhere better, a closed monastery which he would never come out of because they bury their own in the grounds. It was far better that he was off the streets for the rest of his life than spending a few years in prison.

At last, I was learning to take control of, and own, my voices. The voices no longer belonged to doctors, to psychologists, nurses, social workers, carers, support workers or even my family – the voices belonged to me, and it was only me who could deal with them. After visiting some clinical psychologists I was able to apply the technique of "focusing" onto my voices. I learnt how to structure time, to give the voices their space, but equally to demand my own space. And this was hard because it is much easier being a victim. Taking control of my life meant not running to the hospital anymore. I could not run away anymore, nor could I hide in my madness.
Finally, I had to stop taking the medication, and this was the hardest thing. All the time that I had been on medication I still heard the damn voices, so what was the point of being on it? At the time I was on four different drugs, including Lithium and Clozaril. I came off them all overnight.

At first it was hell, and my friends had to look after me. I had hallucinations I had never had before, including out-of-body experiences and visions. I flew through walls, and up into the stars visiting Scotland. But I succeeded in coming off the drugs, leaving me with just one more section to get through. When that was finally lifted, and I got out of hospital I celebrated by dancing on a pub table. I had freed myself from prescribed drugs and had taken control of my voices...at least for most of the time. Three years on my voices are mostly positive.

But where was I to go once I had given all that up? Having given up my madness, I needed something to replace it, and I found that within the Hearing Voices Network. I helped the mushrooming Network find an office, get a grant from the Mental Heath Foundation, and I acted as national co-ordinator. For three years I worked as a training officer. I had given up being a victim and had become Ron Coleman again."

Recovery

Making Miracles – An Exploration into the dynamics of self-healing compiled by American physician, Dr Paul Roud, tells the stories of "eleven incurable patients who battled illness and won." Most of these patients are cancer survivors who lived against long odds, and their stories are painted as testimony to the wonderful fortitude of the human spirit when up against a prescribed terminal end. Mind over matter, self-analysis, inner resolve, self-belief, psychospiritual transformation and positiveness are attributes celebrated as being the key to saving the body from malignant self-destruction. But one of these model "miracle makers", Lindsey Reynolds, was an ex-schizophrenic who, after years of hospital admissions for acts of self-harm was given a poor prognosis by doctors. Her "miraculous" recovery saw her eventually become a psychotherapist and manager of a mental health centre, and the two ingredients for her recovery according to Dr Roud centred around a persistent self-determination and an open, trusting relationship with her doctor. In contrast, Coleman's exchange of status from a shuffling, dribbling schizophrenic – whose tardive dyskinesia (a side-effect of neuroleptics) was so severe pint glasses rattled on pub tables he leant over – to an international figure on the mental health circuit, had little, in his eyes, to do with any particular supportive psychiatrist or therapist. One might say that it had a lot to do with an inner resilience which nearly a dozen years in the psychiatric system failed to dilute. It certainly had a lot to do with friends in the Network prepared to back him unconditionally.

The time Coleman decided to come off Clozaril exemplifies the power of such support and collective self-help. This new wave wonder drug of a neuroleptic, although not losing Coleman of his voices, certainly succeeded in dampening down their ferocity. But, as Coleman stated in an interview for *Asylum* magazine, they flattened his emotions and made him impotent. ("At 35-years-old I am not prepared to be a monk"). The drug was also a danger on his life because it damages white blood cells which in turn effect the body's ability to fight off infection. "Eventually I came to the view that Clozaril was too dangerous and the side effects were not acceptable to me, so I came off it." In the eyes of orthodox psychiatry this was unacceptable, and Coleman's psychiatrists were concerned of an almost immediate "relapse" of acute "symptoms", and they were also unprepared to support him in coming off them gradually. It was in this way that medicine had a reluctant and resistant patient cornered.

Coleman had discussed the consequences of coming off Clozaril with his new friend McLaughlin, and together they did not expect that his psychiatrist would section somebody who, although still hearing occasional abusive voices, appeared so well otherwise. In fact, as evidence of his good heath, Coleman was lecturing to clinical psychologists and CPNs at Manchester University on the subject of voice-hearing the same morning he came off the drug. It was when he went to Manchester Royal Infirmary afterwards for a routine blood test to monitor the effects of the Clozaril that Coleman told the senior registrar there was no point in the test because he had stopped his medication. The registrar replied by telling Coleman he was a fool and warned him he would go into a crisis. "She asked me what the voices were saying and I told her that the voices were saying what they normally say, which is 'kill yourself - you are not worth it,'" remembered Coleman. But by the time the taxi, which Coleman ordered, had arrived to drive him home, the registrar had gone through the process of sectioning him. "They put me straight on a Section Three," remembered Coleman, "which I thought was outrageous because Section Three is a treatment order which did not even allow for a period of assessment. Also, the interesting thing about it was that under Section Three it takes about nine weeks to get an appeal whereas under Section Two, it is 14 days. So, I immediately felt that all my rights were being stripped away....they could do with me what they wanted.....so I promptly escaped." This was when the police were called in.

Immediately following this first escape (there were four under this section) he telephoned Julie Downs, Mclaughlin's wife, asking her to contact her husband and pass on the message that he would be hiding out in a nearby pub. As her husband was uncontactable at the time, Downs rang round Coleman's friends asking them to go and meet him in the pub. Ironically, McLaughlin was at the time presenting a seminar at Prestwich hospital on psychotherapy for people who hear voices, the very service that Coleman had been denied throughout his spell as a patient. "The reason why I was not contactable," says McLaughlin, "was that during the middle of the seminar three fire-engines came and we had to evacuate the place. Prestwich patients, I'm told, are always setting the place on fire. But this time it was the duty psychiatrist on the room above us who had burnt his toast!"

Together Coleman and McLaughlin succeeded, with almost cheeky provocation, to set off the psychiatric service in a chase of its own tail. As Coleman had put Mclaughlin's name down as his next of kin, it was expected that the police would then telephone him, asking for Coleman's whereabouts. As it was they rang McLaughlin's home at two o'clock in the morning, but Coleman was not there. He was with some friends. McLaughlin, as smart as a jester, gave the police an answer they would certainly not have expected. "I explained to them that they should be getting the psychiatrist out of bed because it was he who had given Ron the wrong diagnosis. I don't suppose they ever did" On a later occasion the police actually came round to Coleman's house looking for him. Coleman himself answered the door, welcomed them in, and with characteristic audacity, told them that the man they were looking for was out, and showed them his own empty room to prove it. He got six more hours of freedom after that until one of the hospital night shift staff telephoned Coleman's home and recognised his Scottish accent. The police returned to take him back to hospital.

Freedom as well as recovery – and the formation of Action Consultancy and Training

Coleman emphasises freedom rather than simply recovery in his training and lectures. He argues that releasing oneself from all of psychiatry's shackles including the stigmatising diagnoses, medication, sick notes, disability living allowances and other welfare benefits are all important in the road to freedom, and the transformation of a victimised schizophrenic to an empowered voice-hearer. "I stated in a paper recently," said Coleman, "that I no longer want to be empowered by professionals in small things, I want to take power in all things that are to do with my life." Coleman was taking an increasingly political perspective in relation to the mental health service and the role of psychiatry.. Together with the support of Baker and McLaughlin, Coleman formed Action Consultancy and Training (ACT) in 1995, where he could advocate his left-wing politics without his views being understood as those of the Network. "I also wanted to get back to work and wanted to remain in mental health," recalled Coleman. "I did not think that I would suit a job within any other of the services as they stood. I also wanted to be in control of my destiny."

Coleman, and other users who came on board, such as Sharon Lefevre (see chapters eight and nine), turned ACT into a substantial enterprise – not just in a commercial sense, but as a source of user-led ideas in mental health rooted in a radical political philosophy. ACT's training has built on Coleman's reputation, and, as well as securing training contracts for one month, rather than half days as with the Network, ACT also found its way into academic institutions. For example, *Psychosis: mapping the maze,* is a five day course accredited by the University of Wales and also features in a course at Manchester Metropolitan University. Most recently ACT has earned a contract with West Midlands Health Authority to train its staff. ACT also publishes a total of eight books, pamphlets, and has produced an educational CD on issues of children and mental health. It also hopes to get the rights to what Coleman calls "the first third world user's publication" as well as Romme's next book and a publication entitled, *Schizophrenia, The 100 Years War*.

In Coleman's own words

Because Coleman's personal story is so dramatic, and because of the important developments that he leads in the mental health field and the user movement, a further clarification of his views can be best drawn from a read of the transcript of an interview I had with him. We began by discussing his role in the Network, and went on to talk about his involvement with ACT, and his thoughts on psychiatry and medication.

Adam: Ron will you tell me how you got involved in the Network?

Ron: I suppose my involvement began when I attended my first group. This really convinced me that there was more to what was happening to me than anybody else had said up till then – that my voices were real. It was almost a Paul on the road to Damascus scenario for me. I had spent years having it thrashed into me that I was ill. The Network finally allowed me to go back and challenge the doctors in a different way. For the first time I had a bit of evidence. Up till then it had always just been a gut challenge to the doctors. Once people in the Network, like Anne Walton and Helen Heap, started speaking to me, it became clear to me that I wasn't mad, and that the voices were there because of what happened to me in the past.

Adam: You then became very involved in the Network. What are your opinions of how the Network progressed?

Ron: I think all along we maintained our links with the psychiatric system. I think, in one sense, this was useful and necessary because we were able to pinpoint what we were trying to do. But the result of this was that we did not attract enough people around us who had never been part of the psychiatric system. This meant we lost a whole layer of people who could have taken us forward in a different direction. Bearing in mind that probably two thirds of voice-hearers don't get in touch with the psychiatric system, we actually lost quite a large number of people. Professionals like Nigel Rose and Paul Baker tried desperately, by putting adverts in the papers, to get non-psychiatrised people to the first meetings. Perhaps it would have made a difference if we had had somebody with the reputation of Romme making a TV programme. I think the Network was treated with tremendous suspicion by the system from the very beginning, and it was seen as a direct challenge. The British are resistant to change in a way that, for instance you don't find in continental Europe. Yet you do find the same resistance in Eastern Europe where, although there is a real hunger to get information, there is still a resistance, especially on the part of the professionals to allow any user-led control.

Adam: Tell me about your role as a trainer in the Network and subsequently with ACT.

Ron: I was involved in a lot of training with people like Anne Walton and Terry McLaughlin and I spent time discussing directions we should take – about ideas and concepts. We started developing training in a very systematic way, rather than simply being users who went and shared their experience. We then went beyond that. Putting it in a medical way, if you like, we offered alternative ways of treating people. But what we were doing was giving people the tools to allow them to develop coping strategies, which is commonly called treatment or therapy, although it was never meant as such.

I feel that people like myself, Anne Walton and Helen Heap were very clear about what the training had to be like – it had to be factually-based, researched, and had to be professionally delivered in order to gain credibility. So we worked hard on developing our training. Although when I train I don't use notes it may look as if I'm doing everything from the top of my head. I'm not. There's loads of reading, thinking and writing. I also feel more comfortable talking without notes, because it allows me to engage my emotions rather than just gazing at a piece of paper, and I think Anne and Helen are exactly the same way. Because of the amount of reading and research we put into what we did it meant that we got a good reputation as being deliverers of quality training.
I think the professional allies were not only essential for bringing the Network actually together, they also allowed us access to where they worked. For instance, I remember managing to do some work in north Manchester because of Mark Greenwood. He got me access to this team of psychiatrists who were quite anti what I was saying. They were always saying "what if?" and created scenarios that never happened. But the point really was that we were able to get in there, and I think the thing that always shook them up was that we could hold our own in a debate. In all the time that I've done training, the nearest I came to losing it was very recently in a training session when a psychiatrist

interrupted every third or fourth word. At one stage she jumped up and said, "I object!" I couldn't think of anything else to say other than "over-ruled!" and she stormed out. I later found out she storms out of every training session as she just wants to cause trouble! But you don't know that at the time.

But I think that what was happening was that the Network was being seduced into the system in a very real way because by that stage I suppose people like myself, who were in the national office, were totally ignoring non-psychiatrised voice-hearers, and were not trying to make any contact with them. I think we have got to take responsibility for that. It was something that we didn't do, and we didn't set out to do very much. I think this reflected the background that the voice-hearers came from. We all came from the same psychiatric system, and we had seen abuses in the system and felt abused by it so we wanted to challenge it. I think that was right, but I wish sometimes that there had been a non-psychiatrised person there who would have stopped us from going too far down the road of psychiatry, psychology and the clinical framework. We did try to put checks and balances in. I think the idea of making the Network democratic in terms of regionalisation and delegates' meetings was an important step, because we were opening the executive to every member, where members can decide policy at a national meeting. I think we went one stage further from organisations like Survivors Speak Out and The United Kingdom Advocacy Network who meet once a year. We set up a structure where there would be four delegate meetings a year, so people would be accountable quarterly.

I think within the Network there were typical personality clashes that go on in every organisation. It certainly happens within the professionals' organisations. So I don't think there's anything unique about that. I think a lot of the battles of ideas were really good because they forced us all to think and to develop our ideas. I think regionalisation has not worked as well as a lot of us would of wanted it to, but it certainly worked in areas like Yorkshire which is an extremely strong region.

Adam: Did you have a vision of what the Hearing Voices Network should be about?

Ron: Yes, I suppose at that stage when we were going regional, I was looking to the Network being an organisation where liberty would be the key rather than recovery. I very much wanted this idea of liberation to take over from recovery. I saw in people who had moved out of the system this tremendous freedom to do exactly what they wanted, and I thought to myself well, perhaps, this is really what it's about. It's political, not psychological or psychiatric.

I like the idea of linking with other people – not just voice-hearers, but workers and carers. Not in terms of saying let's be partners, but in terms of saying "we can forge an alliance here on what we see as common ground." I wanted alliances with those parents who didn't like seeing their son lying in a hospital drugged up 23 hours a day in bed – but who wanted him to be free. Sometimes when people have committed suicide I've heard parents say "oh, in a sense it's a blessing, you know, because he just didn't have a life." On the other hand we must recognise that freedom is there, but is denied to us by an oppressive system. My vision – I suppose I could say it was my delusion – was that we would form a mass movement that would smash psychiatry.

Adam: How did the idea of ACT come about?

Ron: I think there were a few reasons behind it. One was that I was getting older and I realised I needed to go back to work at some stage in my life. I'm not saying that I was not working with the HVN, I was! But it was very much a non-paid thing. I mean at one stage when the Network did not have any money, I used my Disability Living Allowance (DLA) to pay some of the bills. It was a weird experience working out how much an organisation owed a volunteer. And the same with John Williams. I've seen John put money in. You mustn't forget that at one stage we only had a telephone with a coin slot and so we would end up having to make coin phone calls to these distressed voice-hearers with pound coins being battered through the slot. That, for me, was the exciting time for the Network because we were living hand to mouth and I suppose that we are going back to that now. I hope that they find it as exciting as we did.

But I resigned in October 1995. I said that I would be there if people wanted me, but I felt I had to move on. I talked it through with Terence McLaughlin, Julie Downs, and others, and told them that what I wanted to do was to develop training/consultancy in a very clear and professional way, maybe not just on hearing voices, but other aspects of psychosis, such as visions, tactile experiences, self-harm and employment. It was deliberately more of a political thing. The agenda was very clear from the beginning with ACT – to allow people to say they were psychotic and proud which is still my dream – that voice-hearers can walk down the street, speaking to their voices and nobody would care. Nobody would be saying "that person's mad". Instead, they would say "that person's talking to their voices. I wish I heard voices." Or for self-harmers to be able to practice safe self-harm without condemnation and judgement. Where we would have a system with self-harm clinics that were not trying to stop self-harm, but were treating what that person wanted treated which was the cut that needed to be stitched back together, leaving as few scars as possible. Psychiatry might exist in this system, but it would exist to serve the people rather than the vested interest of drug companies and the establishment or the knee-jerk reactions of the media.

Adam: Maybe psychiatry should be left to specialise in neuroscience and the chemistry of the brain.

Ron: I think there's another possibility for psychiatry. We might see social psychiatry continue to develop, carrying with it the recognition that psychiatrists should go back to be what they were prior to the 1950s, which were professionals within departments of psychological medicine, where what they dealt with was the mind, not the brain. The brain has always been dealt with by neurosurgeons and so on – that's fine. It's like calling Alzheimer's a mental illness. It's not, it's a physical illness. It's a deterioration of the organic brain, and I've always argued that people with Alzheimer's should never be put in the psychiatric system which treats them like filth in crowded wards where they spend all their time alone urinating and shitting themselves, occasionally being changed by nurses that have not been trained to nurse, but have been trained to be psychiatric assistants. I would put such patients back into the general hospital. I think it's a sad argument that we've never taken on. What to do about the elderly? What do we do about elderly people who hear voices or see visions who are treated as if they have Alzheimer's disease? Why is it not possible for their voices and visions to have a meaning in the same way mine do? Does it mean that at 65-years-old, my voices suddenly become a symptom of Alzheimer's, rather than just part of my experience? This has been a great concern of mine that needs to be addressed at some stage in the future. When I see people like Bob, from Liverpool, who is nearly 70, at hearing voices conferences, I suddenly realise that if he goes back into the system he would be in the geriatric ward. He wouldn't be Bob anymore. Yet he hears voices, and has a clear understanding of where these voices are coming from, and I think to our shame the user movement has totally ignored the elderly. In fact, my conscience was pricked by a nurse who works with the elderly and asked "why do you never do anything about the elderly?" She obviously cared and recognised the scale of the problem.

Adam: What about the role of psychiatric drugs, particularly neuroleptics?

Ron: Perhaps one of the most interesting things is learning more and more about these drugs in terms of how they work and effect the physiology of the person. How they interact with the brain chemistry. For example, Tardive Dyskinesia (a form of Parkinson's disease) is caused by the lack of dopamine, and yet one of our treatments is to inhibit dopamine, so we're actually setting people up to get future illnesses. Or finding out that dopamine is inhibited three hours after the first dose of neuroleptics, not ten days, and that's why sometimes we see an amazing change in people in the first day of admitting them. Because probably it's worked. For whatever reason they have over-produced dopamine, and the first dose has been enough to bring them back into context.

Then we have this silly idea that drugs have side-effects. They don't have side-effects, they have *effects*. You can have stiffness, blurred vision, dry mouth and Tardive Dyskinesia – that's not the side-effects of medication, it's the *effects* of medication. Studies show that it doesn't matter how much dopamine you inhibit, it doesn't correlate with the person's behaviour. Then you have to actually challenge psychiatry when it comes up with strange terms like "drug-resistant" which is applied when you've got all the "side-effects" but none of the benefits. This does not stack up. I don't blame drug companies. It appears to me that drug companies don't write prescriptions, psychiatrists do. Drug companies might give them information on what the drug does, or what it's meant to do, but it is still the psychiatrist with the pen in his/her hand

Adam: It's feasible that a drug may come up on the market with no effects other than getting rid of an abusive voice.

Ron: If a drug works for somebody then go ahead and use it. But I still think that the person has to decide themselves whether to use it. We need to get rid of all compulsion in psychiatry. I've never been convinced that people don't know what they're doing. Certainly in the height of my madness I was aware of what I was doing, and other people that I've talked to talk about the things in a way that makes it clear that they knew what they have done. They may have a different reason for doing it which is unacceptable to society, but they know what they've done, why they've done it, and whether it was right or wrong. This idea that people don't have any notion of right or wrong is not correct.

Adam: This brings us to the medico-legal concept of "diminished responsibility", which is psychiatry's way of saying, "this person is ill, they can not be

104

responsible for their actions". Then of course, someone like Thomas Szasz says that this idea of diminished responsibility is unfounded.

Ron: Yes, I would go along with Szasz to a certain extent. My view is very clear. For instance if you look at violence, all the notorious psychotic murderers such as the Yorkshire Ripper, and people who have committed multiple rapes supposedly because they're schizophrenic. It's a lot of nonsense. When you actually look at how such people pre-planned and got rid of all the evidence, and how it took the police ages to catch them, it shows very clear planning and pre-meditation. The motivation was there. Rape was about power, and not about their illness. Their murders were gratification, not about illness. Now to me they should just be locked up – but not in a psychiatric unit, but a prison. The real case for psychiatry in terms of forensic medicine should be around the situation where, for example, two brothers have a massive row and in a second of insanity one brother kills the other – that second of pure madness after which that madness is gone, and they have to live with the remorse. Yet, we have a system that says "life" and they go to prison. They're the people that need treatment. They need treatment to be able to live with the guilt and remorse, to be able to understand what they've done and the fact that it was a second of madness. They shouldn't be in for life they should be in for months, and the ones like the Yorkshire Ripper should be away for life. The other scenario is where the woman who's abused and battered by her husband and, in a moment of madness caused by provocation, finally deals with it, and we then have a system that says "life". (Although that's now changing since women are beginning to win appeals.) But you have this system that denies their madness, which is real madness, it's real insanity. They're the people who should have treatment. Then there would be no criminal psychiatry, just real psychiatry dealing with people who offended because of circumstances.

Adam: Going back to the creation of ACT, it was set up as commercial company wasn't it.

Ron: Yes, I suppose in one sense it was a commercial company. But it's a company that's never really made that great a profit for individuals. I think that it has made profits for groups of people in terms of setting new things up and allowing things to develop. My commitment is still for people taking control, and money is one of those things that allow you to take control. How you get that money also matters – it is easier to retain control from money without strings. So, for instance, if I was doing training for the Ashton Hearing Voices

105

group where there would be 15 to 20 people paying £75, the group would receive £1500 but with no strings attached. Money that its members controlled because I certainly don't put any strings on it.

In the first period of ACT I didn't have enough work to come off benefits, but the starting point was when the bank approved our business plan, and not only gave us an account, but gave us an overdraft because they saw us as a real business. We struggled, we still struggle as a business. Our lives are not comfortable because so much of the money that we earn goes into projects like the cafe and the bookshop (see below). So I think what we've done is involved ourselves not just in the philosophy and the oppression of psychiatry, but we've also involved ourselves in the economic structure of psychiatry, where people don't need to be dependent on the state.

ACT does not receive any grants. I think it would be wrong for us to apply for grants on the basis of mental health when we're not really talking about mental health. We've applied for grants for financial development but that's been through the Welsh Office which supports industry and is therefore a totally different ball game. It's based on business rather than being a charity or a mental health organisation.

Adam: How has your training with ACT been able to progress compared to that with the Hearing Voices Network?

Ron: I don't think you can compare it to the HVN as what we're doing is something different. It's different because not only are we starting from the approach where Romme would say that hearing voices is normal, we're also saying that there's no mental illness. That's our foundation – that there is no mental illness. There is distress and we deal with these people's distress. So, yes, there are consequences to hearing voices which are distressful, but the voices are no way symptomatic of a mental illness. Although people believe they are ill, we can't change that, so we accept it and work with it. But where we're fundamentally different is that we are geared to the achievement of freedom. ACT is not geared to treatment.

Adam: What about your general knowledge of psychiatry, psychology and research papers. Where have you picked all that up from? Because without being part of an academic library, it's very difficult to get the information.

106

Ron: From people like Terry McLaughlin, Marius Romme, Alec Jenner [retired Sheffield psychiatrist and author], Asylum magazine, and also because of the training I do for psychologists like Lucy Johnstone from Bristol and Paul Chadwick from Birmingham, and talking to Ian Parker from Manchester – they're all people who have written anyway, and they just send me information. I find myself with masses of papers and I do read through them. I quite happily take four or five on the train with me, work through them on the train and glean them for information, especially studies on dopamine and biological models. So often I go into leading workshops better prepared than psychiatrists who have not read these papers, and when I quote these papers and give them references, they're shocked. In a sense research is a bullet. I accept that professional research is a tool useful in the battle against those same professionals.

Adam: It is like what the author and psychiatrist Peter Breggin said in *Toxic Psychiatry* about genetic work. What he said is that these studies actually end up giving evidence supporting the environmental hypothesis for the cause of schizophrenia rather than the genetic one. So what you are doing is, on one hand, accepting the papers for what they are, but changing the interpretations.

Ron: In ACT we have also become sophisticated in applying science to papers that are really non-scientific when they proclaim to be. Also, if you look at how quickly psychiatry is bringing out papers now, almost as a knee-jerk reaction to every argument from researchers putting forward a social view. It quickly publishes a very clear piece of scientific literature which is just as easily criticised. I see my greatest enemy as not the Royal College of Psychiatrists, but organisations like SANE. This charity is more dangerous than the scientists of the Royal College, because they have no science. SANE is a very sophisticated campaigning organisation which wants to oppress me, and, like a charity, do it by being nice and saying drug treatment and compulsory treatment is for my own good. They have a wonderful PR machine, whereas The Royal College does not have such a good one.

Adam: With the formation of ACT, you moved from Manchester to Wales. How did it go from there?

Ron: I did work with Phil Thomas (see chapter eight), and Ian Murray (a psychiatric nurse), and I started getting invited abroad. We did a lecture tour of America to professionals. The first voice-hearers group in America started because of that – it was an amazing feeling to know that you were part of the creation of a Hearing Voices Network in another continent. I then went to Finland with Marius Romme, Sondra Escher and Paul Baker, and I was invited back the following year to the inaugural meeting of their National Hearing Voices Network and was one of their signatories. I think that was a high point for me – that I would actually be the godparent of their organisation.

Adam: What about the cafe and the bookshop. How did they come about?

Ron: The cafe started in a funny way. I was walking through the village of Penryndeudrath when I saw a notice in what used to be a cafe window. It was in Welsh so I didn't understand it. I went into the pub, grabbed one of the lads and asked him, "what does that say?" – I had no idea it read "to let". It transpired that the owners wanted new people to run it. Anyway, we told them up front what we wanted to do – about the fact it was service users who would work in it. We argued the rent down, and also got a rent-free period. We then talked to people who were using services in the area and we opened it. Then we wanted a bookshop, and one day there was a notice in a butcher's shop which read "shop to let next door". There was no window in the shop, just a doorway and so we called it The Book Cave. The owner came over and showed me round, told me what the rent was and I said "OK here's a cheque for the first month." We employed Bill, who is an ex-service user now, put shelves up, went to auctions to buy books, rifled through our own book supplies and started a second hand bookshop. It was a massive drain initially on our finances. For example, four fifths of the income of one of our workshops went on carpeting the bookshop. But it is now breaking even and our targets are being met everyday now.

These projects represented a real move because the message has been "yes, we're right, we do not have an illness," and we are now helping people to achieve independence, economic independence, through owning their own labour. Rather than a boss owning the means of production and labour, they own their own labour and their destiny is with them. I think that's what people are asking for, freedom.

Adam: You talk a lot about the Soviet psychologist, Vygotsky. How does he fit into it all?

Ron: The inspiration I got from Vygotsky were the concepts of social interaction and integration. We interact at a social level and at employment levels, and as we interact and integrate our self-esteem is built up, and as our self-esteem builds up we take more and more control of our lives. We grow more confident about our lives. For me Richard Bentall's work (see next chapter) proved that self-esteem was an important factor. A person of higher self-esteem had voices which tended to be manageable and they didn't have problems with them – they were able to get on with their lives. While the opposite was the case for those with low self-esteem. We live in a capitalist system that says self-esteem is measured by people's productivity. If you put "schizophrenic" on your job application, you're not going to get the job. Unless it's a job application for our organisation where there's a good chance you'll get the job! And so one of the ways to help people's self-esteem to grow is to allow them to be productive. Not through the supportive employment schemes where the only thing that these schemes do is employ professionals to nurse-maid users who don't earn anything, while everybody pretends they're working. I'm fundamentally opposed to sheltered workshops where there is not a real wage for a person they employ.

Adam: When you go to Bradford, you should visit the Cellar Project. On one hand it is a paternalist set-up, but there's a lot of skill there, and they do produce fantastic carpentry.

Ron: Yes, what they should do is become a social firm or a business. That's how you turn things round. Then ownership is given to the user. But you try putting that to the board of management!

We shall probably become more involved in political activity in terms of trying to get recognition that the Mental Health Act, and some of the Tories' amendments, were knee-jerk reactions to very bad reporting in the press and didn't actually reflect real issues and real situations. What we need is a government that's not frightened in the early stages of it's administration to look at this. I think we'll have some strange allies in this battle, like the gay movement did. We'll have both right-wing libertarians and left-wingers, and people who will vote for totally different reasons. That's something we have to accept. I've also given thought to the possibility of stopping all this travelling and making speeches. But it's been pointed out to me that I'll probably be wheeled on a wheelchair at conferences! I suppose where I get the real feeling that I'm achieving something is when I make a key-note speech at a conference, addressing a whole conference, holding it and convincing the audience that you are right. I've had many high points in terms of conferences.

The first was the very first one I did, which I've got a video tape of. I was still drugged up to the eyeballs, my speech was very hesitant and very deliberate, but I was still saying the same things – that there is an oppressive system. Not as well as I would probably say it now, but I was still saying exactly the same thing. I was consistent about it. Then the next high point was in London when Romme was there. (He'd heard me speak the first time and practically ignored me except to say hello.) He heard me the second time, and immediately came over to me at the end of the speech and asked, "will you come to Maastricht and speak at our conference this year?" That was a high point. Another memorable occasion was speaking at Edinburgh, in my home country, and debating against Robin Murray, who's a professor of psychiatry, and getting the upper hand during a debate on the biological concept of schizophrenia. That was the conference where I became totally sure of most of my arguments against psychiatry. Not totally sure of my answers, but totally sure of my arguments. Then going to Derry in Northern Ireland and being given 20 minutes to an audience that was made up of roughly half users and half professionals, and sitting down after 20 minutes, and for the first time in my life seeing the whole conference get on it's feet, instead of the few people who supported me. I also particularly remember being shouted out at a MIND conference for saying I was "psychotic and proud." Ironically this is now something that people are rushing to claim. Of course, I've made many mistakes along the way – like anybody I'm a human being. The problem is you are never forgiven for your mistakes. That's OK as long as you do not make them again.

Adam: Ron, I wonder what your life would had been like if, during your period of madness, you had not gone into the psychiatric system that you experienced, but one with a different approach?

Ron: I probably would have gone back to my career, which is what should have happened. I didn't go into psychiatry to make a new career, I went into psychiatry to get back to my own career – that's what never happened. So that's why I call it a bad career move. It is a bad career move to go into psychiatry.

Chapter six

Cognitive psychology and hearing voices

"In the name of Jesus of Nazareth, I command you, evil spirit, to leave this person and go to the place allotted for you and never return again." **Reverend Canon Dominic Walker, Vicar of Brighton and co-chairman of the Christian deliverance study group, during a 20 minute exorcism of a man, diagnosed schizophrenic, who believed he was possessed by the devil. (As reported in the *Sunday Times* magazine in September 1996.) It is thought to be the most recent exorcism performed on the National Health Service.**

At about the same time the Hearing Voices Network appeared on the UK mental health scene, there were some progressive developments in clinical psychology and psychiatry. Led by Newcastle psychiatrist Douglas Turkington, and Birmingham psychologists Paul Chadwick and Max Birchwood, clinical psychology was finally addressing its role in the treatment of psychosis and voice-hearing by applying the theory and practice of cognitive behaviourism. Ever since the Trethowan report of the seventies gave UK psychologists a recognised role in the NHS the profession had increasingly encroached onto psychiatry's professional territory. It started with psychology as good as taking over the field of learning disabilities from psychiatry, and then as psychologists secured footing and respect in mental health teams psychiatrists began to refer psychotic patients to psychologists. Up to then they had always maintained responsibility for such patients Now psychologists can take psychotic referrals directly from GPs, although this is rare. Despite most psychologists idealising about working in an equal partnership with psychiatry, the increasing confidence and emergence of clinical psychology represents a strong challenge to psychiatry's power in the mental health system. Perhaps the passing of time will see psychiatry's dominant medical biological model of psychosis being usurped by psychology with a very different approach to conceptualising and helping voice-hearing patients.

The psychology profession has also succeeded in reaping support from some within the Hearing Voices Network and the hearing voices movement because cognitive behaviourism does advocate less of a biological-based model of mental illness and voice-hearing. However, cognitive behaviourism has been criticised by radicals for both its philosophical mediocrity and adherence to a scientific model with the associated use of elitist professional jargon (the two mouthful words 'cognitive behaviourism' are intimidating enough). Although I turn to such philosophical inadequacies later on in this chapter I want to start with describing the basics of cognitive behaviourism, especially as it relates to the experience of voice-hearing. I believe that once you have waded through cognitive behaviourism's technical language and seen through its mystique, it is no more complex than bangers and mash. And this, of course, has been one of its attractions.

What is cognitive behaviourism? And how schizophrenics think, feel, and act just like anyone else.
Cognitive behaviourism is a study of how people think and behave, and in cognitive psychology parlance thoughts are labelled "cognitions". So, the thought, "I am no good at socialising with people", is in psycho-speak a cognition. Cognitive psychology is interested in the cognitions we have about ourselves and the world because emotions or feelings, such as happiness or sadness, are judged to be a result of how we think. Therefore, if I *think* I am a hopeless socialiser I may as a result *feel* sad, or even depressed, about my inadequacies. Generally in cognitive psychology, *thoughts* lead to *feelings* and not the other way round as psychodynamic practitioners are more likely to advocate. Cognitive behaviourism trys to unravel how people come to think about their experience, or how they process information about the world – hence the common use of the term information processing in cognitive behaviourism.

Up to the 1980s NHS psychologists (most qualified adult mental health clinical psychologists work for the health service) only really plied their trade on the cognitions of depressed, "neurotic" or panic attacked patients. Psychotics meanwhile were left with psychiatrists and neuroleptics on the presumption that such severely ill patients were beyond the help of psychologists' "talking therapies". But as psychology grew more powerful in the mental health service the professional challenge facing the discipline was whether it could also deal with the cognitions of the psychotic schizophrenic? Whether it could treat the person whose thoughts and cognitions have, supposedly, become irrational, incomprehensible and beyond the rescue of reason? Whose views on the world had become reduced to a DSM IV symptomised "odd belief", "delusion" or "magical thought".

There are an infinite number of such colourful delusions, odd beliefs and magical thoughts that circulate in psychiatric wards – some of which are more historically contemporary than others. For example, we can say that the "delusionary" conspiracy theory that the CIA are plotting against an individual only came into existence after the American intelligence agency was established. Other run of the mill "delusions" have been around for hundreds of years – like the notorious belief that "I am the Son of God". Indeed, what better example of the archetypal madmen; the lunatics who either publicly rant and rave that they are the Son of God or hold their belief in humble silence? Throughout history people have been punished or demonised for holding such beliefs (Jesus being the best example), and when the cross and stake became outdated, nineteenth century psychiatry chained people up for madly proclaiming such a heresy. As the philosopher and psychologist Michel Foucault related in *Madness and Civilization*, one of the prisoners released from the Bicetre hospital in 1792 by the French liberal psychiatric reformer, Pinel, was a former ecclesiastic who believed he was Christ – and he had been in chains in the hospital for 12 years. But now, two centuries later, how would cognitive psychology apply its theory and practice to the "cognitions" of these hundreds of sons of God who have popped up throughout history, as well as the thousands of other "deluded" individuals roaming the domain of statutory madness?

The Son of God

As the story went in the Old Testament it was God who saved Daniel from the lions when King Darius cast him into a pit full of the beasts. More than 2000 years later in September 1994 Tony Sarumi had his picture splashed on the front page of national papers after scaling the 22 foot safety screen of London Zoo's lion enclosure to prove to his disbelieving pastor that because he was the Son of God the Lord would protect him as he did for Daniel. Sarumi told newspaper reporters in September, 1994: "When I arrived [at the zoo] a voice in my head told me to jump into the lions' den....The voice was saying: Today the world will recognise you are the Son of God." Unfortunately however, Sarumi was badly mauled by 40-stone Arfur and two cubs. Remembering the occasion Sarumi said: "All three of them were on me, but I didn't feel any pain or fear. But I could see them crushing my bones and ripping my flesh. I lay there for about 20 minutes with Arfur's teeth clamped round my throat. Then I heard people coming and hitting things to distract the lions. I had my Bible in my breast pocket and that was bitten as well. I take my Bible everywhere with me. All the time I was conscious. I realised God had saved my life. Now I believe I can't ever die. I am indestructible. I want to move forward now and make people believe who I am. I can heal AIDS and cancer. I want people to believe there is a living God."

From what Sarumi said it appeared that his voice hearing experience fuelled his thought (cognition) that he had special powers. If Sarumi had been referred to a cognitive psychologist during his subsequent stay in a psychiatric hospital he might have tried to help Sarumi think differently about the world compared to how he saw it through his bible-tinted view. The psychologist might have encouraged Sarumi to entertain the thought that Arfur did not kill him because of distractions from the crowd rather than the blessing of any deity. Ideally this might have made Sarumi *think* differently (stop thinking that he is the Son of God) which would result in him *feeling* differently (not saddened by the fact that no one believed it was God who saved him from the lions), and ultimately *behave* differently (not jump in with lions again).

Delusions or beliefs?

Richard Bentall, Professor of Liverpool's Department of Clinical Psychology, is internationally renown in psychology circles for his cognitive behavioural work with people diagnosed schizophrenic. (He also became the first contact for the Hearing Voices Network in Liverpool when in 1988 Mike Greenwood from Manchester got to talk to him about Romme's work in Holland.) Bentall is behind moves led by a handful of psychologists to *reconstruct* or redefine schizophrenia, and stands out from his less audacious clinical psychology colleagues because he emphasises that schizophrenic "delusions" – which voices may be implicated in – are in fact similar to more conventional everyday "beliefs". He argues that in the same way one can unravel the processes that leads someone to hold the more socially acceptable belief that only Jesus was the Son of God, so one can reveal the processes that leads someone like Sarumi to hold the "deluded" belief that he is also a Son of God. So, for Bentall, rather than such a schizophrenic delusion being a meaningless product of a biological dysfunction, it is as comprehensible as any other belief. But what is important for Bentall is to find the "abnormalities" in how patients' minds process information about the world which allows them to arrive at such a belief. Bentall demonstrates how he believes people come to hold a belief or delusion by refering to a box diagram of the mind as shown below which is divided into "data", "perception", "inference", "belief" and "data search". Using the hypothetical cognitions of someone like Sarumi whose beliefs lead him to throw himself to the lions we can illustrate the processes that lead to the creation of such an unconventional belief. As Bentall describes, exactly the same processes are involved with the formation of conventional beliefs, the only difference being, according to cognitive psychology, is that somewhere along the line information has been processed incorrectly by the likes of Sarumi.

Data	Perception	Inference	Belief
Jesus, Abraham and other Hebrew leaders heard voices	The bible said they were the voices of God	Hebrew leaders can hear the voice of God	**People who hear voices could be a Hebrew leader**

..........*leads to **data search**......Pastor agrees that all the Hebrew leaders communicated with God.*

Data	Perception	Inference	Belief
I hear voices	Hearing voices is a religious experience	It is the voice of God I hear	**Because it is the voice of God I hear I am a Hebrew leader**
The voices say I am the son of God	It is the voice of God I am hearing	What God says is true	**I am the Son of God**

The above table illuminates how a "delusion" such as "I am the Son of God" can be constructed. To begin with I, as a voice hearer, have some information (data) e.g. I read the bible which said Jesus and Abraham heard voices. I may then understand this information in a certain way (perception) e.g. the bible stated it was the voice of God that Jesus and Abraham heard. I may then make a conclusion (inference) from this perception e.g. Hebrew leaders heard the voice of God. This will of course back up my attitude (belief) that it is Hebrew leaders who hear God's voice and consequentially, as a voice-hearer myself I could well be a Hebrew leader. So, if a voice advised me to proof this by leaping into a den of lions I would be inclined to do it believing as I do that it was an instruction from God. Yet we must remember that being mauled by the lion or being put in a psychiatric hospital may still not be enough to alter my belief that I am the Son of God. Indeed, for Sarumi, the fact that he did not die under Arfur's jaws *confirmed* he was protected from death because his grandiose self-belief of indestructability was supported. God really was on his side, and because he survived the ordeal he showed to the world that he was not a fraud. The big problem for Sarumi however was that the rest of the world failed to see it like that. Nevertheless, the important point that cognitive psychology is making is even though others may not share a belief the processes leading someone to hold the general belief that they are the Son of God can be constructed and understood logically. Bentall and other psychologists would probably share the conventional view that, in fact, Sarumi's voice was not that of God. They might point to the "abnormalities" in his thinking, stating the voices Sarumi heard were not those of God but his own audible thoughts (see later in this chapter). They might also conclude that Arfur chose not to go for the kill and plunge his incisors into Sarumi's neck not because Sarumi had the powers of a deity but because either Arfur was insufficiently hungry or the crowd were putting him off with their noise.

So, I think we can see why the theory of cognitive behaviourism is popular in the West's materialist scientific era. Not only is it inclined to reject spiritual/religious explanations for voices it states that feelings and behaviour are logical consequences of thoughts. Cognitive behaviourism's principles have become so popular they are regularly used professionally across the whole spectrum of mental health problems, including panic attacks, phobias, obsessions, depression and self-harm. The flood of self-help books on the market to boost self-esteem, confidence, depression and so on swim in cognitive behaviourist ideas. It is DIY therapy that can be handed out over the counter, and all the better for that. Also, as mentioned, Bentall and co's introduction of cognitive behaviourism into the arena of psychosis and voice hearing is a radical move for a conservative mental health service because it promotes discussion and conversation with people about their voices which are not just condemned to the status of a by-product of an unfortunate neurochemical mix-up. In fact psychologists are now conversing with their patients about the meaning of voices in the same way they might debate politics back home – the only, but highly significant difference, is that they debate with their clients in a clinical setting. Cognitive psychologists call discussing the meaning and content of voices, "focussing", and it is this therapeutic technique which Sarumi would have probably experienced if he had come into contact with cognitive behavioural psychologists. But, the example of such focussing that I would like to cite is that given by Chadwick and Birchwood in the book, *Cognitive Behavioural approaches to Psychosis.*

Selling your soul to the devil – the voices of DD.
DD (Chadwick and Birchwood's chosen pseudonym), aged 41, was an unemployed economics graduate with a 10 year psychiatric history. For three years she heard mainly commanding voices which lasted for half an hour usually in the morning or evening. DD believed she could transmit thoughts telepathically, and said the voices were those of the devil whose aim was to destroy the British economy. DD believed the devil tried to do this by using her as a go-between between itself and the Prime Minister. The devil's voice would issue an economic command to DD, such as to raise taxation. DD would, at first, resist the command by saying the opposite, but her resolve would weaken under the pressure of a very persistent devil and she would then repeat its order. DD believed this instruction would then be telepathically picked up by the Prime Minster who would

act upon the instruction. DD followed the economy religiously and was angry, guilty, and depressed when it dipped because she felt responsible.

During the 13 clinical sessions that Chadwick had with DD a number of themes were "focussed" on to challenge the validity of her beliefs. Firstly, DD was asked to reflect on how she would feel if she met up with the Prime Minister (then John Major) who told her he did not hear her messages. Secondly, DD was encouraged to examine alternative explanations for the dipping of the economy, such as that economic indices fluctuated regularly and bore no relationship to her telepathic powers. Thirdly, discussions between Chadwick and DD centred on the occurrence that on most days which DD repeated the devil's commands, the economic disaster failed to materialise, and also the question of why, if the devil was so omnipotent, did it not communicate directly with the Prime Minister rather than going through DD? Fourthly, in order to test DD's compliance to the voices and their meaning she was encouraged to stop saying the opposite to the voice's command, and to instead repeat the commands many times. If her beliefs were true then the results of her commands to the Prime Minister, such as a taxation increase, would appear within a fortnight At the end of the sessions Chadwick reported: "In all cases the test had no effect [on the economy] and this appeared to weaken DD's beliefs about the consequences of compliance and about the meaning she attached to her voice"

Despite the fact that we are given no indication of what DD herself thought of this whole enterprise this case is a good example of focussing on voices. By challenging the validity of DD's beliefs, suggesting alternatives for economic movements and by opposing the commands of the voices, DD was encouraged to find different ways of viewing her voices which would make her life less painful and traumatic. Focussing can be a beneficial experience for a psychiatrised voice hearer, especially if no one has previously taken an interest in their voices and beliefs. If stuck in a culture that defines you as mad, to sit, analyse and discuss your outlook on the world can be extremely valuable. This is why cognitive behaviourism has its supporters, especially if all a patient has been given before was a packet of neuroleptics and glum expressions as soon as he mentioned a belief in satanic plots.

However, whatever belief you have, it can take a lot to change it. It could be argued that most adults will have developed a core of beliefs which will not significanlty alter over time. In addition, however much evidence we may find that contradicts our beliefs we may always find something that does support and feed them. Political persuasions are a good example. This adherence to a belief applied not only to Sarumi but also for DD because there were economic events which actually *supported* her belief about the

117

devil's efforts to disrupt the British economy. During the summer of 1992 interest rates rose and fell by five per cent on one infamous Black Wednesday, and although Chadwick ended his report by writing, "DD's voice activity is now far less frequent and, perhaps most importantly, DD is no longer resisting the voice by saying the opposite to the commands," the question that remains is what of the devil? If it was not the voice of Lucifer himself that DD was hearing who or what, in the view of clinical psychology, was it?

Turning up the volume – voices as inner speech.

"Let us blame ourselves and not the devil". **John Proctor in Arthur Miller's play** ***The Crucible*. Proctor was calling for an end to the witch hunts in a 17th century Massachusetts town.**

Imagine you are preparing for a job interview. It is your dream job but the competition for the post is intense. People have advised you to "just be yourself". This is fine, but you know you have to predict and prepare for the questions that the interview panel will fire at you. You are stressed out by the thought of the interview and you are pacing up and down your bedroom reciting answers to probable questions. In your head you can picture the scene: two interviewers looking inquisitively at you as you sit opposite them, cross-legged, in your smartest gear, trying to be amicable and relaxed. Because you are nervous, you play over and over again the questions they might ask. "So what do you consider are your best attributes for this job?" "Are you profficient at working on your own?". They might even throw in a trick question, such as "When was the last time you lost your temper?" If you concentrate and listen carefully enough you might even be able to *hear* the voice of your imagined interviewer. Psychologists call these voices inner dialogue or inner speech because you are having a conversation "in your head" where your voices and those of your interviewer are "in your head". But hang on. What do we mean by "in your head"? Are the voices in your brain? In your mind? Or in the air somewhere above your head? Is, in fact, the voice of the interviewer your own thought or *really* her voice which you are just repeating? The boundaries are, I suggest, not all that clear.

Cognitive psychology works on the presumption that the voices of a voice hearer are thoughts where the volume has been turned up. One consequence of this is that the voice hearer may believe these loud thoughts are voices of an external entity, such as spirits, aliens, the television, radio, objects or neighbours. Cognitive psychology would say that in this situation something has gone wrong with how the voice hearer perceives or believes where the voice is coming from. Whereas many scientists have said the reason for having the "delusion" that voices are coming from an external source is due to some faulty mechanism in the brain. Bentall suggests that understanding voices as coming from outside the person is a deficit in the ability to "monitor reality". So, to hear the question "When was the last time you lost your temper?" as a voice, and to believe that it was the interviewer's voice being telepathised to you would be an inability to realise that in fact you were just hearing your own thought.

During cognitive therapy spiritually-inclined clients are encouraged to think about the possibility that the voices they hear are actually self-generated and do not come from some external source. "An individual who believes his voice to come from a powerful and vengeful spirit may be terrified of the voice," claimed Chadwick. "This may lead him to comply with its commands and to harm others: if the same voice were believed to be self-generated, however, terror and compliance would be unlikely." Distress caused by voices can, according to cognitive psychology, be considerably alleviated if the voice-hearer accepts the voices to be his own thoughts – a form of inner speech.

These are the basic working principles of cognitive therapy for voice-hearing patients, and because of user demand to have more counselling, psychotherapy or other "talking therapies" available on the NHS cognitive therapy has received some good press. As more psychologists have the opportunity to introduce their cognitive therapy into the clinical setting we will increasingly hear (predominantly from psychologists) of its benefits in enabling people to cope with distressing voices. Cognitive therapy is the up-and-coming treatment for psychosis. As I have discussed, not only is it based on a scientific, logical, materialist, non-spiritual philosophy, the practical technique of focussing can be extremely valuable for a voice hearer in a psychiatric ward barren of such therapies. There are some other attractions of cognitive behaviourism which I turn to next, afterwhich I will outline some concerns about the theory and practice of this form of treatment.

For and against cognitive behaviourism
"By not giving cognitive behavioural therapy to me I think psychiatry has taken a large number of years out of my life by saying I was schizophrenic and that I should keep on taking these tablets – it was only by accident that I found my way out. I could still be sitting in Bridge House Drop-In three or four days a week just drinking tea and coffee and asking, 'what kind of medication are you on?' and swapping all sorts of stories – and still believing myself to be ill. I no longer believe that I am ill." **Micky De Valda, author, and Hearing Voices Network member, 1998.**

"There are very few examples from the history of psychology where the production of knowledge has consistently and unambiguously been in the service of the majority of ordinary people, of the poor and unemployed, of the working class, or of the mad," **South African writer, Grahame Hayes, 1996.**

You don't have to be ill to hear voices
Cognitive psychology does go some way down the line of depathologising voice hearing. As Chadwick said: "Attributing voices to illness is such an impersonal explanation that it rarely satisfies people." Those psychologists leading the drive

behind cognitive behaviourism have also openly criticised the concept of mental illness, and particularly schizophrenia. For example, Bentall has stressed the uncertain scientific validity of schizophrenia, and, in a paper he wrote with fellow psychologists Gillian Haddock and Peter Slade, he also addressed the inadequate living conditions with little social support of many patients. He wrote: "Unless their material and social needs are addressed first, the success of psychological therapies is likely to be very limited." Such talk echoes the message of Romme and Escher and many in the hearing voices movement which advocates that as long as voice hearing is viewed as a symptom of a disease, and treatment is focused on the disease, then problems in a person's experience as expressed by the voices will never be solved. In the same vein, Bentall recognises Romme and Escher's observation that many people who hear voices have never had contact with psychiatry, and he also appreciates the influence of culture on the voice-hearing experience. Bentall also differs from biological psychiatry by asserting it is a *moral*, as opposed to a *clinical*, decision to diagnose someone schizophrenic. He says: "It seems to me that the decision about what counts as illness and what counts as sanity is essentially a moral one...Suppose when your appendices became swollen your IQ doubled – appendicitis would no longer be considered an illness. It depends on whether the associated behaviours are ones that we value or not. Happiness can be a mental illness. The only reason why we don't see happiness as an illness is that we value it."

Cognitive behavioural therapy as democratic?
Another attraction of cognitive behavioural therapy is that focussing purports to be a democratic exercise in discussing the meaning, content and validity of voices between a psychologist and a voice hearer. This claim has to be seen in light of the different power dynamics between psychologist and voice hearer and a voice hearer and psychiatrist. A voice hearer can refuse and walk away from any services offered by a psychologist (though it may not be easy) whereas to say no to the intervention of a psychiatrist carries with it a risk of being sectioned and compulsorily treated. A psychologist does not carry the same degree of statutory responsibility and obligation as a psychiatrist. So, psychologists can have the luxury of being non-coercive and more laissez faire in their clinical sessions, and the only professional obligation they have is to demonstrate to their NHS managers that cognitive therapy "works", and is cost-effective. At The Hearing Voices International Conference in Maastricht, Douglas Turkington and his colleague Ronald Siddle presented a cognitive therapy case study of 28-year-old Carl. Even though Turkington, as a psychiatrist, has unparalled statutory powers bestowed on him, his work with Carl does demonstrate some of the democratic principles (theoretically at least) of cognitive behavioural therapy.

Carl, for the six months subsequent to being referred to Turkington, was an in-patient in an acute psychiatric ward. Carl had been tormented by voices for years, and when Carl was outside the hospital, the voices would tell him to rape, kill and eat women who came to view. Understandably, Carl was terrified by these voices, fearing that, one day, he would do what the voices ordered. Medication was of little effect. Working from the hypothesis that "both the form and content of voices are intimately related to the persons life history and key personal events", Turkington embarked on a "critical collaborative analysis of voice origin", and looked at ways of enhancing Carl's coping strategies, changing the negative attitudes he had about himself and, finally, finding ways to prevent "relapse" should the voices seriously trouble him again.

Turkington explained that when they first started discussing the origin of Carl's voices, Carl believed that they were of an ex-friend who lived in London, 300 miles away. Based on Turkington's self-confessed rudimentary knowledge of physics, he and Carl had discussions on the mechanics of sound and its likelihood of travelling long distances. Turkington reported that this led Carl to have doubts about his voices, and that subsequently he was prepared to entertain other explanations for the voices' origin, considering they might be the voices of God, the Devil, aliens or his mother. "He also, to a much lesser degree was able to consider the *possibility* that the voices might be some sort of internal thought process," wrote Turkington. During the course of their sessions, the pros and cons of medication and suicide were discussed. Carl also kept a diary of what the voices said and, as "homework", "gathered information" and prepared questions for the subsequent session.

In addition, an essential ingredient of democracy is diplomacy and tact. Returning to the case of DD, although Chadwick in his write up of DD's case study labelled DD's belief that she could transmit thoughts using telepathy, a "delusion", during his actual clinical sessions with DD he said her beliefs were not labelled as delusions, "but were discussed as being a reasonable and reasoned attempt to understand what was a puzzling and alarming experience." This is another of the attractions of cognitive behaviourism because, in the literature at least, practitioners have prioritised the promotion of engagement and trust between psychologist and client. To avoid confrontation and a subsequent rejection of the therapeutic service psychologists are encouraged to avoid saying anything that arrogantly invalidates any of the client's beliefs. Bentall gave a personal example of this during a talk in Manchester. One man who Bentall used to see as a client believed he was being surveilled and bugged by the Home Office. During a session in Bentall's clinic, he said to Bentall, "OK, no one else is here. It is just you and me. You can tell me honestly now that you work for the Home Office, don't you?" Rather than give a yes or no answer to his client, Bentall replied, "It must be very lonely when no one shares the belief that you are being bugged." By not refuting the man's suspicion that Bentall works for the Home Office and by not labelling DD's telepathic belief as delusionary the psychologists have diplomatically avoided confrontation with their patients.

Turkington wrote to me about his ideas of the democratic principles of cognitive therapy. "The whole idea of cognitive therapy of voice hearing is based on collaborative empiricism...and power should be equally shared beween the voice hearer and the therapist," he said. Although I believe Turkington is glossing over his *extremely* powerful position as psychiatrist and doctor, I think that we can see where he is coming from because he has given some ground to his patients by allowing them to join him on exploratory conversations and discussions on the nature of voices. (I should add that Turkington is unusual in that most psychiatrists do *not* practice cognitive behavioural therapy with patients they have diagnosed psychotic.).

So, to its credit, it appears that cognitive behaviourism can be a progressive psychiatric practice because (i) it goes someway to depathologising the experience of voice hearing, and (ii) also allows open empirical discussions between doctor and patient or psychologist and client. However, in order to broaden the analysis I think that we should take a look at the politics of mental health in this country, particularly the future of clinical psychology which, at present, is mainly responsible for carrying the mantle of cognitive behaviourism.

Who partners who?
In the acute wards of psychiatric hospitals up and down the country psychologists predominantly play second fiddle to psychiatry. As mentioned clinical psychologists are only beginning to make a mark in the arena of psychosis, and they tend to only be consulted when a psychiatrist believes it to be appropriate. The future for psychology is therefore open to a range of possibilities, and David Pilgrim, a clinical psychologist and lecturer in Health and Social Welfare with the Open University, highlighted one way forward for clinical psychology. In *Clinical Psychology Observed* he wrote: "A future role for the profession...is to ally itself with progressive forces 'from below' in mental health politics...At present psychologists have rarely come out and aligned themselves directly with users organizations. There is little current evidence that there is much support from psychologists as full-blown activist-allies within the mental health service users movement. Having said this, psychologists may still be able to encourage a more user-sensitive service, whilst remaining within their professional boundaries." I think that this is a real challenge to the psychology profession because historically it has been governed by the ideal of working in partnership with psychiatry rather than with users.

Back in 1950 when the profession was born, Professor Hans Eysenck, a key player in the development of psychology as a distinct discipline, was prophesising that the more effectively psychology was able to ally with psychiatry the more this would benefit psychology's prestige and status. And aspirations for such alliances with psychiatry are still echoed by the likes of Bentall who hopes that psychology will share professional territories with psychiatry. But what would such partnerships look like? Could we see a fairy-tale three-in-a-bed partnership of users, psychology and psychiatry? Or, would one (or two) get turfed out in an ensuing kick-about?

One future scenario is that psychology continues to linger in its position as a side-kick of a psychiatry-controlled "multi-disciplinary team". A second, as already mentioned, is that psychiatry sucks up cognitive behaviourism into its own treatment remit, leaving psychology to make something out of the crumbs. If, as Pilgrim hypothesises, psychologists do not actively ally with users, then I believe we will probably see some version of these two possibilities. In *Accepting Voices*, Bentall attempted to define the role of psychology: "The task of cognitive psychology is to investigate the mental processes associated with particular kinds of experiences and behaviours. It is up to others to determine whether those experiences and behaviours should be regarded as pathological or not." I believe it is such laissez faire messages which will restrict psychology to passively and opportunistically latching on to any favourable political developments in the mental health field, rather than taking the initiative itself. When Bentall says it is "up to others" to determine whether experiences (such as voice hearing) are to be regarded as pathological, the question begging to be asked is, who are these "others"? Politicians? Psychiatrists? Neurophysiologists? Citizens in a democratic society? I fear psychology is guilty of historical short-sightedness because, I suggest, the politics of psychiatry of the next 20 years will demonstrate that political developments determine whether or not voice-hearing is conceptualised as a pathological experience. Again psychology should remember that it was a political, not a clinical, decision that the American Psychiatric Association Board of Trustees took when it voted to take "Ego-dystonic Homosexuality" off its list of mental illnesses. And, although such developments have not prevented geneticists from searching for – and proclaiming success in finding – the gay gene, it was the *political* achievement of gay activists that influenced psychiatry, and not visa versa. (Interestingly, it took the American Psychological Association another two years to follow psychiatry's suit and likewise depathologise homosexuality.) But will clinical psychology take heed of history? Will the discipline continue to distance itself from these illusory "others" and lie dormant while the rest of society – particularly the establishment of psychiatry – continues to energetically pathologise voice hearing as a disease symptom? If this psychological passivity and moderateness continues I believe psychology will never become much more than one of psychiatry's side-kicks. Or can psychology ally with the political concerns of the user movement and some in the hearing voices movement? If psychology takes this option it might thrive in unexplored alliances.

However, another possibility is that if psychology was to ever take over control of psychosis from psychiatry it would become an image of the master who it usurped. With power comes responsibility, and, as psychiatry demonstrates, the onus of being responsible has brought with it the practice of control. If psychologists are given the right to prescribe drugs, as has already been discussed in psychology's higher circles, this would lead to an emphasis on medical training, and then would we be able to differentiate psychology from psychiatry? Probably not, and I think the tools of the trade that psychology would use if this third unfortunate scenario developed are already being learnt. Let us go back to the case of DD.

In a respect DD was a model client because Chadwick was able to report positive results in this intervention. (Again I emphasise we do not know whether DD was equally positive). But let us imagine that DD had not been such a "good" client, and that she maintained her beliefs despite Chadwick's proposal of alternative explanations. What if DD believed the reason the prime minister would say that he did not hear her telepathic messages was not because he did not hear them, but it would be damaging to his political status to admit to hearing them. Also, what if DD insisted that the movement of economic indices were not entirely independent of her telepathic messages, and she kept to her view that, to the contrary, they were actually directly influenced by the devil. Finally, let us suppose DD could not summon the courage to repeat, rather than say the opposite, to the devil's commands because she believed colluding with the devil to be too dangerous. What then for the cognitive behaviourist? And what does the cognitive behaviourist do when a client insists in believing the voices they hear are not audible inner thoughts but telepathic communications with the spirit world?

Bentall's response is: "It's important not to be dogmatic. If someone wants to believe in telepathy that's fine, but as a scientist I do not believe in it. There's a real world out there, a world of facts. If you are my patient I would make a great deal of effort not to show disrespect and I would encourage you to look at it in many different ways as possible. But, at the end of the day one of us is right." Cognitive behaviourism retains its cohesion as long as the client goes along with his role despite his different beliefs, and is willing to empirically test his beliefs such as DD was asked to do. This is a legitimate democratic process. But what of pre-empirical and non-empirical questions? Is psychology going to be able to accommodate alternative "psychologies" to its own and different understandings of the nature of the mind and relationships with a spiritual world?

Joan of Arc, a most famous apparent voice hearer, was burnt at the stake in 1431. Right up until her last moment the authorities tried to make her confess that the saint's voices she claimed to hear were not real. However, Joan of Arc burnt and did never confess. If psychology was to reach the top eschelons of power in the mental health system voice hearers should not suffer as rough justice as Joan of Arc. But, if psychology looks outside its professional institutions and journals it will see a society that is mopping up alternative psychologies of the mind to the ones that it offers. In every city throughout the country there is an increasing number of spiritualist churches hosting crowds of mediums and clairvoyants where spiritual experiences such as telepathy and communication with spirits (or the world of the dead) is very real. In addition, there are dozens of alternative psychotherapeutic techniques being practised privately up and down the country – from clairvoyancy to hands on healing to Buddhist meditation to Yoga to shamanic or Reiki healing. So, when a client comes to a psychologist with a spiritual understanding of his experience the principles of such beliefs will be shared by thousands of others. To make a comparison, whereas 20,000 copies of the Psychologist magazine are distributed every month, Psychic News, the most popular spiritualist paper sends out 60,000 a month. It would be a safe gamble to predict that more people would be able to articulate the philosophy of spiritualism than they would of cognitivism. As mentioned in chapter three the Hearing Voices Network recognises the pervasiveness of alternative psychologies and endeavours to incorporate a diversity of explanations for voices. Meanwhile, if the official discipline of psychology is to build allegiances with users, it may well have to address whether it keeps to a strict materialist scientific model or whether it can take the bold step of incorporating such alternative psychologies and philosophies. If psychology cares *about* people in distress, rather than *for* them, then it will listen to their explanations of who the voices are. If people in trouble with their voices are to empower themselves over their voices then the alternative ways of helping people deal with these voices must be supported. In addition to cognitive behaviourism this may mean anything from deliverance to meditation to Bach flower remedies to psychic defence. I believe that only if it takes this step can psychology begin to work in partnership with users. If not, there will continue to be an uncrossable gulf between the two. Maybe psychology should start by freeing itself from the ethnocentric philosophy of cognitive behaviourism. If not Pilgrim envisages that: "the public, as potential clients, will suffer a double mystification. They might be encouraged to believe that clinical psychologists really are experts in human misery, instead of practitioners who have a partial, confused or uncertain understanding of their fellows and a fairly modest set of current proposals for the amelioration of their distress."

The problem is that the discipline of psychology aspires so much to earning scientific credentials that it is in danger of prioritising its own professional standards above the experience of the client. I once heard a critique of the psychology discipline say that psychology is more concerned with its own model than the experience of the person seeking help. He may be right. Even accepting that how a professional works in the privacy of her own clinic can be at odds to the theory she publicly endorses (to get research published in psychological journals usually means conforming to a scientific methodology and discourse) I would suggest that if cognitive psychology is ever to become the dominant discipline in mental health it will have to attend to its allegiance to a scientific model. Time and time again users say they do not want to be put under a scientific microscope but be related to.

An alternative practice

Ron Coleman and ACT (see previous chapter) recognised these deficiencies of clinical psychology. Although acknowledging that cognitive behavioural approaches to voice hearing are "quite a good start", Coleman, echoing the above criticisms, says: "Bentall and others claiming to *reconstruct* schizophrenia have got it wrong, because if you reconstruct schizophrenia into the same scientific paradigm you are going to end up with the same mess. Pscyhology needs to let go of its pseudo-scientific status and stop treating people as if A + B always equals C otherwise it will end up being as dangerous as psychiatry by trying to reduce everything to the same clinical framework."

Because Coleman used the principles of cognitive behaviourism to aid him in his own recovery he will always have an appreciation for the profession. Although Coleman does very little one-to-one work with voice hearers, when he has been requested to do so his stance exemplifies what it may mean to work with other voice hearers without the baggage of scientific methodology. It is worth documenting his work with a woman called Jenny (a pseudonym) to demonstrate an approach which does not resort to technical jargon, does not vigorously define voices as a form of "inner speech", and which is prepared to accept the voice hearer's definition of what the voices represent.

Jenny

Jenny had heard Coleman speak at a conference. She asked him to help her with her voices, because as someone who had been abused as a child, Jenny felt that she could build up an understanding and rapport with Coleman, also someone who had experienced abuse. Over the next few months they spent many hours together either at Coleman's and Jenny's house. Unlike standard one hour therapy sessions they spent whole weekends discussing her voices and trying to resolve the negative effect they were having on her life. Jenny told Coleman how she heard four voices, all of which had different characters. One was abusive and hostile, one was distressed and demanding, one was calming and reassuring, and the other took a disinterested, objective role.

Because Jenny had been sexually abused as a child by her step-father, she came to see the abusive voice as representing him. She decided that the demanding child was that of herself when she was a child at the time of abuse, and the consoling voice represented her grand-mother – the only person who sided with Jenny and supported her during her frightening childhood years.

Coleman's approach in helping Jenny with her voices was to view all of her voices as interacting in a social network, reflecting Jenny's traumatic time as a child. In effect Jenny's step-father was still abusing Jenny with his taunts and denigrations, and Jenny as a child was still screaming in distress. It could be suggested that Jenny's unresolved mental anguish was still haunting her. Coleman and Jenny decided that one way to relieve this continual pain which the child was experiencing was to make practical efforts to resolve Jenny's situation. Coleman explained: "Anyone who has been abused has to at some point confront their abuser in some way in order to put right what had gone wrong. Because Jenny's abuser was no longer on the scene the only way that she could confront him was through her voices." Whereas psychologists, for example, would talk directly to Jenny to help her deal with her situation, Coleman found that the best way to work with Jenny was to actually negotiate with her voices.

Coleman believes in the psychological concept of "dissociation" – an experience when the personality fragments or splits as a defence mechanism to the pain of trauma such as sexual abuse. Jenny and Coleman came to accept that when Jenny was a child her personality had split (into voices) as a result of the abuse, and that Jenny's voices had never had the chance or space to integrate back into a "whole" personality. In effect, the abuser was still abusing. So, as one may decide to deal with such an unbearable situation in "real" life Coleman and Jenny decided the best strategy was to try and get the grand-mother's voice to ally with the distressed child. As the grand-mother was the only support which the child had, it was essential that the child had her as an ally. If this was achieved the child could rely on the support of her grand-mother to confront the abuser. So, reflecting what it really means to treat someone's voices as *real,* Coleman communicated to Jenny's voices using Jenny as a go-between. As the child's voice only really trusted her grand-mother Coleman's main point of contact was with her, and he would discuss how to confront the abuser's voice with the voice of the grandmother. Remembering the encounters Coleman said: "The child's voice spoke to the grand-mother who spoke to Jenny who spoke to me. There were a lot of dynamics going on!"

Finally, the child, with her grand-mother's support, did confront the abuser's voice. And, as would be in a "real" situation it was pretty mucky and nasty. At times Coleman never knew whether Jenny would kill herself because of the tormenting memories, and the effect the whole process had on her self-esteem. The child and the grand-mother told the abuser what damage he had caused, how he had abused his position within the family, how the child hated him, how she could never forgive, and how the abuse was not *her* fault but *his*. Through this process of confrontation some kind of revenge took place. Jenny had mustered up the courage to deal with what had happened to her in a way that she had never been able to before. Although Jenny still hears voices subsequent to her work with Coleman they now play a different role in her social network. The abuser's voice remains but has less of a hold on Jenny, and it is the friendship of the grand-mother's voice which has taken more of a leading role in Jenny's life. As for the screaming child, it has disappeared.

Distancing himself from clinical psychology, Coleman believes working *with* the framework of the distressed voice hearer is more important than adhering to the philosophy of psychological science advocating voices as "inner speech". This may mean accepting a meaning for the voices which he does not himself agree with. He says: "My job is not to try and change a person's framework it is to let the person explore their own framework." With Coleman's strong Catholic roots he adds: "Indeed, I could probably quote the scriptures better than most priests...but when I work with voice hearers if I say to them that I do not believe their explanation for the voices and I can not work with it then I am as guilty as any psychiatrist. So, for example, if someone has a spiritual explanation for their voices I will talk to them about what they have read because often this is a good way of coming to an understanding of their core beliefs about voices." Coleman believes there is nothing extraordinary in working with a person's voices in this manner. "Prior to psychiatry becoming psychiatrised priests cast out spirits from people all the time, and that was never seen as a problem," he said. "By negotiating with the voices you are resolving conflicts with dialogue. The problem is that voice-hearers have been denied that constructive dialogue, and if people are not given the option of this dialogue then they are liable to crack up. The fact that the dialogue I had with Jenny was through her voices makes no difference. It was a dialogue conducted in different space. In effect it is external dialogue as opposed to internal dialogue. But it is still the same process."

Chapter seven

Who's a monkey? Patient or psychiatrist?

"For a long time, there has been only one version of my life story. According to this version, I had a psychiatric disorder which had landed me in an institution. I had received treatment there and although I was never entirely 'cured' I was able to live with the remnants. This is not my story. I do not believe in it and it is of no use to me." **Wilma Boevink, research worker at the Netherlands Institute for Mental Health, speaking at the *Self-harm, abuse and the voice-hearing experience* conference (1996) organised by Action Consultancy and Training.**

An important role of Action Consultancy and Training (ACT), is to circulate not only alternative understandings of disturbing voice-hearing experiences but other distressing experiences such as depression and visions (or visual hallucinations). ACT achieves this via its own publications, training seminars, and conferences. And because self-harm is a personal experience of Coleman he has developed a particular professional interest in it. Under the umbrella of ACT he partnered up with Sharon Lefevre, a dramatist from Wales who has also self-harmed, to develop training sessions focussing on the experience, and how it may be connected to hearing voices.

In 1996 ACT organised a conference entitled *Self-harm, abuse and the voice-hearing experience* held at a conference centre and hotel in the mountains of Snowdonia National Park in Wales. The event was attended by a group of 30 or so social workers, community psychiatric nurses, psychiatrists and representatives from voluntary organisations. It was an opportunity for victims of self-harm from the UK and Europe to give their own interpretations of, and meaning to, self-harm.

The conference was also marked by the launch of Lefevre's book *Killing me Softly* which tackled the issue of self-harm unreservedly, shockingly, and radically. I shall turn to her work later in the chapter not only because of her involvement with ACT but also because it exemplified the kind of different perspectives on self-harm that came out of the conference. But firstly I think it is interesting to examine orthodox psychiatry's latest theorising on the subject. Written by two Australian psychiatrists Jones and Daniels the editorial, *An ethological approach to self-injury,* appeared in the British Journal of Psychiatry at about the same time that ACT was holding its self-harm conference. I would like to discuss it in some detail because it represents the kind of medical perspective and discourse that those at the conference criticised.

A clinical story of self-harm

In one respect *An ethological approach to self-injury* begins encouragingly. As Marius Romme did with voice-hearing, it elevates the practice of self-harm from being just one of a list of symptoms of a psychiatric illness such as schizophrenia, to an experience worthy of examination in its own right. As Romme's work demonstrated this can have enormous potential in developing a whole new way of understanding an experience. But, unlike Romme, the Australian psychiatrists chose not to discuss self-harm based on the existential experience of self-harmers, but in the world view theory of sociobiology. And because a characteristic of this Darwinian theoretical off-shoot is to emphasise the pervasive influence of genetic make-up on human nature, they looked to animals, humans' genetic predecesors, to find clues to understanding human behaviour.

In accordance with sociobiology, Jones and Daniels turned to self-injury (self-harm) in the animal world, and wrote: "Self-injury has been reported in non-human species including macaques, marmosets, squirrel monkeys, leopards, lions, jackals, hyenas, rodents and opossums...Severe self-injury is often preceded by confinement of the animal and occurs when it is in a high state of arousal. In the macaque monkey the injury may be inflicted by teeth and claws, by gashing the limbs, trunk and scrotum and biting accessible areas of the body." Jones and Daniels called these examples of animal physical self-harm "redirected social aggression". They argued that social aggression i.e. fighting off threats, is vital for the survival of a successful species. But if an animal is provoked and unable to direct its aggression towards the provoker it may redirect this aggression towards itself. Again it is tormented laboratory macaque monkeys who provide evidence for such assertions. If, for example, a macaque is threatened while in its cage it may direct aggression towards itself because it is unable to attack its provoker. Early separation from parents, isolation, disturbed sexual bonding and even failed copulation are also cited by the psychiatrists as situations resulting in macaques harming themselves.

When Jones and Daniels then switched their concerns to self-injury in humans they followed the same line of thought as they did with animals, looking to the traumatic social situations that humans may face which lead them to harm themselves. So, rather than building an explanation for self-harm around the bricks of genes and neurochemistry, as is predominant in most psychiatric literature, the writers sought analogous threatening *social* situations in humans associated with self-harm. They report self-harm amongst institutional populations of prisoners and violent youths, suggesting it is an act of "redirected social aggression" because the physical (cells) or non-physical (rules) barriers prevent such frustrated individuals from directing their anger outwards. "Inadequate parenting", particularly "maternal deprivation" are also

132

given as examples of such traumatic social situations which have been associated with self-harm. They also quoted an American study which claimed that parental separation, family violence and physical or sexual abuse was linked to self-harm. "We suggest that while the humans may not be physically isolated, the feelings of isolation and abandonment which arise from experiences of separation from parents, abuse and violence are similar to those experienced by individuals of other species which have been physically isolated," concluded Jones and Daniels. Although they did regard the phenonemon of aggression as a fundamentally genetic trait, they suggested it is the social situation – or life events – of the person that ultimately brings on self-harm.

This attention, from mainstream psychiatry, to the *social* situation of self-harmers is encouraging. But, as if to ensure that this talk about self-harm being linked to life events does not drift dangerously from psychiatry's medical roots, the writers asserted that organic or neurochemical abnormalities may predispose a person to self-harm. They mentioned correlations between the brain's serotonin levels and self-harm, and organic disorders, such as neurosyphilis, with which self-harm is associated. Nevertheless, that is about all they have to say about neurobiology for the writers increasingly wander onto the territory traditionally belonging to clinical psychology and start referring to "emotions" and "cognitions" linked to self-harm. They wrote: "The most common associated emotion (with self-harm) is unbearable tension; the patient cuts, often painlessly, and the tension is relieved. The patient may report other evidence of high arousal, for example, feelings of depersonalisation before the cutting, with the cutting leading to its cessation."

Rubbing up yet closer to clinical psychology Jones and Daniels look to cognitive behaviourism (see chapter six) as the guiding theoretical model for any future "treatment" of self-harm. "Cognitive or behavioural techniques may be used to provide alternative responses to separation or feelings of loss and provide mechanisms for reducing high levels of arousal, coping with frustration and for redirecting aggression other than toward the self." They go on to suggest that cognitive therapy can help modify self-harmers' "cognitive schemata" such as "My psychic pain is so intense that I can not bear it", and, "My anger controls me: I can not modulate my behaviour."

Interestingly then, although this editorial is guided by the generalisations of sociobiology, the message – like Romme's with voice-hearing – was not to delve further into the brain's chemistry but into an individual's experience of trauma, abuse or violence. Jones and Daniels have identified one of the symptoms of a supposedly underlying physiological disease (schizophrenia) and rewrapped it as a symptom of a non-physical event (redirected social aggression) Also, in suggesting that self-harmers' thoughts about themselves are the target for "treatment", Jones and Daniels are mimicking the maverick theoretical side-stepping of American psychiatrist Aaron Beck. In the 1970s it was his publication of cognitive-behavioural techniques for depression that paved the way for clinical psychology to work with the "cognitions" of depressed and neurotic people. Cognitive behaviourism helped the psychology profession gain respect and referrals from GPs and psychiatrists, and for it to eventually carve out territory of its own within the UK's National Health Service. Ironically, I believe that the psychiatrists Jones and Daniels are offering psychologists the carrot of "self-harm" with their editorial. With clinical psychology asserting itself on the professional realm of voice-hearing as discussed in chapter six, we may be witnessing medical psychiatry shooting itself in the foot – amounting to as good as a profession can get to its own form of self-harm. Radicals may not see this as such a bad thing,

The self-harmers' story

*''The table is set, hand towel, tissues, larger towel for the floor, razor blades. I sit at **my** table, it is **my** table in **my** house. I have cleaned the house, I am very concerned that my house is clean; my chores are complete. I am up to date with the laundry, there is food in, the plants are watered. My son has clean, freshly ironed clothes. His room is tidy, my room is tidy. My work is up to date, I have completed all that I possibly can at this point in my life. May be I could have phoned someone, family perhaps, but I don't think so, not really, for that would mean talking, possibly telling lies and possibly being manipulated. I do not let external influences come in unless I am in a post-set state. I am not, I am in a pre-set state. I look at my watch, it is ten thirty p.m. My son is in bed, possibly still awake **but**, he is fairly predictable, once in bed he nearly always goes to sleep.*

*I have cleaned my teeth, freshened up. I roll up my sleeve. I pick up the razor blade. It is a new blade. I rest my arm upon the table and I involuntarily flex my arm. I take the blade close to my plump flesh and it hovers there, waiting, as I decide to cut clean, unscarred flesh. I then confidently guide the blade upon my upper arm, I position it, I do not hesitate it and carefully **slice it across, quickly, sharply!**... and a stream of red blood appears, shimmers upon my skin. My heart beat increases, my breathing becomes deeper, louder, my teeth are clenched but there is only a loud melody in my head and like a demonic voice, it wails and urges, orders me to continue. I take the blade again, position the corner of it into the stream of blood and I press the blade down and tear it across the ready scratched skin. I pull it now and feel the flesh splitting open. Yes, I have broken through. I have opened the seal and now I must go deeper. The blade takes over now, my hand merely follows instructions. I cut again and **sure...yes**, now the blood gets deeper, redder and it pours out and down my arm, falling suitably upon the towel on the* *floor. **No mess on the carpet please**. My eyes glaze over for a second, my ears thud and I feel momentarily faint. I lean down, steady my breathing. I hear the rain outside. I concentrate on the noise. My pulse is racing now and I must continue . . ."* **Sharon Lefevre in Killing me Softly, Handsell Publications, 1996.**

"Practicing safe self-harm is not seen as an option, indeed most clinicians still believe that it is para suicide or attention seeking," **Ron Coleman, co-ordinator of Action Consultancy and Training.**

"We can not do what the users say and that is the frustration. Sometimes I feel very helpless," **Sara Smith, psychiatrist, Bushey Fields Hospital, Birmingham, and participant at the *Self-harm, Abuse and the voice-hearing experience* conference.**

The speakers at ACT's conference did not look to the animal world to theorise about self-harm. There was no talk of genes, ethology, sociobiology, or "re-directed social aggression". And victims of self-harm were not framed as humanoid descendants of frustrated caged macaque monkeys, but as their own experts of self-harm. Linking the early experience of physical or sexual abuse with abusive voices and harming oneself – be it by cutting, burning or refusal of food – the talks at the conference centred around the struggle to de-psychiatrise and to find personal meaning in self-harm. The request to professionals was to become discussion partners. One of the speakers was Vera O'Shea of the Bristol Crisis Service for Women who supports women, aged 16-25, many of whom hear voices and self-harm. She viewed voice-hearing (or what she calls "dissociation") as a creative coping mechanism, where the voices must be understood, identified and de-pathologised. I think her words summmed up the feelings of those at the conference. ''We do not treat people as mad or bad, but we ask relevant questions like what are the voices, what are they saying and will they speak to us? We help to empower the individual and we work with, not against disturbances,'' she said.

As mentioned the conference also marked the launch of Lefevre's book, *Killing Me Softly: Self-harm – survival not suicide*. Written in four weeks by Lefevre, from Dolgellau in North Wales, it was both a personal testimony of, and theory about, self-harm. Lefevre was a voice-hearer diagnosed with personality disorder and spent time as a psychiatric patient at Gwynedd hospital, Bangor. Like Louise Pembroke's edited book, *Self-harm*, Lefrevre's killing me softly recounted some of the problems of orthodox treatment, especially behaviourism, towards people who self-harm. It also signposted the reader – and professional – to a path to understand self-harm which is based on valuing the victim's subjectivity, their reality (and conflict of realities), and how life events, such as abuse, can be related to self-harm. This path does not lead the reader through a theoretical model for "treatment", but to follow it does involve engaging in an open supportive relationship with someone who self-harms. "For the family, friend, employer or whoever, being involved with the self-harmer is tough. I cannot dress it up, pretend that it is easy for them. It isn't. In the case of such people the self-harmer can only ask for patience, understanding, maybe even a little compassion, but if it is too tough then so be it for self-harm is not *curable*," wrote Lefevre. This may sound disheartening to those who have a professional or personal relationship with someone who harms him/herself, but if you are uplifted by accounts that find answers and meaning to distress in people's experience then *Killing me Softly* is a golden can of worms to open.

I want to discuss Lefevre's ideas because they symbolise what the ACT conference was about. *Killing me Softly* also highlighted the connections between child abuse and self-harm later in life. And when you consider that Dutch research estimated that between 50% and 75% of psychiatric patients are abuse victims the fortress of taboo that protects abuse and abusers deserves to be stormed.

The identity of an abused child.
Anyone who has worked in child-care will be familiar with the torrid times some youngsters have had to endure. Such a life is no fairy tale for a child, but, as Lefevre suggested, it is their only known reality. It will be the basis from which they learn to understand all later relationships. Enclosed within the confines of the home, violence and abuse may be the foundations of their entire world, identity and truth. It is the child's language of love and she has no power or ability to choose another. She can certainly not run away from it because there is no where else to run, and no other language which she is aware that she can be part of. Lefevre explained: "If there is physical pain connected to the lingual understanding of love through the love of a dependent (i.e. a child and parent) then the child only understands this physical pain being connected to love (*and not necessarily just to the person who gives it*) and to further this argument, the child is set up to respond to pain as an identity of love." She argueed that if a child is being sexually abused and does not know that it is sexual abuse, the child is not (in theory) being abused.

But as the child grows older, maybe at the time of early adulthood, she may encounter and learn of another language of love and relationships – a world where being denigrated, violated or hurt is not part of it. With hugs and no hitting. Or just simply no hitting. The problem facing this person is that they have no idea how to speak this new language or to engage in, what for her, is a bizarre, foreign culture. Using a computer analogy to clarify her point Lefevre explained that if a computer engineer loads up a computer with particular hardware enabling it to read certain software, and a second engineer then tries to load up software that the computer has not learnt to recognise, it will spit it out. It is unable to incorporate or understand it. This is how a world of non-abuse can be to the person who has been abused: "The new language is in conflict with the person's knowledge. This conflict creates a disturbance in the patterning of the person's development," said Lefevre.

But why can the person simply not choose to accept the preferable world of cosy, respectful relationships with other people? Well, Lefevre might have said, it is like asking a Christian European to choose to become a Tibetan Buddhist. To speak the language, and live the culture, without maintaining any remnants of Europeanness. But you can not just *be* someone else. Existentially and experientially this is not possible because we are no Aladdin's genie, able to magically transform in to somebody else.

The dilemma confronting an individual trapped in a language of abuse is that they may have to *try* to learn a language of non-abuse. "When the child becomes old enough to be aware of *another language*, through the child's development, the child has to reappropriate the first language. However, there is now the problem of translation." But this "translation problem" need not necessarily arise from just being "aware" of another language. For example, the abuser may have left his/her victim, or the victim may have left a hostile home or an aggressive partner. But the problem is that if the perpetuator of abuse leaves, the victim is alone, bereft of anyone to share with them the only world they know. Like a Tibetan Buddhist being dumped in Trafalgar Square.

Tending to your wounds – self-harm as survival not suicide
But where does self-harm come into the equation? Keeping to our cultural analogy, in trying to learn the ways of a Tibetan Buddhist the European needs to take on a whole new cultural language. To do this will inevitably involve the European slipping in and out of her European identity. Immersed in a strange culture, she is likely to telephone home, eat Western food or go through periods of feeling ambiguous about Buddhism's codes of self-restraint. Of course, she can always get on the next flight back to Europe. But, for the European, telephoning home, indulging in an occasional McDonald's or not blindly acting out Buddhism's codes is a way of coping with the alien culture she is up against. It is what Lefevre called the "intermediary language", or a step, between the two cultures. And for an abused person, self-harm can be that exact same intermediary language. "To maintain your sense of identity," wrote Lefevre, "which is of course essential to one's *sanity*, you cleverly create a diversion and through this diversion you create another language" – the language of hurting yourself as others have done before you. "The self-harm, although seen by most professional carers of self-harm victims as

137

an extremely negative and self-deprecating behaviour, becomes the protection and surety of your welfare, your own care and control which will be maintained for as long as it takes you to realise that you can actually speak both languages and then choose which one you wish to speak." Self-harm is a way of relating to a past truth. "It may appear very negative, but it is very positive. The language of self-harm is keeping the person alive."

Killing me Softly was significant for two other reasons. Firstly, because it theorised about self-harm without using the resources and language of standard psychology or psychiatry. Not only were the medical and behavioural treatment regimes criticised for their insensitivity in supporting the world of a self-harmer, *Killing me Softly* did not side with any other cognitive or psychodynamic theory. But what it did do was to encourage the reader to appreciate the life and reality of the victim. And more prevalent practices can make it more difficult for a victim to progress towards a new language. For example, under the guise of a punitive behavioural programme it may be said to a self-harming patient – "I will not speak to you if you cut yourself". Lefevre wrote that this was control, not support, and that it denied the personal importance of self-harm. It made life yet more distressful. It kicked a self-harmer when they were already down. It *killed them softly*. Such taunting hurts and what better way to express it than cutting yourself with the nearest object – the exact behaviour that the programme was designed to prevent.

Secondly, and to conclude this chapter, it is worth acknowledging the avenue that has enabled Lefevre's analysis of self-harm to be in the public domain. Although not stacked on a WH Smith bookshelf, *Killing me Softly* is now a public message. While Lefevre was supported by many professionals, the book was published as a result of a history of ideas and movements rooted in a radically different perspective to medicine. From voice-hearer Patsy Hage's influence on Professor Marius Romme, to the founding of The Hearing Voices Network, to the formation of ACT, to Coleman inviting Lefevre to stay in his Welsh cottage to concentrate on writing the book. This is one shred of the history behind *Killing me Softly*, and it is a very real space that radical ideas have established and occupied. In the end it will be political decisions that determine whether work such as Lefevre's stays on the bookshelves of a minority or end up encouraging a new way of thinking about self-harm. Whilst macaque monkeys are wonderful under the scrutiny of Attenborough, maybe a source for doctors' ideas are staring right at them from across their desk. "In essence, the professional must liberate themselves before they can expect to liberate the practice of psychiatry and ultimately their patients," said Lefevre. It is a look at such "self-liberation" that I turn to next.

Chapter eight

Grooming maverick psychiatrists

"I occupied myself with filling in records and firing questions at the bewildered newly-admitted 'patient', a procedure followed by the completion of the 'diagnosis', a sort of christening on which a lot of psychiatrists expended much time and energy. Tranquillisers had made their appearance: I prescribed them. From time to time I pressed the button of an electroshock apparatus." **Dutch psychiatrist, Jan Foudraine, from European best-seller,** *Not Made of Wood – A Psychiatrist discovers his own profession.* **Foudraine called for a complete overhaul in the training of psychiatrists.**

"There is a very popular view outside of these walls that psychiatrists are nasty bastards who are just there to slam people up. I don't believe that is true. I believe that most of us come in to the job because we are genuinely concerned and want to help people – that is why I came in." **Consultant psychiatrist Dr Phil Thomas addressing trainee psychiatrists during a seminar at Birmingham's Queen Elizabeth Psychiatric Hospital, 1996.**

Learning a new script
In a kitchen of a psychiatric hospital. It is 10.30pm.
Male Psychiatrist: "Let me do it!" (He looks nervous as he takes the razor blade from the hand of the female psychiatric patient and pulls up his sleeve. She stops and look at him, blood is running from her arm but neither of them take any notice of it). "I think I can do it," (he begins to scratch his arm, but immediately begins to shake).

Female psychiatric patient: (she panics) "Oh.....oh..... you don't have to do this to understand your patients. You cannot do it because you have not got the other voice have you."

Scene from the play, *On the Edge of a Dilemma,*
by Sharon Lefevre

A psychiatrist and a patient
On the Edge of a Dilemma is a gripping drama. It tells the story of a soul-searching discussion between a psychiatrist and his patient who, in the midst of terrible confusion and psychological crisis, periodically inflicts terrible physical self-harm by cutting herself, usually with razor-blades. Written by Sharon Lefevre (see previous chapter)

On the Edge of a Dilemma is not meant as a form of drama therapy. Instead its aim is to expose the short-comings and deficiencies of orthodox biological psychiatry which is so often inadequately equipped to relate to the subjectivity behind such actions. For two years the play was performed up and down the UK and abroad to mental health audiences. It was 45 minutes of provocative and compelling "in-your-face" drama, intensified not least by the fact that Lefevre, herself a voice-hearer and self-harmer, played the patient. To add further intrigue, her consultant psychiatrist at Gwynedd hospital, Dr Phil Thomas, played the psychiatrist. By using this reality-mix, with each performer playing him/herself, it dawned on the audience that they are witnessing an important chapter in both Thomas's professional career and Lefevre's history of self-harm. It was also a remarkable partnership between a psychiatrist and former patient, pushing even more boundaries than those surpassed by Joseph Berke and Mary Barnes in their 1971 *Two Accounts of a Journey through Madness*. Because of its message, as much as the identities of its performers, the play may have stirred up uneasiness amongst traditionalists. But it had support from those pushing for progressive changes to the mental health system.

The play was set in the cold and clinical surroundings of a kitchen in the ward of a psychiatric hospital during the early hours of the morning. Apart from one patient – Lefevre – no others are present. The solitary patient is joined by Dr Thomas, a psychiatrist fed-up and disillusioned with his profession. He tells Lefevre of his difficulties of working as a psychiatrist, and how he feels plagued by what he sees as his failure to help his patients. He is yearning to discover a new way to relate, understand and assist them. In a subversive exchange of roles the confused psychiatrist is the sufferer helplessly harrowed by his dilemma, while the self-harming patient tries to teach him of ways to contact the distressed person underneath the patient, rather than simply treating a diagnosis.

On the Edge of a Dilemma has an assortment of memorable lines and scenes, none more astonishing than when the psychiatrist, so desperate to help his patients, makes a move to cut himself with a razor blade in an attempt to existentially "experience" the predicament and reality of his patient. You will not see a record of this extraordinary moment in psychiatric journals. But to those indignant of the ways of orthodox psychiatry it surpasses in its impact any dopamine hypothesis, family genetic study or CAT scan finding. You can almost hear the thud of bricks that build psychiatry's prestige, power and status crashing to the stage when the psychiatrist makes this gesture with the razor blade. What is this psychiatrist doing mimicking a symptom of a mental illness? What is this man doing questioning the roles which construct a patient/doctor relationship? What is he doing admitting disillusionment with his profession, its inability to listen to patients, its failure to "cure", its relentless preoccupation with biological determinism? What is he doing revealing his personal vulnerabilities to his patient? In light of psychiatry's conservatism it is like a warden unlocking a prisoner's cell, freeing the inmate, and then ambling in to the cell himself, while handing the keys back to the prisoner.

But Dr Thomas, who has continually supported the work and ideas of the Hearing Voices Network, is not your conventional psychiatrist. Whilst having trained in medicine to specialise in psychiatry in Edinburgh, his objections to the dominant biological approach to mental distress stand him out from most of his colleagues. "I have probably been different from most psychiatrists because I have always been interested in matters such as philosophy which has not been very fashionable in my profession," he told me. Listening to one of Thomas's talks it is evident that here is a psychiatrist who endeavours to understand and make sense of a patient's speech, beliefs, behaviour or voices not in the language of medicine but their experience. This is certainly refreshing.

Thomas, who at the time of writing works for Bradford's innovative Home Treatment Service, would aspire psychiatry to work less on a model of biological determinism and more on a paradigm which reflects users' social conditions. "Users complain that all we have to offer is medication, when what they want is a job or decent housing," he wrote in a 1996 British Journal of Psychiatry editorial, *Psychiatry and the Underclass*, co-written with Marius Romme and Jacobus Hamelijnck from Ysbyty (Hospital) Gwynedd, Wales. What he called for is his profession to accept and reflect on the political dimension to mental health. As the public health movement earlier last century improved the health of the poor by establishing causal links between poverty and health, so, argued Thomas, must psychiatry attend to the relationship between poverty and mental ill-health. He quoted a 1987 World Health Organisation Study in Nottingham which reported that schizophrenia clustered in the poorest inner-city areas. Psychiatry's medical model might explain such statistics by suggesting that the mentally ill "drift" to society's gutters. For Thomas this interpretation – that psychosis causes homelessness – is flawed, and reflects how biological psychiatry is working in harmony with right wing philosophy which lends itself to society being absolved of a responsibility for mental distress. In his speech at the First International Hearing Voices Conference in Maastricht, Thomas proclaimed: "What better news could there be for right wing politicians to hear from the research institutes in UK and the USA, that schizophrenia is a genetically determined biological disorder? In one dramatic *coup*, biological psychiatrists have cut society out of the list of possible causes of mental illness. Unemployment, poor housing, poverty, racial discrimination, oppression of any kind no longer enter the frame. The fault lies with the *individual*."

Lefevre, meanwhile, first had contact with psychiatry as a result of her self-harm. Diagnosed with personality disorder by other psychiatrists, when she had her first appointment with Thomas there was no indication that this everyday psychiatric consultation would eventually spark off an unique and bold partnership between a psychiatrist and patient. "Initially I did not see Phil as anyone different," remembered Lefevre. "I think he thought, 'Oh no! Not another bloody cutter!' That's how he saw me – as a cutter and not as a person. But he used to ask me what I thought about things. He would listen. He did not patronise me and showed respect for me. He seemed to care about me and my distress. He looked for my qualities."

Lefevre wrote *On the Edge of a Dilemma* while studying drama at Aberystwyth University. Inspired by Antonin Artaud, poet, playwright and theatrical theorist, Lefevre understood drama as a potent art of communication when adopted as a teaching tool. This was borne out by the varied audience's reactions to the play. After a performance at Thomas's Department of Psychological Medicine there was a stunned silence. Other audiences have been fascinated and intrigued by it, and one consultant psychiatrist admitted having no time for "cutters" until he saw the play. "Because professionals are watching their own experience happen in front of them, they are seeing themselves being challenged. It allows them to spectate on their own behaviour," commented Lefevre. Both Lefevre and Thomas shared the view that essentially *On the Edge of a Dilemma* addressed the nature of psychiatry: "We want to educate professionals to go beyond their biological training. The play demonstrates the importance of working with the person and not with their behaviour, and highlights the barriers that exist between the professional and the patient," explained Lefevre. "The psychiatrist in the play is clearly wanting to change alot of the orthodoxies and the relationship between psychiatrists and patients," echoed Thomas.

Teaching an elephant to dance?
Lefevre and Thomas took their play to a number of audiences. But one memorable occasion was on an October afternoon when *On the Edge of a Dilemma* was performed to 20 trainee psychiatrists at Birmingham's Queen Elizabeth Psychiatric Hospital. It had been included as part of their psychiatry training programme, and these junior doctors who were working in hospitals around the Midlands, had just started in psychiatry as their chosen speciality. Their training was supervised by consultant psychiatrist, Dr Christine Dean, a self-confessed "maverick" psychiatrist. It is thanks to such professional courage that *On the Edge of a Dilemma* has been included in the psychiatrist's training schedule at all. And this particular performance of the play represented an unique opportunity to gauge the reactions of a group of raw medics to this most provocative and innovative user/psychiatrist partnership.

Following the play's performance, there was a 90 minute discussion focusing on the roles of psychiatrists, and what the trainee psychiatrists talked about resonated strikingly with Lefevre's message from the end of the last chapter ("the professional must liberate themselves before they can expect to liberate the practice of psychiatry and ultimately their patients"). For here were 20 representatives of future psychiatry, and what they had to say was certainly revelationary if not revolutionary. It pinpointed the real dilemmas facing trainee psychiatrists when they are encouraged to relate to their distressed patients while wearing the traditional doctor's mask of detachment and objectivity. I would suggest that physicians specialising in more traditional medical conditions such as cancer, AIDS or tropical diseases, would never have reflected on their roles with as such emotive concern as these psychiatrists did. Be the focus of interest a cluster of malignant cells, a virus, or bacteria, an aim of most doctors is to alter in some way the physiological characteristics of the body. As demonstrated below, these Birmingham trainees were evidently aware that psychiatry does not have such a typical remedial relationship with a biological entity.

Their discussion told a story itself. Although it ebbed and flowed to and from different themes, concentrating on some while flirting with others, there were a collection of narratives which when tied together reveal the archetypal dilemma of working in a hierarchical institutionalised discipline such as psychiatry – to either accept your training or to resist it in whatever way possible. A trainee psychiatrist, supervised under the umbrella of the Royal College of Psychiatrists and the hospitals in which she works, is really no different from anyone learning the trade or skills from a professional institution. They face similar pressures of whether to conform to the orthodox ways of the profession or to resist it and follow either an alternative ethos or a revised one. Psychiatry sets ways of working and behaving, and trainees are moulded in the image of the profession. I believe the discussion that followed the play revealed the workings of the profession that led these particular trainee psychiatrists, who I have given pseudonyms, to express an acute (but suppressed) discontent with how they are trained.

(Andy, Jayesh, Razia and Imran are the contributing trainee psychiatrists. Dr Christine Dean is consultant psychiatrist and senior psychiatry lecturer at Birmingham University, and Dr Phil Thomas and Sharon Lefevre perform in *On the Edge of a Dilemma*.)

Diagnosis
Let us imagine an anxious student of medicine embarking on her first placement in psychiatry, her chosen speciality. Fuelled by both an academic interest and a commitment to helping people, the eager to impress junior doctor looks forward to practicing her new skills of conducting a diagnostic and symptoms interview with her

patients. As the first admissions come rolling in, some possibly even brought in by the police, she welcomes with pleasantries her new patients into her consultation room. With possible reference to the DSM IV, she rehearses her skills of recognising and classifying symptoms, and making a diagnosis. But she is pressed for time, and after a consultation lasting any time between 10 minutes and an hour, either she prescribes no medication to her first patients, or perhaps with a copy of the National Dispensary Formulary at hand, she offers a suitable drug. She may even suggest a spell in hospital for the most serious of cases, or she may even decide there is nothing clinically wrong with her patients, suggesting instead some life changes and another appointment for a few weeks. The Birmingham trainees are well in to their placements, and this, astonishingly, is how Andy summarises his: *"You have to huddle someone into this category in a limited time frame in order that you can give out this tablet, which meanwhile everyone says doesn't work anyway! It just seems sort of crazy to me! And all this talk about biological receptors. All this is being forced on top of psychiatry and dealing with people. It doesn't seem to sit right for me. And courses like this where you have to pass exams which don't seem to bare any relevance to dealing with patients anyway...I feel under pressure from being a psychiatrist – because I've got a limited amount of time to cram what the person says into a diagnosis which fits a classification which then chucks out a treatment which I then give to that patient. Now, I feel immensely uncomfortable with that because a lot of times I don't know what's been going on in the patient's life and time is running out and...that's it – just some kind of diagnosis has come out of it."*

Andy is evidently uneasy about the diagnostic/treatment situations he acts as an agent in. He said: *"I feel that this is just totally inadequate and I am feeling...look I don't know what's going on! I kind of feel there's a sort of conflict in my mind between myself as a person who hasn't got the framework of a psychiatrist while dealing with someone's problem – and then as a psychiatrist."* Andy is expressing a painful discrepancy between how he behaves as a professional and how he would want to behave as Andy the humane individual, stripped of this medical persona. The ability to relate to someone in distress humanely, non-judgementally and with empathy is not part of a psychiatrist's training because they have been encouraged to perform another purpose – to diagnose and treat according to set procedures. But ironically, it appears that because orthodox psychiatry fails to officially value and recognise such human interpersonal abilities that "conflict", or indeed distress, is experienced by trainees like Andy.

Pressure from seniors
Moreover, if the pressures of the unwritten medical role of a psychiatrist are not compromising enough to a trainee's ideals, professional superiors throwing their weight

around is equally disheartening, Jayesh recalled: *"On three occasions three separate consultants told me it was an inappropriate behaviour for me to actually say anything about myself to the patient – so after that I stopped saying it...And if you're looking to get some form of reference from your so-called consultants, and they have pointed this out to you once, you just sort of detach yourself more or less."*

Psychiatrists as victims

What we are perhaps seeing here is the grooming of trainees to conform to a certain behavioural dictate. This is when the seeds of the dilemma to accept or resist psychiatry's intellectual and behavioural code are sown. The trainees are being offered a hand to shake, and they can either grip it firmly, half-heartedly or reject it outright. (All these trainees will probably continue to become consultant psychiatrists). Andy and Jayesh talk of conflicts and pressures which turn them into aloof, impersonal, psychiatric doctors "chucking out" diagnoses and neuroleptics when treating their patients. And all this is contrary to their feelings as compassionate fellow human beings. They sketch a picture of a coercive profession. That these trainees are able to identify and share with Thomas and Lefevre a contempt for such behaviour speaks volumes of the power of psychiatry to continue determining the terms of the relationship between doctor and patient in spite of these grievances. And the patients are evidently not the only victims of this medical behaviour. Despite dissatisfaction with their training and disapproval of the rules of medical behaviour, if trainee psychiatrists succumb to such conditioning they are likewise victims of the same depersonalising regime. If they are unable to resist this victimisation process their professional behaviour will probably end up being no different from those whom they disapprove.

Social constructionism as resistance

But on what foundations and justifications does psychiatry base these behaviours and ways of conducting itself? With its concept of biologically-determined mental illness continually attacked by critiques from both inside and outside the discipline of psychiatry, mental illness remains for many as nothing more substantial than a convenient social construct, or "scientific delusion" as Boyle has dubbed schizophrenia (see chapter 10). Although it would be difficult to envisage orthodox psychiatry, with its biological foundations, to ever modify itself and base its clinical practice on the idea that mental illness is a culturally and historically specific phenomenon, Thomas used a social constructionist discourse to understand much of psychiatrists' behaviour. He described the barriers separating patient and doctor as being entirely socially constructed: *"These barriers are to do with the rules that are passed on from generation to generation of doctors. There are certain aspects of our behaviour and ways we behave which are completely determined by the social context in which we are trapped."*

To hear a psychiatrist framing his profession's rules and behaviour within a social constructionist model is evidence of Thomas's intrepidity in contrast to most of his intellectually conservative peers. Assessing psychiatry within a social constructionist paradigm can be a useful and powerful tool to criticise the profession as there is always the underlying implication that such rules and behaviour can be constructed differently i.e. less oppressively. To assess behaviour as being socially construed by the culture and society we live in is a tool to *resist* the unspoken laws that the psychiatric institution sets its trainees. By performing in the play, Thomas, as a consultant psychiatrist, set an example to the trainees on where discontent with their role can be channelled – he sign-posted a path which deviated away from the training doctrine.

The system needs changing
Many a psychiatric patient has spoken of the damage they feel the psychiatric system has inflicted on them, inciting them to press for changes. When a trainee psychiatrist states the same it is reassuring. *"If you are on call and are expected to admit six or seven patients in one hour, you can't do that – you need much more attention and commitment to that patient – it's just a commercial thing,"* says Imran. *"I mean you just write four or five pages on the patients mental state – it takes about five or six minutes. Then there's the legal aspect. You are always worried when the patient says he is going to kill himself. Although you are not convinced, you always feel insecure as a trainee not to admit them. You have to admit them. You don't want to face the coroner. So I mean it's really the system. The whole system needs to be changed,"* said Jayesh. Thomas shone more light on this system: *"We are being governed by fear, let's be honest about this, we're governed – our decisions, our behaviour – by fear of a paternalistic authoritarian professional structure"*.

To listen to psychiatrists complaining collectively about a "commercial" and "authoritarian" system under which they work is not something often heard in public. Whether these particular trainees accept or resist this system during their career is a separate question. Certainly the pressures on them to conform will be weighing down on them throughout their working life, and all that is really left to them, if they want to make any difference to the culture within which they work, is to take risks. *"There will be no change until you stop being afraid of the user, until you stop covering your own backs,"* said Lefevre passionately to the trainees. *"These boundaries have got to be crossed and I say you must take risks. Until you, as professionals, start taking risks nothing is going to change, and that's what it's all about. You must take risks. You can stay safely in your professional clone-like mind, your conditioned mind, you can stay there forever.....Surely we* [Phil and herself] *are an example that you can take risks – just believe in yourself and do it. Go for it!"*

146

A psychiatrist's choices

The choices for an apprentice psychiatrist are clear. Either you are vulnerable to be moulded like putty through your career into a medical automaton, or you become a maverick psychiatrist taking risks and breaking a few rules in an effort to create a more humane and respectful practice. What Lefevre and Thomas did on this autumn afternoon was to actively change the agenda for relating to the patient – they offered an alternative language to the medical one. They kick started psychiatrists to reflect on their roles, and it was echoes of resistance that filled the lecture room for 90 minutes rather than a subservient curtsy to the established way. The voice of the psychiatric text book had either momentarily disappeared or had been sedated by this upstart of a substitute language. Although short and sweet on this occasion, it is such an alternative which the hearing voices movement, and all other critics of traditional psychiatry, have been advocating in some form for decades.

There is not only the worry about suicide. Psychiatrists are also singled out for blame if they fail to prevent violent incidents involving their patients. For example, in November 1998, Dr James MacKeith of the Bethlem and Maudsley Mental Health Trust spent five days being quizzed by an inquiry team on why he did not insist that his patient, Michael Folkes, take monthly injections rather than oral medicine which Folkes preferred. Folkes, diagnosed paranoid schizophrenic, was later convicted of the manslaughter of Susan Crawford, supposedly because he had not taken his medication and as a result became unwell. The report on Dr MacKeith's conduct read: "Even the most eminent can be tested to the utmost of their skill – and occasionally fail."

Chapter nine

Advocacy at the deep end

"Imagine a campaigning group
With the members,
Drugged into a submissive state.

That is the fate, of the mentally ill."
Carol Batton, of Manchester Survivors Poetry Group, March 1997.

As well as supporting voice-hearers in their efforts to find a more harmonious relationship with voices, another practical role in the movement is assisting patients to develop a more mutually appreciative relationship with psychiatry. Usually because of their dishevelled state of mind psychiatric patients are not best equipped to articulate their needs to a psychiatrist, and possibly they are even lost to define what their needs are. Almost always they have little knowledge of how the psychiatric service operates and the treatment it has to offer. Concerned relatives are often equally naive participants in the consultation process. It is in light of this, plus concern for "user empowerment", that there has, over recent years, been a mushrooming of mental health advocacy projects across the country, with the remit of articulating the needs of users to mental health professionals. Many within the Hearing Voices Network participate in such advocacy, either through one of these projects, or offering informal assistance to a friend or colleague. Such advocacy work introduces differences of interpretation and perspective into the arena of pragmatic struggles in assisting those unfortunate enough to seek, or be admitted to the psychiatric services.

This chapter centres on the story of one long-suffering patient Sarah Devrin, her family, and the unpaid efforts of Network member Terence McLaughlin (see chapters two and five) to support them when Sarah had the need to be cared for by psychiatry. Although laden with misery and sadness, because of this telling of Sarah's story it is now at least in the public arena, as opposed to being consigned to one of the hundreds of untold struggles in our psychiatric hospitals which have degenerated into fierce battles of opposing interpretations. What made Sarah's story so more intense is that throughout her time as a patient McLaughlin and Sarah's mother, Jane, were prepared to challenge the accepted, and often harsh procedure, for working with a woman who resisted the treatment she was prescribed. It also reveals highly dubious psychiatric practice, exemplifying the subjective horrors of compulsory treatment and detention. Like Coleman's experience of chapter five, Sarah's story documents the antagonism which can stain the relationship between a distressed victim[1] of misfortune and a powerful psychiatric authority. The psychiatric service found Sarah's reluctance to conform to its interventions extremely hot to handle, and Sarah, forever resistant but vulnerable, found the system equally as disagreeable. While the 26-year-old was forcibly injected with neuroleptics, prescribed compulsory electric-shock treatment, and the by-stander of efforts to see her transferred to a medium secure unit, she also had to deal with a system that often disapproved of her having access to her new-born baby. In return Sarah – usually while distraught and muddled – physically fought back. The whole saga proved to be messy and unpleasant, with the sad irony being that Sarah had willingly seen a psychiatrist in the first instance in the hope of being prescribed medication to help her sleep.

McLaughlin meanwhile, with a political radicalism nurtured by a background in trade union politics, coupled by a doctorate in psychology, has an alert and critical knowledge of mental health issues, psychology and psychiatry. As the Coleman story demonstrated he used such insights and experience in his significant part in Coleman's subsequent recovery/"freedom". McLaughlin tapped into such faculties while helping Sarah during her rocky journey through psychiatry.

Sarah's story

Sarah first approached her Stockport GP in 1996 after having not slept for two weeks. She, her partner Raymond, and their six-week-old baby, Christine, shared a house with three male students and one young woman and her 18-month-old child in Hereford. In a noisy, dirty environment not conducive to bringing up a baby who screamed day and night (it was later discovered that Christine had colic), Sarah was breast-feeding on demand, and her sleeping pattern was continually disrupted. Because Sarah's family had become concerned about her predicament, Sarah's brother, Stuart, drove his sister and Christine back to Stockport for respite care with her mother so she could help look after Christine while back in Hereford Raymond looked for improved accommodation. Jane and Sarah both visited their GP on March 11 in the hope that Sarah would be prescribed sleeping tablets to enable her to return to a normal healthy sleeping pattern. But Sarah had a previous psychiatric admission following illicit drug-taking three years before,

---

[1] I use the term "victim" because I understand anyone distressed to such extent that they seek psychiatric help as a "victim of misfortune". I do not want to imply that an individual is a victim throughout their distress, but the term does convey the sense of an individual's hopeless powerlessness I accept attempts can be made to move on from victim status.

and the doctor thought it wise that Sarah visit a psychiatrist at Stepping Hill, the local hospital. Although a blood test revealed no traces of illegal substances, the psychiatrist, Dr John Christie, assessed Sarah to have a "post-natal psychotic development" and she was admitted to the acute psychiatric ward of the hospital where her clinical notes mentioned symptoms of "sleeplessness" and "hallucinations". Dr Christie wrote: "On admission she [Sarah] was observed to be emotionally labile, her moods frequently alternating between being tearful, cheerful, suspicious, perplexed or blank when she would stare into the distance. She was unable to give any adequate account of herself." Sarah, evidently unwell, was prescribed neuroleptics which initially she took willingly. While Sarah stayed in Stepping Hill, Jane brought Christine to see Sarah each day, and no-one seemed to regard the visits as a problem.

On March 22 at 5pm Dr Christie sent Sarah and Christine, with Jane accompanying, to a social services mother and baby unit. The primary aim of the exercise was to assess Sarah's parenting skills which her psychiatrist obviously had become concerned about. It was here that matters became more serious for Sarah because her relationship with the unit's nurses immediately set off on a wrong footing. Jane recalls: "One of the nurses picked Christine up and started feeding her. And because Sarah was feeling a bit paranoid she challenged the nurse, asking what she was doing with Christine and what she was feeding her. She said she felt that she herself should be feeding Christine." Because Christine was constantly crying, Sarah preferred to stay with her baby in the unit's nursery. But this was judged to be inappropriate, and a verbal confrontation between Sarah and the nurses ensued.

The unit's staff were obviously highly sceptical about Sarah's ability as a carer, and later on that evening, just after Jane left, Sarah was detained under Section Two[2] of the Mental Health Act, the procedure used when someone is believed to be either a danger to his/herself or someone else, and was later transferred to the unit's acute psychiatric ward. Over the next five days Sarah was denied access to her baby daughter, apart from for between five to ten minutes a day.

However, by now the tranquillising effects of Sarah's high dose of neuroleptics meant she was sleeping almost constantly, and not eating properly. She was so sedated that she only has snatches of memories of what then unfolded at Stepping Hill Hospital, to where Sarah was transferred from the mother and baby unit. Understandably, she became reluctant to take the medication, and in the first evidence of the compulsory

---

[2] Section Two is for an assessment period of 28 days. During "assessment" a patient may also receive compulsory treatment.

assessment/treatment powers she was held under, nurses ominously informed her that if she did not take it voluntarily she would be injected intravenously. Jane was desperate like any mother to see her daughter improve. But, in her judgement and to her disappointment: "Sarah just started being pumped full of all these drugs – she started getting worse and worse."

Two days later Jane went to visit her daughter with Christine. She remembers: "I was told by the nurses that Sarah was not allowed to have the baby. There was no reason given except that they had just injected Sarah and so she was asleep." Obviously it was still felt inappropriate for Sarah to have contact with Christine. About half an hour later Jane managed to see Dr Christie who had prescribed Electro-Convulsive Therapy (ECT) for Sarah. "I asked him whether Sarah had agreed to it, but he said that he did not need her consent," said Jane. Of course he was right, because Sarah was held under a Section Two[3] and Jane, like any member of the public, was not read up on the Mental Health Act. "I started getting most upset, and said to Christie that I thought he did need her consent." She was wrong, but Christie said he would seek a second opinion from another Mental Health Commission psychiatrist, as the law dictated. Jane could protest as vehemently as she could – but in the eye of the law her opinion mattered no more than.....well Sarah's. And the medication had conveniently silenced her. By all accounts Sarah was in no state to object to a lobotomy, let alone ECT.

Jane immediately contacted Sarah's GP who, with the backing of her surgery partner, voiced her concerns directly to Dr Christie, stating she was fully opposed to Sarah being prescribed ECT. Sarah's uncle, also a GP, phoned Dr Christie to inform him of his objection. In addition, Jane telephoned McLaughlin who visited Sarah for the first time in hospital on March 30. During the ward round he suggested to Christie that there was an alternative to ECT, including psychological intervention. Christie's response – not an unusual psychiatric one – was that he did not believe in talking to patients as it only prolonged their misery, emphasising that ECT was his treatment of choice and he had enough confidence in it to prescribe it to his own children. By now he had also claimed that the beneficial effects of ECT would help Sarah bond with her baby. Despite psychiatry's obvious doubts about Sarah's capabilities as a mother, Jane and McLaughlin did not share the professionals' angst about Sarah's "bonding" ability, because Sarah had breast fed Christine for her first six weeks. Admittedly, during this turbulent time in her life, Sarah did need support with child-care duties, but Jane had more than proved her willingness to provide this.

---

[3] Once a Section Two procedure has been completed a patient has no right to refuse drug treatment, and a nearest relative also has no right to stop such treatment. A second opinion, however, is required from another psychiatrist to administer ECT.

After losing an appeal against the section McLaughlin tried a different tactic: "It had come to the stage where, in a diplomatic way, I had to use the threat of a judicial review. The second opinion which Christie had to get in order to carry out the ECT – which, basically he was going to do any minute – was carried out by another psychiatrist sitting on Sarah's bed as she was waking up. I pointed out that this was not a particularly appropriate time to assess a patient." All in all the combined pressure pulled off, and Christie said he would not proceed with the ECT.

Another important factor in the whole unfolding fiasco was that Christie and Sarah were unable to strike a sufficient degree of inter-personal communication, leading Dr Christie to conclude that Sarah was "insightless into her changed mental state", and "unable to give any adequate account of herself". Looking back on the power dynamics of the situation, Sarah saw it differently: "After being given drugs to sedate you it is really nerve-wracking in a ward round with a room full of professionals that have the authority to control your life – it is very difficult to think straight." In addition, McLaughlin had a far better quality communicative relationship with Sarah, explaining how she made complete sense to him. "Sarah was able to explain to me that her condition had come on due to her not having the opportunity to sleep," he said. "When Dr Christie asked Sarah if she thought she was ill, she responded that she felt her condition was due to sleep deprivation, accepting she was ill, but she was terrified at the prospect of ECT. This is the basis of Christie's observations of 'insightless'," said McLaughlin.

Nevertheless, it was agreed that Sarah could make home visits which, as well as getting her out of Stepping Hill, would give the young mother time to be with her daughter. Everything went successfully and according to plan, and so a longer weekend visit was organised. But, Dr Christie's subsequent manoeuvre caught everyone off guard. "Ken Smith, Sarah's social worker, was waiting for me on my next visit to Stepping Hill," remembered Jane. "He told me Dr Christie was planning to put Sarah on a six month section [Section Three treatment order], and that he was to give her electric shock treatment – even though he knew that the visits had gone well. For Jane and McLaughlin the whole situation had become frighteningly out of control, and they felt there was an urgent need for Sarah to get out of Stepping Hill if her daughter was to avoid electric shock treatment[4]. So when Jane went to the hospital the next day she asked whether she could take Sarah out for a coffee. The hospital agreed, but Jane brought her daughter straight back home. And when the Section Two had expired, Jane returned to Stepping Hill, thanked staff for their efforts, and asked them not to concern themselves about

---

[4] Theoretically, Jane could have gone through the procedure of appealing against Section Three via a civil court.

Sarah. Considering the disgust and disappointment she felt at how her daughter was treated under their care this was remarkably courteous.

However, there was plenty to worry about. For a start Sarah's condition was infinitely worse than when she was first admitted to Stepping Hill, possibly due to the high doses of medication. To be out of Stepping Hill's reach was also considered a high priority. So, using McLaughlin's contacts in the Network, it was decided to go to Wales in April, and for Sarah to be under the care of Gwynedd Community Health Trust, with Dr Phil Thomas (see previous chapter) as her consultant. Until Dr Thomas had made the necessary transfer arrangements with Stepping Hill, Sarah could use Coleman's home in Penyrndeudrath as a refuge. In the meantime Raymond would look for somewhere more appropriate for the three of them to live, so they could again begin some semblance of family life. Those closest to Sarah recognised her needs as a mother even if the statutory services were either reluctant to do so or did not have the resources to organise support for Sarah, even though during all this time Jane had been willing to help care for Christine.

Sarah then became a voluntary patient at Dryll y car, an innovative community support unit based on a more non-medical philosophy to mental health. Sarah had always recognised that she was not well during this period, citing her "nervous disposition". Quite possibly this was not helped by the fact that at Dryll y car all her medication was withdrawn at once, rather than gradually. Dr Thomas described Sarah as being "heavily over sedated and over medicated" from her time in Stockport, hence the decision to come off the medication. But Sarah claimed she was not told of the probable effects of coming off the drugs. To what extent this was a factor in Sarah's "scuffle" with a nurse remains controversial. The incident happened one afternoon after Raymond, who usually visited with Christine everyday, did not arrive. Sarah said she thought a nurse was laughing at her. "I barged past her and she pushed me, so I pushed back," she recalls. "She then grabbed hold of my hair, so I grabbed her hair. I then let go and apologised, and went back to my room. But they asked me to leave." Although the nurse involved admitted it was nothing serious, the ward was not staffed to deal with such physical incidents, and so Sarah was once again transferred. This time to the Hergest Unit of Bangor hospital, where she remained under the consultancy of Dr Thomas.

Meanwhile Raymond had by now found a flat in Porthmadog in North West Wales. Good news on one hand. A pity though it was an "absolute hovel" according to McLaughlin. "When I moved Raymond and the baby down to the flat, I realised how bad it was," he said. "There were no carpets, and it was absolutely filthy, with no running water. The next day I was supposed to go and fetch Sarah to bring her over. I was getting concerned." Despite the conditions, Sarah believed it would be better than their Hereford place. But unfortunately it did not work out because within a few days Sarah, still struggling with life, was sectioned again.

She committed no criminal or dangerous offence to warrant this latest compulsory detention in hospital. Rather, it seems her behaviour was perceived as distastefully odd, inappropriate and alarming by Porthmadog residents. It appears that following an argument with Raymond, Sarah had left the house to buy some cigarettes, and when she returned the house was locked leaving Sarah unable to get back in. Crying, and in a distressed state, Sarah wandered the town all night, periodically walking back to the house to see whether she could get in. "I could not even climb over the back gate because it was too tall – it was about an eight foot high gate," remembered Sarah. With only a vest on her top she evidently caught the attention of her concerned neighbours who called the police, who in turn summoned Sarah's psychiatric nurse, who then initiated the section. In hospital Sarah was put back on medication. Her relationship with Raymond, already sour, also took a dive for the worse, and he visited with Christine less frequently. The staff at Bangor, although supportive of Sarah having contact with her baby, were frustrated because they did not have the facilities. And despite her poor mental state and confusion Sarah still cared for her youngster, and was concerned for her safety. Matters soon came to a head

Sarah at the Hergest Unit
"Sarah frequently required restraining to be given prescribed medication." **Internal inquiry report on treatment of Sarah at Bangor Hospital's Hergest Unit (January, 1997)**

Whereas in Stockport Dr Christie had diagnosed Sarah with a "post-natal psychotic development", Dr Thomas took a more rounded analysis of Sarah's mental health. More inclined to understand the young woman's breakdown in relation to her life's events, he wrote: "Sarah presented to us with a complex mixture of emotional problems and at the end of our detailed and complex assessment we decided she was not suffering from a formal psychiatric disorder, but that she was experiencing severe emotional difficulties relating to traumatic experiences in her life, which had been re-awoken following the birth of her first child, within the context of a very difficult and stressful social environment in which she was living when the baby was first born."

So here was a young woman with no "formal psychiatric diagnosis", but who evidently needed care and support. The problem was that Sarah distrusted the culture of the psychiatric ward where she was once again held against her will. Under the Mental Health Act she was forbidden to leave, and she had no right to refuse medication. Sarah had committed no criminal offence, but was denied her freedom. Not only was she compelled to stay in the Hergest Unit, she was also seeing very little of her baby. If Raymond did not himself take Christine to see her mother Sarah had no opportunity to see her child at all. And because Sarah's relationship with her partner was in a steady decline it meant he was hardly visiting. How long was Sarah to be in this unhappy predicament? Sarah had little idea – it could be indefinitely. Although the hospital felt confinement was the most suitable treatment procedure, Sarah, however helpless, still had a thirst for freedom. The whole situation was in a chaotic spiral, and Sarah, without the intellectual or psychological capabilities to do otherwise, resorted to the most basic of reactionary drives – to physically escape.

Her clinical notes made many references to Sarah's attempts to escape from the Hergest Unit, which included trying to ram down locked doors. But all her efforts failed, and nurses reacted to her flights for freedom by placing her in solitary confinement ("seclusion"). Jane remembered one occasion when she went to visit her daughter following such practice: "When I asked the nurses whether Sarah was in solitary confinement as an act of punishment they said no. So I asked them why she had been locked in there. They replied that she had made herself a cup of tea in the kitchen, and that one of their nurses had gone to say something to her – I can not remember what – but he said Sarah had a funny look in her eye and *looked* as though she might throw this cup of tea. So he took the cup of tea off her, injected her and put her into solitary. It is absolutely crazy because nothing happened." Sarah, by all accounts an "uncooperative" patient, also does not have favourable memories of her relationship with staff, which had evidently reached a new level of mutual mistrust.

And what about the nurses forcing tranquillisers on Sarah? The same nurses who restrained her when she tried to escape; the same nurses who placed her in solitary confinement. How should have Sarah reasonably felt and behaved towards them? Whereas a more compliant patient might respect their actions Sarah challenged them and the regime they worked under – in so doing allegedly earning her the reputation as a "bad" patient and even an "animal"[5]. Ever since her teenage years Sarah had resisted what she regarded an unjust authority, and now facing such powers which frightened her she fought back to protect herself.

Sarah's clinical notes list 63 cases of violence or aggression, almost all of which she directed at staff. Having got to know Sarah, I am astonished that such a number of

---

[5] Allegations of staff's "poor attitude" towards Sarah was part of the later official complaint which the trust investigated through internal inquiry.

incidents involved her. But on the other it does perhaps reflect her pit of desperation, and the overwhelming worry she had for the whereabouts and safety of her daughter. Certainly Sarah was experiencing a tornado of psychological horrors, exacerbated by her resistance to compulsory treatment and fortuitous desire to be out of the hospital.

Because of their concern at how Sarah was treated at the Hergest Unit Jane and McLaughlin submitted a detailed complaint to the hospital on October 24. In response the trust carried out its own internal inquiry into its treatment procedures – the results all came down in favour of the methods used by staff to deal with Sarah's behaviour. In reply to accusations of "poor staff attitude" towards Sarah the inquiry stated staff "had dealt with Sarah in a sympathetic and non-judgmental manner and conducted themselves professionally". In fact, out of all Jane and McLaughlin's complaints – such as lack of privacy for Sarah, Jane's curtailed visits, searches on Jane, nurses acting provocatively to prevent Sarah from absconding – the only complaint felt to necessitate a review was that of Sarah allegedly losing two stone while in the Hergest Unit. The internal inquiry read: "It is considered that it would be good practice in future to weigh patients on admission and on a regular basis during their inpatient stay". Other than this relatively minor complaint staff were judged to have behaved in an entirely professional and appropriate way.

As for Sarah's complaints of being forcibly pinned down and injected, the report concluded: "Staff have confirmed that these incidents occurred and that, because of her behaviour, Sarah frequently required restraining to be given prescribed medication.....Most staff stated that, even during restraint, Sarah would continue to struggle. There is evidence that staff used appropriate techniques and ensured that the medical staff were called to review Sarah's physical and mental well-being after each incident." The report, unsurprisingly, did not question the practice of compulsory medication which had provoked Sarah to such an extent.

Sarah "the criminal"
Sarah has no criminal record, but because of her behaviour while in the Hergest Unit she almost received one. Gwynedd Trust proceeded with prosecuting Sarah on two separate charges of assault on nurses during her stay in the unit. What was happening here? Although acting correctly in the eyes of present law it seems somewhat puzzling for a hospital to deprive an individual of their freedom via a section, force medication on them, and then charge them with assault if they physically resisted. Bangor solicitor, Aled Jones, who defended Sarah, has acted on behalf of other Hergest Unit patients who have appeared in court because of similar actions. Jones recognised the contradiction of the trust's policy, which is an increasingly common one in the UK, and wrote to the

trust's manager, Alun Davies, saying: "More often than not patients do not have a history of criminal offending prior to their admission and detention, and it does seem rather strange for demonstrating this kind of behaviour whilst in the trust's care, which is symptomatic of the problems which lead to their admission in the first place...From a purely therapeutic point of view it surely cannot assist a patient's recovery to have to go through the rigors of a criminal prosecution."

Alun Davies replied by telling me that for some patients it was "clinically appropriate" for them to be charged with assault or damage. He said: "Patients are accused when it is felt to be appropriate and for their own well being." Davies went on to write in a letter to Jones that his trust has a responsibility towards its own staff: "The duty requires the maintaining of good order at the unit, and the minimising of incidents of violence on the ward" he wrote. And, in making an unusual comparison with other hospital wards, he went on to say: "The interests of all patients and staff are ultimately served by the knowledge to all concerned that behaviour, which would be entirely unacceptable in any other hospital setting, will be equally unacceptable in the Hergest Unit when it is considered to be voluntary on the part of the patient, and potentially criminal, and will then be treated as such." Even though Sarah was on a cocktail of therapeutic/mind-altering drugs she still admits her actions were voluntary. But it is limp to compare the predicament of a sectioned psychiatric patient with a patient in any other hospital ward without further qualification. Quite simply a patient can walk out of any other ward, with no threat of being dragged back in and treated under compulsion. They have certain freedoms which Sarah, as a sectioned psychiatric patient, did not share.

Interestingly, in the penultimate paragraph of his letter, Davies wrote: "We are sure you will agree, on reflection, that not to prosecute a patient in such circumstances, when a patient knowingly and willingly commits such acts, would amount to a licence for all patients in the unit to behave exactly as they wished, free from any threat or fear of sanctions, to the ultimate detriment of the well-being of everyone concerned.[6]" But we should remind ourselves that patients are detained because frankly they would prefer not to be, and for this reason a ward of sectioned psychiatric patients will never be a haven of tranquillity. Compulsory medication will further aggravate antagonism, and while the

---

6 I am reminded of the film, One Flew Over a Cuckoo's Nest. Jack Nicholson (playing a sectioned psychiatric inmate) breaks out of hospital and takes all the other patients with him. He steals a boat from the nearest harbour, and the whole nutty crew have the best – but illegal – fun for years of their pitiful lives. It was a glorious escapade when the patients did "exactly as they wished". Later Nicholson did "exactly as he wished" when he attacked one of the nurses a few days later. The price he paid for that action, however, was to be treated with a frontal lobotomy. The hospital made an example of him – and thus prevented Nicholson from "giving a licence" for disruptive behaviour to all the other weaker-willed patients.

practice may be perceived to "work" for some, it failed to for Sarah, adverse to psychiatric medication which has never appeared to improve her mental health.

If the sectioning process became more open to the civil courts, and if compulsory medication was prohibited, I think Davies's argument of patient responsibility would hold more water. But if you deny someone of their right to defend themselves against enforced physical intervention, you surely can not judge their actions from the same moral pulpit as you would an individual able to walk the streets in relative freedom. The trust's guidelines are more a reflection of efforts to protect the interests and working conditions of staff fed up with having to deal with patients' physical dissent when they may not necessarily be trained to deal with such resistance. But dissent from a free individual is different to that from a young woman feeling she should neither be detained against her will nor have medication forced on her. The Bangor magistrates were evidently unhappy with the prosecution and threw the two assault charges out of the judicial window.

Sarah's discharge from the Hergest Unit

Because Dr Thomas recognised that Sarah's mental health was not being improved by the hospital culture, and by her also being separated from her daughter, the agreed discharge procedure was that a mother and baby unit at Bangor would be made available until all was ready for Sarah to return to Stockport. It was agreed that Christine could also stay at the mother and baby unit. Unfortunately this never happened, and when McLaughlin returned from Holland after one week he found that none of this discharge procedure had taken place. Raymond had not only failed to turn up with Christine, he had pretty much faded out of the picture entirely. Sarah was alone in the hospital, uncertain of the whereabouts of her child, and the discharge that did go ahead followed a radically different protocol. Recollecting the occasion Sarah said: "I remember the nurses coming in to my room and holding me down and injecting me. There was a nurse on each arm, and one giving me a headlock." (The trust's internal inquiry defined this "headlock" as a "controlled arm lock".) Nurses "escorted" Sarah into the back of an ambulance for the drive to her mother's house in Stockport where she was "discharged."

In her confusion, Sarah mistakenly supposed she would also find Raymond, and more importantly Christine, back in Stockport. But her daughter was not there, and Jane was told that Raymond had taken her on holiday to Cornwall to visit her grandmother. This spiral of broken agreements, misunderstandings and puzzlement over the whereabouts of Raymond and Christine, together with her unpleasant memories of Bangor only served to pummel Sarah's mental distress further. She was in a state of panic which proved to worsen her predicament.

The day after returning to Stockport she wandered into a play group asking for a job. A friend had given her a name of an employer at the toddlers group, and Sarah went to visit her in the hope of finding some kind of employment.[7] This was certainly not a clever thing to do because not only was Sarah physically effected by her medication, but her psychological presence was hardly going to impress a potential employer. Shortly after walking into the nursery, and without introducing herself, Sarah casually got talking to two children. One of the assistants became alerted to the fact that a complete stranger had ambled into the nursery, and predictably it all ended up with everyone getting their wires crossed, and Sarah being whisked away by the police. Nothing seriously untoward happened in the nursery, and Sarah on later reflection was able to accept that the nursery staff's behaviour was totally reasonable considering that they had no idea who she was. The police did not charge Sarah with any offence, and she returned home.

But still not knowing the whereabouts of Christine was distressing for everyone involved. It was in this collective angst that Jane, Sarah and Stuart headed back to the mother and baby unit in Bangor. They also visited Porthmadog only to find no sign of Raymond. He had taken Christine with him, and seemingly left no indication of where he had gone. Jane phoned his parents but there was no reply. Sarah was now homeless and she had lost her child. "She went berserk," recalled McLaughlin, "and was banged up in a cushioned room in the hospital. She was incontinent and apparently aggressive." By now the hospital's staff decided they could no longer deal with Sarah, so they tried to find her a place in a medium secure unit, particularly after what had happened in the Stockport nursery. This meant that she could be sent anywhere in the country.

But Thomas, known as a maverick by his colleagues, was in the familiar position of differing with them, because he recognised that it was the hospital culture and the uncertainties of Christine's whereabouts which seemed to be causing Sarah most problems and aggravation. But in light of the nurses' intentions, it seemed he would have to go through section appeal procedures via a Mental Health Tribunal for Sarah to be discharged, rather than sent to a secure unit. McLaughlin, present at the hearing, said: "This was a strange situation because if a consultant supports discharge, such a procedure is usually proceeded with. But the appeal against the section had to take place because of the nursing management's opposition to Sarah's discharge." The tribunal consisted of Thomas, a second psychiatrist, a lawyer and a retired social worker. Describing the hearing's tense atmosphere, McLaughlin said: "The second psychiatrist was really hostile to the discharge – there was a terrible argument between him and Thomas. This second psychiatrist did not take to Sarah, and even came out with the statement, 'You mean being a retard isn't a treatable mental illness?' – imagine how

---

[7] Sarah has always aspired to working with children.

Sarah felt about these people talking about her as a retard. I don't think Thomas knew what to say at all in reply to that!" But the social worker and lawyer backed Thomas and on September 18, 1996, Sarah won the appeal

But Sarah and Raymond's relationship by now had fallen apart, and they became embroiled in an unpleasant and drawn out custody case where the accusational daggers of Sarah and Raymond's solicitor dug deep into each others reputations. While Sarah's solicitor had many a line of attack against Christine's father, his main aim was to convince the judge that Sarah was not "mentally ill". Of course it was in Raymond's solicitor's interest to convince the judge that she was. The pressure took its toll on Sarah's vulnerable constitution and she struggled to stay mentally fit. Although Sarah still had no officially recognised mental illness, to have psychiatrists standing in the witness box casting their judgement on the working order of Sarah's mind was of little benefit to her cause. Like any adversarial custody hearing, the court heard vicious allegations and counter allegations, each party trying to degrade the character of the other. The decision went Raymond's way, and he was granted continual custody of Christine.

Conclusion

At the time of writing Sarah is, in between a prolonged spell at home, being held in a privately-run medium secure unit more than 100 miles away from her home in Stockport. She hardly sees Christine at all and is still on a large cocktail of medication. Jane, who feels her daughter has "become institutionalised", is almost her only visitor. Sadly there is, at present, no happy ending.

Yet what makes Sarah's experience so revealing is the practice and culture of care which, I would argue, characterises many of our psychiatric hospitals. It also rings with serious problems which are acknowledged by other mental health charities and campaigning groups. Some of these problems, reflecting themes discussed in earlier chapters, include:

- The practice of quickly embarking onto a course of physical treatment, including ECT and medication, without recourse or consideration of other methods of therapeutic assistance.
- The abusive practice of compulsory physical treatment, and lack of acknowledgement of the pain, fear and trauma of receiving such enforced treatment.
- Psychiatrists and nurses who, because of their training and background, ally to a medical model of distress, which risks blinding them of other avenues of intervention with a patient.
- Difficulty in establishing communication, and hence empathy, towards patients.

What makes Sarah's experience so emblematic of such problems is that she had the steel-strong support of those prepared to challenge such a philosophy of treatment, and also to propose alternatives, even though they were not taken up. Psychological intervention and committed social support has still yet to be tried with Sarah.

The differences Sarah's family's, McLaughlin, and to some extent Thomas, have with the service which Sarah received (and continues to receive) centres on (i) a concern about the excessive use of tranquillisers to subdue/treat Sarah; (ii) an opposition to enforced ECT; (iii) a recognition of the oppressive nature of compulsory detention and treatment; (iv) a recognition of Sarah's confusion of not knowing the whereabouts of her child.; and (v) the lack of *social* support for Sarah and her family.

Some readers may claim I have conveniently focused on Sarah's story to reinforce such criticisms. But, for me, it is not a matter of convenience to highlight such dubious practice. Sarah needed help and initially accepted this, but that the psychiatric service provoked such resistance and retaliation from Sarah and her family is sad indeed. To resolve the roots of the problem of such intervention would involve addressing the philosophy of care for the distressed. But, referring to the criticisms as listed above, I do not think it is demanding too much professional and political commitment to (i) increase focus on social and psychological support as much as neuroleptics; (ii) legally enshrine a right to refuse ECT and all forms of physical treatment; and: (iii) recognise that separation of a mother from a new-born child is going to concentrate anxiety. By reforming psychiatry's authoritarian tendencies and insensitive culture patients may end up getting a great deal more from the service.

N.B Dr John Christie was asked for his comments on parts of this chapter. But he chose not to comment. *The names of some people in this chapter have been changed.*

Chapter ten

The genetics of schizophrenia – science or hocus pocus?

"A large body of evidence collected over more than 60 years and culminating in recent studies applying refined methods including standardised diagnosis strongly suggests a genetic contribution to the aetiology of schizophrenia." **Dr Michael Owen and colleagues, authors of *The Strength of the Genetic Effect* in The British Journal of Psychiatry, 1994.**

"If there has been a revolution in genetic psychiatry, it has been in the opposite direction – toward discrediting the old studies and casting scepticism on the few new ones" **Dr Peter Breggin, psychiatrist and author of *Toxic Psychiatry*, 1991.**

"It has long been my impression that lying is one of the most significant phenomena in the field of psychiatry," **American psychiatrist, Thomas Szasz, author of *The Myth of Mental Illness*.**

In many ways what I have written in the previous chapters invalidates the need for this chapter where I look at the genetic research into schizophrenia. Because the message of the hearing voices movement in itself challenges the whole idea of the existence of schizophrenia as a medical disorder why examine the scientific credentials of such research? In addition, many people quoted in previous pages are diagnosed schizophrenics who are themselves pioneering a new way of understanding the whole concept of schizophrenia, and how hearing voices is related to it. However, in spite of this I must confess that I keep an avid interest in genetic psychiatry because, I am intrigued to know what researchers do claim to find. Who knows, possibly they are genuinely on to something, and will eventually prove to be right? Maybe the geneticists *will* one day find a schizophrenic gene, and put it under a microscope for us all to see. I belief however, that the day they do this will be the day they find a gene that determined me to advocate the belief that they will *never* find this gene! Nevertheless, as a personal and final act of investigation into the psychiatric discipline, I would like to critique the genetic work into schizophrenia, and evaluate its scientific merit. While the hearing voices movement endeavours to question the medical concept of schizophrenia, geneticists still lean against the shoulder of scientific research when advocating their point of view. I would like to put all other critques of psychiatry aside for the duration of this chapter, and examine schizophrenia from the perspective that psychiatry knows best – science.

Genetic power

To advance the notion that schizophrenia is not a genetic disease is making a stand against the power of 21st century psychiatric science – and there's a lot of power out there. Ever since the quest to demonstrate the genetic basis of schizophrenia began there has been a voluptuous history of research and summary papers found in periodicals such as the British Journal of Psychiatry, the Schizophrenia Bulletin, the Archives of General Psychiatry, Biological Psychiatry, and Critical Opinions in Psychiatry. These papers which, if not directly stating a genetic basis to schizophrenia, all share the geneticists' medico-scientific discourse.

Other bastions of psychiatric science's power are the multinational drug companies which fund and support much of the biological research, placing glossy adverts in the journals; psychiatrists with seven years medical training; psychologists with three years clinical training; approved mental health social workers; community psychiatric nurses and ward nurses – most of whom will have been pushed the medical model. Psychiatry also has a towering physical presence with buildings such as London's Institute of Psychiatry; journalists attend psychiatrists' conferences writing front page stories on their latest "findings"; psychiatrists get awarded Nobel Prizes and appear in court as "expert witnesses"; they act as voices of authority on day time TV and the Oprah Winfrey Show; the charities such as Schizophrenia A National Emergency (SANE), Space, The National Schizophrenia Fellowship, and The Schizophrenia Association of Great Britain (SAGB) all tow the genetic line to so some degree. And so the tunes whistled by these pied pipers of "schizophrenia as genetic illness" seep in to the public consciousness. This is the efficiency of power. But the question I would like to pose is whether the studies into the genetics, and associated neurophysiology, of schizophrenia are in fact based on good science? I want to ask whether it is a valid hypothesis to claim that a causal factor for schizophrenia lies in an individual's genes?

The first generation genetic studies – cracking the egg

In 1972 Irving Gottesman and James Shields published a study of what were then the five most recent international twin studies supposedly demonstrating the influence of genes on becoming schizophrenic. Modern psychiatry quoted this work ever since as, at worst indicating and, at best, irrefutably revealing a genetic determination to schizophrenia.

These studies traced – primarily through hospital records – a twin who had been diagnosed schizophrenic, and then traced his/her co-twin to discover whether s/he had received the same diagnosis. The main finding was that genetically identical monozygotic twins who grew from the same maternal egg were more likely to be diagnosed schizophrenic than dizygotic twins who came from two different eggs. This difference was believed to be due to the genetic differences between the two sets of twins, and the book published on the research, *The Genetics of Schizophrenia*, was revered to be the ultimate in studies demonstrating schizophrenia's genetic base. At the time it was the biggest investment the medical model had in it's bank, and any student reading this academic pillar of genetic psychiatry can be excused for being seduced by its findings. This is how you can see them in the Gottesman and Shield book:-

	Concordance rates for Schizophrenia in never twin studies					
Country/Year	MZ Pairs			DZ Pairs		
	Total	Pairwise rate (%)	Probandwise rate (%)	Total	Pairwise rate (%)	Probandwise rate (%)
Finland 1963/1971	17	0-36	35	20	5-14	13
Norway 1967	55	25-38	45	90	4-10	15
Denmark 1973	21	24-48	56	41	10-19	27
UK 1966/1987	22	40-50	58	33	9-12	15
Weighted Average			48%			17%
United States 1966/1987	164	18	31	277	3	6

These tables are impressive and persuasive in arguing for a difference in schizophrenia concordance rates between monozygotic and dizygotic twins. (The library copy I referred to was graffitted with pencil scribbles conveying how impressed a previous reader was – "Look! Powerful Figures" was daubed beside one table.) Gottesman and Shields' findings are backed up by statistical analyses and scientific discourses – all neatly packaged in genetic theory. But what about the study's scientific rigour? Remembering that we are judging this study from a scientifically critical perspective, how does the Gottesman and Shields study look after an examination of its reliability and validity, the two ingredients essential for good science?

Mary Boyle, head of clinical psychology training at the University of East London, has already provided such a critique. Her book, *Schizophrenia: a Scientific Delusion,* lists the methodological flaws of Gottesman and Shield's study. The most important point she made is that what makes Gottesman and Shields' concordance rates so much higher is the introduction of the term "schizophrenic spectrum" instead of "schizophrenia". Gottesman and Shields have, in fact, compared concordance rates not for DSM-IV-R "schizophrenia" but a "schizophrenic spectrum". This spectrum includes diagnoses such as "personality disorder", "psychopathic personality", "affective disorder" "schizoid personality" "schizophreniform" and "paranoid" or "atypical psychosis". So, for example, one disruptive twin who heard voices was diagnosed as having "affective disorder". The co-twin felt someone was "taking part of her brain away" and was diagnosed with "schizoactive psychosis". Under the schizophrenic spectrum umbrella they were classified as concordant, although they did not share the same diagnosis. In addition, each study had different criteria for what behaviour satisfies concordance.

What we have then in these many cases of schizophrenic spectrum concordance is, in fact, concordance of twins behaving oddly or expressing what may appear to be unusual beliefs, without necessarily being DSM-IV-R schizophrenia. To clarify the point, Boyle said: "If we call a pair of twins who share one or two of these vague 'symptoms' concordant for schizophrenia, it is almost like calling concordant for cancer a pair of twins where both report that they sometimes get headaches or feel nauseous." I would add that it is as far fetched as claiming that being fined for speeding on the motorway is evidence of a "criminality spectrum" gene. Of course geneticists have arguments to justify such a use of "schizophrenic spectrum", such as that there are different manifestations of one same gene. But the essential point is that the twin studies in *The Genetics of Schizophrenia* do not study "schizophrenia", but a cluster of behaviours and beliefs which have been regarded as sufficiently odd to warrant a psychiatric diagnosis.

Another look at Gottesman and Shield's tables shows an increase in concordance when the term "probandwise" is used. What is this term, and is it legitimate? A proband is a schizophrenic twin found in the original search (independently) for twins for the study, rather than during the later process of tracing co-twins (dependently). So, it is possible that some of these proband twins, though found independently, will be each other's twin – i.e. that a set of concordant twins will be counted twice. It is a statistical tool and can be used validly "if a researcher ensures exhaustive sampling and traces every person in a large population who has a twin and who fulfilled criteria for inferring schizophrenia," commented Boyle. Because Gottesman and Shields' twin-study samples were often from *hospital* samples there is no evidence to suggest that these samples are representative. It is feasible that twins who behaved aberrantly enough to earn a psychiatric diagnosis, but did not come into contact with a hospital, had quite different concordant rates to those recorded on the above tables. If, for example a twin, George, comes to the attention of a hospital after complaining that people in the street are laughing at him, it is probably *more* likely that his co-twin, Patrick, who is mute and apprehensive will also end up being seen by a psychiatrist, and gaining a "schizophrenic spectrum disorder" than it would be for any other member of the public. This is because friends, relatives or interested psychiatrists may encourage such a referral. This is another alternative explanation which eats away at the justification of bringing in the "probandwise" measurement, and ultimately the validity of Gottesman and Shield's study. If we also consider that many of the twins were dead in some studies (32% of the Danish sample), and the researchers were not always acting blind, knowing of the twins' zygosity (e.g. the Finnish and Norwegian studies), the floodgates of methodological error are opened yet further.

Boyle highlighted another example of dodgy scientific conduct – the selective criticism of studies reporting low-rate concordance. For example, when the Finnish researchers did an extension of their 1963 study they reported a pairwise concordance rate of 15% for monozygotic twins. Yet, Gottesman and Shields excluded this study (apart from in a footnote) because they said the report lacked case detail. This is in spite of other higher concordant rate studies also lacking case detail – for example, the Danish study only reported the case details for monozygotic twins, and not the dizygotic twins. If amount of "case detail" is judged as important in evaluating the validity of studies, you can not have a rule for one, and another rule for the rest. Secondly, Gottesman and Shields assessed that some of the discordant monozygotic twins in the Finnish study featured an organically (as opposed to functionally) psychotic twin. They left these discordant twins out in their probandwise analysis, again in light of the fact of the unreported information on which other researchers based their diagnosis. Thirdly, if you look at the above table, it appears that the USA study, with pairwise concordance of 14-27%, is one study. In fact it is two. The original researchers reported a monozygotic concordance rate of 14%. It was actually *another* study by another group of researchers who reported the 27% rate. (Although they used the same case material they only included twins of known zygosity, and used wider diagnostic criteria.)

A huge amount of research went into Gottesman and Shield's review. Considering their social status as prestigious scientists it is easy to except their word on the matter. But, in fact, I would say that their review suggests no genetic link to schizophrenia. In light of (a) the unreliable data from which they based their review and (b) the impact it had on the psychiatric discipline, it is unfortunate that they ever put pen to paper in the first place. That the report is entitled the *Genetics of Schizophrenia* is, in itself, misleading.

167

Firstly, because it was a cluster of psychiatric diagnoses that was measured and not "schizophrenia", and secondly – and more significantly – because there is no evidence to claim that genes, as opposed to anything else, caused these diagnoses. Whilst accepting that the evidence points to a difference in psychiatric diagnosis between monozygotic and dizygotic twins, it is scientific suspicion to hypothesise that this difference can be explained by reference to genes. Feasibly, this *may* be the case. But what about other possible explanations for the differences between the two sets of twins that may lead to a diagnosis of schizophrenia – such as variations in the subjective experience and social environment between monozygotic and dizygotic twins (are identical twins more likely to experience the world similarly?), variable rates of physical, emotional or sexual trauma (are identical twins more likely to *both* suffer from physical abuse?), scapegoating (is one non-identical twin more likely to become a family victim?) , the likelihood of feeling "odd" or "different" (are identical twins more likely to share odd beliefs?), parental treatment, bullying at school, identity confusion, shared wild imagination and empathy towards each other and so on. Perhaps such factors could equally lead to a different rate of "schizophrenic spectrum" diagnoses between the two sets of twins. But Gottesman and Shields have made no efforts to control for, or measure, such variables. Such scientific rigour should have been adhered to if a genetic hypothesis is to be supported.

In conclusion, I would say that Gottesman and Shields' twin study goes no further than supporting the hypothesis that more monozygotic than dizygotic twin pairs are admitted to psychiatric hospital. To cruelly twist the academic knife, I think the book should have been given a more accurate title such as, *Trends in twin hospitalisation rates.*

The adoption studies – good science or hocus-pocus?
In 1975 some of the top minds of western psychiatry published what has become the most cited research in support of the genetic theory of schizophrenia. Seymour Kety, Professor at Harvard, colleagues from the American National Institute of Mental Health, and Danish psychiatrists, tracked down and assessed relatives of children who were adopted early in their infancy and were subsequently diagnosed schizophrenic. An aim of this study was to make it unlikely that the social environment could be used to explain the causation of schizophrenia. So the study compared the schizophrenia diagnoses in the biological families of the schizophrenic adoptees with the diagnoses in the biological families of a control group of adoptees who were not schizophrenic. If the biological families of schizophrenic adoptees were found to have a higher rate of schizophrenia than the biological families of non-schizophrenic adoptees then the researchers believed this difference must be due to something other than the environment because none of the adoptees were brought up by their biological families.

The explanation for the difference must lie in the genes. Their book, *The Transmission of Schizophrenia*, suggested that 9% of the blood-relations of adoptee schizophrenics had a schizophrenic diagnosis compared with 2% of the relatives of non-schizophrenic adoptees.

Peter Breggin, American psychiatrist and author of *Toxic Psychiatry*, located a report of Kety's study, and this was his reaction: "I was shocked by what I found. There was no increase in so-called schizophrenia among the close biological relatives, including the mothers, fathers, full brothers, and full sisters. Thus the studies actually tended to *disprove* the genetic origin of the presumed illness." Breggin then asked: "So what data were they using to prove a genetic tendency?" He went on: "They had made a most strange finding: *the half brothers and half sisters on the father's side did have an increased rate of "schizophrenia"*. In other words, we have a miracle gene that skips the biological mothers, fathers, brothers and sisters – and even the biological half-brothers and sisters on the mother's side – and strikes only the half-siblings on the father's side." What is more, this increased diagnosis on the father's side was dependent on one large family with six offspring who were all classified as suffering from schizophreniclike disorders. Breggin, during a public meeting, was fortunate enough to question one of the study's researchers psychiatrist Fini Schlusinger on the large effect this one family would have had on the study's results. "Did he produce some statistics to prove me wrong" asked Breggin? "To the contrary, he conceded the point. Yet the whole genetics of schizophrenia rests on this house of cards. What hocus-pocus!" Breggin concluded.

The in-vogue "schizophrenic spectrum" category was also used for Kety's adoption study. What questions the validity of the category yet further is that 14 of the 18 schizophrenic paternal half siblings were actually diagnosed with "latent schizophrenia", a condition which the investigators claimed was for "potential schizophrenics". Although this category existed in the DSM-II at the time of the study, it has since been dropped.

And what about the adoptive homes that the schizophrenics and non-schizophrenics ended up in? Was there any kind of selective placement in allocating families to the adoptees? Well, 24 per cent of the adoptive families of the schizophrenic adoptees consisted of parents who spent time in psychiatric hospital, compared to none of the parents of the non-schizophrenic adoptees. You would expect a Harvard-induced study to report such statistics considering the huge influence they could have on how the results are interpreted. In fact, it was only thanks to Steven Rose, a biologist from the Open University, who managed to get hold of the original unpublished data, and then publish it in *Not in Our Genes* that anyone, other than the researchers, came to be aware of this fact. Rose also observed: "There is no indication that the biological parents of the schizophrenic adoptees have been in mental hospital at an excessive rate. That occurred in only 6% of the families, a rate in fact lower than that observed in the biological families of the control adoptees." Kety and his colleagues carried out another study in 1994 which was a replication of the Copenhagen study on the rest of Denmark where the results were equally supportive of a genetic hypothesis. I was sceptical about the results and wished to look at the study myself. Like Rose, I wrote to the National Institute of Health requesting a reprint of this study. (The research paper in the *Archives of General Psychiatry* advised curious readers to do this). When I received no reply I wrote them again repeating my request. Still now I have yet to hear from the National Institute.

Nevertheless, I believe it is justified to suggest that these twin and adoption studies direly lack scientific rigour. Because of possible alternative explanations to account for the results I would suggest it would be misguided to cite them as examples of the development of *genetic* research in unravelling the aetiology of schizophrenia. It is second-rate science.

Within families
Since these early studies, psychiatry increasingly turned to examining the rate of schizophrenia *within* families. So, taking someone diagnosed schizophrenic researchers compared the likelihood of this person's parents, brothers and sisters (first-degree relatives) being diagnosed schizophrenic compared with the relatives of a non-schizophrenic. In 1993 two American psychiatrists, Kenneth Kendler and Scott Diehl, published a review in the *Schizophrenia Bulletin* of these family studies. They concluded that it is ten times more likely for the first degree relative of a schizophrenic to also be diagnosed schizophrenic than it is for the relatives of a non-schizophrenic. Although suggesting that environmental factors could play a part, genetic determination is cited as the main reason for this difference.

But once again we find ourselves asking whether these family differences could be explained by a non-genetic hypothesis? Could these family differences in schizophrenia also support the hypothesis that traumatic life experiences leads to schizophrenia. But, to examine such a hypothesis requires knowledge of the life experiences of such schizophrenics. Yet the family studies quoted by Kendler and Diehl, like the twin and adoption studies before them, gave no such information. A reader has no idea of the life experiences these research subjects had prior to their diagnosis of schizophrenia because the studies did no such investigations. Once again I feel it is legitimate to suspect that geneticists may be barking up the wrong tree. But, as psychiatry is a medical profession we should not be really be condemning it for failing to examine non-biological factors that may lead to the development of schizophrenia. We may, however, hope that the profession of psychology would. Yet in the UK there has as yet been no such study on the scale of the American twin or adoption studies. All we have is anecdotal evidence, and the story of the Genain quadruplets which I turn to next is the most compelling, fascinating and horrifying anecdotal evidence one is likely to find.

Dreadful genes, dreadful parents or dreadful science?
Noris, Iris, Myra and Hester were four American identical sisters born in the early 1930s. All of them ended up with a diagnosis of schizophrenia by the time they reached adulthood and by the sixties all four had been admitted to The Institute of Mental Health where they became subjected to probably one of the most intensive psychiatric interventions ever carried out on one family. To this day there is nothing comparable.

Clinical psychology Lucy Johnstone described the case in a 1996 edition of the psychotherapeutic journal, *Changes*. She wrote: "During these three years the quads and their parents were subjected to every possible physical and psychological investigation, from EEGs and GSRs to Rorschach tests and attitude rating scales. Their relatives, neighbours, teachers, doctors, colleagues and schoolmates were all interviewed." Johnstone then retold the miserable life stories of these four women.

At school-age their father did not allow them to mix with other children, invite friends home, go on school outings nor attend parties. The quadruplets were also resented by their peers for their special status (they attracted wide media attention). Hester masturbated from a young age, and this horrified her parents who resorted to whipping her and swabbing her vulva with carbolic acid. When this failed to deter Hester they found a surgeon who circumcised both Hester and Iris. The surgeon (later employed by a state mental hospital after being driven from private practice) also ordered the girls' hands to be tied to the bed for a month afterwards. As a result the girls wet their bed several times a night and were so distraught they could not eat. Mr Genain was violent to his wife and children, dominant and a heavy drinker. To cap it all he was sinisterly intrusive. By the time his daughters were at secondary school, he allowed them no privacy while dressing, washing or even changing their sanitary pads. He often fondled their buttocks and breasts. The role of the girl's mother in this horrendous domestic culture was to accept it as a legitimate way of "testing the girls' morals".

By the time Hester was 18 she began to show more signs of inner turmoil – feeling insecure, self-destructive and tearful. Her parents response? Mrs Genain attributed her daughter's distress to her sexual activities, while Mr Genain threatened her daughter and forced her face into a basin of water. As the other sisters found secretarial jobs their father's intrusiveness continued, opening their post and forbidding them to go out on dates. Nora next showed signs of distress, when, after an attempted rape, her father told her that the attacker meant no harm. Exhausted and tearful Nora ended up in a psychiatric hospital in a severely disturbed state. Three months later Iris was diagnosed with schizophrenia after hearing voices and was admitted to hospital. Back home, Mr Genain was drinking more and wandered round the house armed with a gun to deter supposed invaders. Hester then made a suicide attempt and Myra, under strain from her sisters' distress, finally broke down. They became classic schizophrenics. "This is a heart-rending tale of extreme child abuse – the emotional, physical, and sexual abuse of four female children who happen to be quadruplets," wrote Breggin in *Toxic Psychiatry*.

Left to ponder on such a horrific family story what should the message have been to society, let alone psychiatry? Breggin explained how David Rosenthal, an American psychologists who edited the orginal book on the Genain quadruplets, presented these "cases" as a scientific study of genetic and environmental influences on the development of the "disease" of schizophrenia, with a heavy emphasis on genetics, including elaborate reviews of supposedly relevant genetic studies. Ironically, that was in psychiatry's liberal sixties era. In addition, when a follow-up was carried out in 1984 it focused almost entirely on biochemical theories to explain the breakdowns of these four sisters. Unsurprisingly no definite conclusions were made supporting a biochemical explanation. Breggin stated that to see such a study as supporting a genetic theory of schizophrenia constituted a form of child abuse in itself. "To fail to underscore or to summarise the outrages perpetrated against the children constitutes intellectual complicity with the child abuser," he said.

But what this Genain study did reveal was the more the life experiences of people diagnosed schizophrenic are seriously looked in to the more non-genetic the whole experience becomes. With knowledge of the girls' domestic life should we be surprised to hear that Nora had hallucinations of her father lying dead in a casket, while Myra heard parental voices controlling her actions? As a clinical psychologist herself Johnstone listed the dynamics that can be drawn out from this Genain study which would support a non-genetical, psychological explanation for schizophrenia. These included a difficulty in establishing one's own identity, blurred boundaries, sexual abuse, emotional and physical intrusiveness, confused communications, and a taboo on expressing feelings such as anger. The question that then overshadowed all the hundreds of genetic studies into schizophrenia was what about the lives of all those thousands of schizophrenic patients the studies based their findings on? If as much time and energy had been spent looking at the lives of these patients what would the researchers have found? If the scientists had paid more attention to their patients' life stories than their genetic relationship to each other what would they have discovered? We just do not know.

Because genetic studies do not publish the life history or subjective experience of their subjects, readers of such studies can only guess as to the lives they led. Gottesman and Shields, however, were generous in *The Genetics of Schizophrenia*. They published a summary of their subjects' hospital reports and interviews. This is how the summaries of two twins appeared in their book.

Psychiatric History of A: At 16 A suffered "mild nervous breakdown"; left his job, went to hospital where he was told nothing was wrong. He was religiously oriented at this time. At 20 broke off his engagement after the announcement party with no reason given. At 31 in the RAF he became engaged to a continental girl (RC). When permission to marry was refused, he left his unit, was picked up because of strange behaviour, and was admitted to the RAF psychiatric hospital: apathetic, poorly orientated, preoccupied with thoughts of "truth, his father, his brother, and an incident when he was accused of stealing something." The diagnosis: acute schizophrenia, with hallucinations, periodic negativism, and paroxysms of violence. After four ECT and insulin coma, he was medically discharged from service, after 38 weeks in hospital. From that point on he was never really well. He married the girl (at 33); a son was born a year later. First seen at Maudsley (at 35) revealing ideas of influence and suspiciousness he was admitted to the out patient ware after giving up work and expressing suicidal ideas, then to Maudsley for four weeks where he was diagnosed as schizophrenic. In hospital, terrified lest he be going mad again. Treated with ECT, refused insulin. Six months later irritable, depressed, would not eat, would not speak to wife. He was a Maudsley inpatient for 20 weeks. Four ECT cleared delusions and hallucinations, but pentothal and methedrine injections revealed schizophrenic thought disorder. (Diagnosis: Depressive psychosis in schizoid personality, changed to schizophrenic). At 36, attacked wife, admitted to Maudsley where still hospitalised at age 49. (Diagnosis: chronic schizophrenic). At admission, solitary, withdrawn, hallucinated, laughed incongruously, harboured persecutory ideas. A few months after admission, escaped and was brought back. Thereafter he was less agitated, dull, self-absorbed, flattened in mood. By age 37, disinterested, unemployable, remained aurally hallucinated. Visited by wife every three weeks.

When interviewed: At 49, co-operated, seemed "out of it"; smiled, grimaced, whispered to himself (?aural hallucinations). How are you feeling? "All right..." How's your appetite? "All right..." How do you sleep "All right..." You sleep all right at night? "Well I don't sleep I dream." When asked if he had ideas that were different from other people's he suggested that his ideas were not "revolutionary". Described inappropriate laugh as "Habit, don't mind..."

This is a classic example of clinical report writing on a patient. There is no suggestion that the clinicians have ever tried to communicate with 'A' on his level. No evidence to understand his voices, his negativity, and his spiritual crises. Above all there was no evidence to suggest that his fear of "going mad" was ever addressed. Cloaked in a language of medicine, it appropriately partners the researchers' emphasis on genetics to explain A's development of schizophrenia. But, following on from the previous chapters, and the Genain quadruplets example, should A not be understood as a confused, distressed, and social pariah of a man, plagued by voices, and past experiences (when he was accused of stealing) which he has never been able to resolve. Gottesman and Shields use A as an example of a man with dysfunctional genes. But with the message of previous chapters in mind we should have a more enlightened view of A's predicament?

Putting schizophrenia onto a slide.

The one over-riding and essential problem for medical psychiatry in all the twin, adoption and family studies has been that researchers have only been able to hypothesise on the existence of gene, or genes, responsible, in some way, for bringing on schizophrenia. While schizophrenia may "run" in families, so, as critics have pointed out, do political beliefs. If the geneticists are to bolster their hypothesis in the genetic basis to the bizarre beliefs and behaviours of schizophrenics, it would help their cause if they were able to "discover" physical evidence for these genes. Something you can see under a microscope.

The development of molecular genetics in the 1980s should have assisted psychiatry in that it enabled researchers to locate "markers" for genes. Such markers are detectable as proteins of a known function, and once a marker has been identified researchers are able to identify where on a chromosome this marker is associated with. This has enabled geneticists to literally see the genetic structure of schizophrenic families (and any other families) by putting a blood sample on a slide and gazing at it down a microscope. High hopes are invested in such research. As Kendler and Diehl wrote, there is "the promise of great breakthroughs in our knowledge of the genetics and etiology of schizophrenia at basic biochemical and physiological levels that may never be addressed by traditional methods."

Over 40 studies based on such developments were carried out in Europe and America between 1986 and 1993. They have also been reviewed and summarised by Kendler and

Diehl. Their conclusions? After reviewing all the studies they wrote: "In summary, no replicated positive findings have yet emerged from efforts to locate individual genetic loci that influence the liability to schizophrenia." Of the 45 studies they listed in their review only one study had "strong support" for linking schizophrenia to a particular chromosomal location. Nine other subsequent studies failed to replicate this finding. "Thus, we remain in the unsatisfactory position of having no adequate explanation for this puzzling and discouraging series of events," wrote Kendler and Diehl, adding that a gene with a significant effect on the liability of becoming schizophrenic probably does not exist in this chromosomal region. To those who suspect science will never find a schizophrenic gene, this review reconfirmed such suspicions. But how do the geneticists explain it? Kendler and Diehl wrote: "The number of genes expressed in the central nervous system almost certainly reaches the tens of thousands, only a minute fraction of which have been identified. If major genes exist for schizophrenia, it is more likely that they will be among the large majority of previously unknown genes than among the small minority of genes already identified." On the one hand this is reasonable speculation, based on interpretations of past research. All science engages in speculation. On the other hand it is a wonderful example of the elaboration of the geneticists' argument. It is the oft-quoted "one day we will get there" slogan; If it is not this gene, it will be one of the genes not discovered yet. Kendler and Diehl summarised: "Schizophrenia is clearly a complex disorder in that gene carriers need not manifest the illness (incomplete penetrance), affected individuals need not have the gene (environmental forms or phenocopies), diagnostic uncertainties cannot be avoided, and different families may carry different susceptibility genes (genetic heterogeneity)." In one swoop the geneticists have covered their back of all possibilities. Another way of phrasing Kendler and Diehl's conclusion is – if you are not schizophrenic then it may be because your schizophrenic gene is too weak; if you are schizophrenic you may not have the gene, or the wrong diagnosis may have been made, and, finally; if you do not have the same schizophrenic gene as some other relative also diagnosed schizophrenic it may be because your gene is different!

It's all in the brain
"Somewhere here in a mere three-and-a-half pound lump of pinkish-grey matter, the answer has to be." **Julian Jaynes caricaturing biological reductionists in *The Origins of Consciousness in the Breakdown of the Bicameral Mind, 1976.***

But still the biggest chink in genetic psychiatry's armour is that it is endeavouring to explain how schizophrenia exists (genetic vulnerability) when there is still no evidence that this "illness" does exist at all. I should stress once again that previous chapters have questioned the "existence" of schizophrenia. But referring to other areas of medicine, how is a diagnosis of illness made? To receive a diagnosis of cancer, AIDS, malaria, heart disease or tonsillitis a patient will complain of particular symptoms, such as sore glands, a roaring temperature, sweating, or a sore throat. From a collection of symptoms a suspected diagnosis can be made, and such a diagnosis may then be confirmed or negated by the presence of biological entities such as malignant cells, a virus, a bacteria or abnormal arteries. But with schizophrenia, or similar psychiatric diagnoses, it is a completely different enterprise. For starters schizophrenic "symptoms" are not based on physiological complaints, but behaviours (e.g. staying in one's bedroom rather than socialising) , beliefs ("I think the Nazis are spying on my parents") or unusual experiences ("A voice is telling me not to trust you"). Secondly, there are no "signs" for schizophrenia as there are for physical illnesses. In other words, there is no specific bodily or neurochemical entity to diagnose schizophrenia. As 1995's DSM-IV itself stated: "No laboratory findings have been identified that are diagnostic of schizophrenia".

So how can a psychiatrist diagnose schizophrenia if there are no physiological signs? "Individuals with schizophrenia are sometimes physically awkward and may display neurological "soft signs," such as left/right confusion, poor co-ordination, or mirroring," advises the DSM-IV. "Some minor physical anomalies (e.g., highly arched palate, narrow- or wide-set eyes or subtle malformations of the ears) may be more common among individuals with schizophrenia. Perhaps the most common associated physical findings are motor abnormalities. Most of these are likely to be related to side effects from treatment with antipsychotic medications. Motor abnormalities that are secondary to neuroleptic medication include Neuroleptic-Induced Tardive Dyskinesia, Neuroleptic-Induced Parkinsonism, Neuroleptic-Induced Acute Akathisia, Neuroleptic-Induced Acute Dystonia, and Neuroleptic Malignant Syndrome..."

There are three points that beg to be made. Firstly, the listed "soft" signs – "left/right confusion, poor co-ordination, or mirroring" are indeed so "soft" that it would be interesting to know whether any psychiatrists actually use them to help make a diagnosis of schizophrenia. Moreover, a diminishing of cognitive abilities often results from distress of many varieties. Secondly, to speculate an association between "subtle malformations of the ears" and schizophrenia is of no worthier scientific standing than relating the colour of one's skin to an IQ score. Thirdly, and ironically, it is diseases caused by drug treatments for schizophrenia that are linked with "motor abnormalities" rather than the manifestation of any schizophrenic disease.

1990s – the decade of the brain
Neuroscience has developed substantially since the mid 1980s, particularly with the introduction of technology enabling scientists to peer non-invasively into living brain

tissue with microelectrodes, CT scans, PET scanners and magnetic resonance imaging (MRI). There have also been developments in molecular biology and pharmacology, allowing researchers to examine individual brain cells. These new scientific tools were assessed to be so important that The US Congress declared the 1990s to be the decade of the brain. Did this new era herald discoveries supporting the idea that schizophrenia was a brain disease? Was psychiatry now be able to find the, as yet, illusive sign for schizophrenia?

Two British psychiatrists, Chua and McKenna, in a 1995 British Journal of Psychiatry article, *Schizophrenia – a Brain Disease? A Critical Review of Structural and Functional Cerebral Abnormality in the Disorder* summarised studies carried out in the late eighties and early nineties which compared differences between schizophrenics and non schizophrenics in overall brain size, size of the basal ganglia and limbic system structures, hippocampus structure, and cerebral blood flow. The researchers concluded: "The only well-established structural abnormality in schizophrenia is lateral ventricular enlargement; this is modest and there is a large overlap with the normal population." Reclining back into the "we will get there in the end" argument they added: "schizophrenia is a heterogeneous disorder clinically and one which will ultimately be found to be aetiologically heterogeneous as well." But a scrutinous look at Chua and McKenna's review casts doubt as to whether such a definitive statement is well-founded. Some of the discrepancies that Chua and McKenna themselves list are (i) in an analysis of the ventricular studies up to 1992, researchers Van Horn and McManus found that the year of publication was a significant determinant of the effect of ventricular size for controls (no reason was given for this curious abnomaly), and (ii) that in one of the largest studies carried out by Owens et al in 1985 there was a significant correlation between the presence of tardive dyskinesia and ventricular enlargement, but not schizophrenia.

Nevertheless, Chua and McKenna went on to state that the studies by University of Iowa's Nancy Andreasen and colleagues in 1990 "place the existence of lateral ventricular enlargement in schizophrenia beyond reasonable doubt". But, to the contrary, I would suggest that it *is* reasonable to doubt. In an Andreasen study previous to the one that Chua and McKenna invested so much confidence in, she mentioned that 20 of her 55 schizophrenic subjects had been given courses of ECT. There was a significant correlation between ECT and ventricular enlargement then, but, it appears, this was not a good enough reason to exclude ECT patients in her next study when she stated this time that no significant relationships were recorded between ECT and ventricular enlargement. Interestingly, in her previous study it was mostly men who had had ECT, and, in her follow up research, it was the male schizophrenic subjects who had a significant correlation with ventricular enlargement, but not females. Andreasen also asserted that her findings can not be explained by the effects of alcohol or drug abuse, or neuroleptic and ECT treatment. Yet, any subjects from the control group who had a history of mental illness or substance misuse were excluded from the study. (Leading to what is known as a "super-control" group i.e. an abnormally normal control group, a category of dubious scientific category). Nevertheless, the interest on ventricular enlargement will probably continue into the 21st century, probably following the course of other psychiatric vogues by dying out and getting superseded when attention is focussed on another physiological phenonemon believed to be associated with schizophrenia.

A wedding to conclude

Yet despite my 'polemic' most medical psychiatrists will still advocate that schizophrenia, and voice-hearing with it, is to some degree genetically determined. They will use counter-arguments against my counter-arguments, possibly refering to one of the hundreds of more recent studies that I have not cited in my analysis. A conversation I had with a psychiatric researcher at a wedding (ironically between a psychiatrist and psychologist) demonstrated the sticky bog which is difficult to get out of when discussing the genetics of schizophrenia. As the two of us went through some of the arguments against a genetic understanding of schizophrenia, she cited a study to support a genetic explanation which I had not mentioned. We started discussing this study – with me fighting from the non-genetic corner, and she fighting from the genetic one. We became embroiled in a discussion as circular as one about religion or politics. There are questions of whether there is a god, whether society runs better on the principles of collective class consciousness or altruistic self-interest? Add to these: is schizophrenia genetic? Because whatever I said to back my corner, the researcher re-interpreted. Whatever she claimed, I counter claimed. This, I think, is the essence of the genetics of schizophrenia. Rather than residing in the domain of scientific certainty or fact, we are dealing with interpretations, frameworks, beliefs, ideologies and politics. And whatever the belief, ideology, politics or framework we can cite evidence to support it, and evidence to negate it. Look at the example of the Loch Ness monster. Most people would say this beast does not exist, yet others might believe it does, and whatever evidence brought up to support the belief in Nessie, others will do likewise to demonstrate that the amphibian does not exist…that photograph of Nessie is a fraud...no it is not; that woman who said she saw Nessie is lying...no she is telling the truth; ultra-sonic radar picked up evidence of a large animal in the loch...it was a drifting log not an animal. Compare this with the genetics of schizophrenia. The twin studies are reliably scientific..no they are not reliable enough; we can not deny the mass of neuropsychological research into schizophrenia...yes we can because they demonstrate nothing concrete; ventricular enlargement is evidence of a schizophrenia disease...this is a highly dubious hypothesis. So it goes on endlessly spiralling upwards. Perhaps what is for certain is that the schizophrenic gene exists as much as Nessie does.

Reading

Anderson, W.T. (ed) (1996) *The Fontana Post-Modernism Reader*. Fontana Press.

Barnes, M. and Berke, J. (1971) *Two accounts of a journey through madness*. London: Free Associations

Boyle, M. (1990) *Schizophrenia: a scientific delusion* London: Routledge.

Breggin, P. (1991) *Toxic Psychiatry*. New York: St Martin;s Press.

Dennett, D. (1991) *Conciousness Explained*. London: Allen Lane.

Foucault, J. (1989) *Histoire de la Folie*. (English) *Madness and Civilisation; a history of insanity in the age of reason*. London: Tavistock/Routledge, 1989.

Foudraine, J. (1974) *Not made of Wood: a psychiatrist discovers his own profession*. Translated from the Dutch by Hubert H Hoskins. London: Quartet Books.

Gottesman, I. and Shields, J. (1972) *Schizophrenia and Genetics: a twin study vantage point*. New York: London: Academic Press.

Hofstadter, D. and Dennett, D. (1981). *The Mind's I: Fantasies and Reflections on Self and Soul*. Penguin.

Honderich, T. (ed) (1995) *Oxford Companion to Philosophy*. Oxford University Press.

Jaynes, J. (1976) *The Origins of Consciousness in the Breakdown of the Bicameral Mind*. Penguin.

Kety, S. and Rosenthall, D. (ed)(1967) *Transmission of Schizophrenia: proceedings of the Second Research Conference of the Foundations' Fund for Research in Psychiatry*. Puerto Rico, June 26 to July 1, 1967.

Klein, M. (1975) *Envy and Gratitude, and other works, 1946-1963*. London: Hogarth Press: Institute of Psychoanalysis.

Laing, RD. *(1965) Divided* Self; an existential study in sanity and madness. Penguin

Mavromatis, A. (1991) *Hypnagogia: the unique state of consciousness between wakefulness and sleep*. London: Routledge.

O'Brien, S. (1989) *Visions of Another World: the autobiography of a medium*. Wellingborough: Aquarian.

Orloff, J. (1997) *Second Sight*. New York: Time Warner International.

Parker,I. et al (1995) *Deconstructing Psychopathology*. London: Sage

Pembroke, L. (ed) (1994) *Self-harm: perspectives from personal experience*. London: Survivors Speak Out.

Pilgrim, D. and Treacher, A. (1992) *Clinical Psychology Observed.* London: Routledge.

Podvoll, E. (1990) *The Seduction of Madness: A compassionate approach to recovery at home.* Harper Collins.

Potter, J. and Wetherell, M. (1987) *Discourse and Social Psychology: beyond attitudes and behaviour.* London: Sage.

Romme, M. and Escher S. (1993) *Accepting Voices.* London: MIND.

Rose, S. (1990) *Not in Our Genes: biology, ideology and human nature.* Harmondsworth: Penguin, 1990.

Roud, P. (1990) *Making Miracles.* Thorsons Publishers Ltd.

Szasz, T. (1990) *Myth of Mental Illness: foundations of a theory of personal construct.* London: Routledge.

Williamson, L. (1990) *Mediums and their work.* Rober Hale.